Missouri State Parks

A Complete Outdoor Recreation Guide for Campers, Hikers, Anglers, Boaters and Nature Lovers

by

Bill Bailey

GLOVEBOX
GUIDEBOOKS
OF AMERICA

To our readers: Travel entails unavoidable risks. Know your limitations, be prepared, be alert, use good judgment, think safety and enjoy Missouri's terrific outdoors. GGOA makes no warranty or guarantees regarding the accuracy of information in this book.

Check with the state of Missouri parks division for the latest details and official park information.

Design by Dan Jacalone
All interior photos by the author, cover photos, charts and other information courtesy of the Missouri State Parks Division.
Edited by Bill Cornish, Penny Weber

Published by:
Glovebox Guidebooks of America, L.L.P.
3523 North Gleaner Road
Freeland, Michigan 48623-8829
(800) 289-4843

Library of Congress, CIP

Bill Bailey

Missouri State Parks Guidebook
(A Glovebox Guidebooks of America publication)

ISBN 1-881139-29-8

Printed in the United States of America

10   9   8   7   6   5   4   3   2

For my sons
Mike and Ryan

Missouri
STATE PARKS

A Guide to Missouri State Parks

Table of contents

Kansas City Region

1. Big Lake State Park 2

2. Knob Noster State Park 8

3. Lewis and Clark State Park 13

4. Wallace State Park 18

5. Weston Bend State Park 24

6. Watkins Mill State Park and Historic Site 31

Northeast Region

7. Crowder State Park 38

8. Cuivre River State Park 44

9. Graham Cave State Park 50

10. Long Branch State Park 56

11. Pershing State Park 64

12. Thousand Hills State Park 71

13. Mark Twain State Park 80
14. Wakonda State Park 88

Central Region

15. Finger Lakes State Park 95
16. Katy Trail State Park 100
17. Rock Bridge Memorial State Park 105
18. Van Meter State Park 110

St. Louis Region

19. Dr. Edmund A. Babler Memorial State Park 117
20. Castlewood State Park 128
21. Hawn State Park 134
22. Edward "Ted" and Pat Jones-Confluence
   Point State Park 140
23. Meramec State Park 144
24. Robertsville State Park 157
25. Route 66 State Park 162
26. St. Francois State Park 168
27. St. Joe State Park 175
28. Washington State Park 182

Lakes Region

29. Bennett Spring State Park 191
30. Big Sugar Creek State Park 203
31. Ha Ha Tonka State Park 206
32. Lake of the Ozarks State Park 214
33. Pomme de Terre State Park 226
34. Prairie State Park 237
35. Roaring River State Park 244
36. Stockton State Park 258
37. Table Rock State Park 267
38. Harry S Truman State Park 275

Southeast Region

39. Sam A. Baker State Park 285
40. Big Oak Tree State Park 301
41. Elephant Rocks State Park 308
42. Grand Gulf State Park 315
43. Johnson's Shut-Ins State Park 319

44. Lake Wappapello State Park 327
45. Montauk State Park 338
46. Morris State Park 353
47. Onondaga Cave State Park 356
48. Taum Sauk Mountain State Park 363
49. Trail of Tears State Park 370

Introduction

Wise Stewardship

Missouri's state parks are the keepers of our cultural and natural history. From important sons like Thomas Hart Benton, and with the places that shaped the state's history like the first Missouri State Capitol, residents admire Missouri's dazzling beauty in Elephant Rocks, Ha Ha Tonka and Onondaga Cave; and they fondly recall spending time with their families at expansive parks like Johnson's Shut-Ins or Pomme de Terre Lake.

This powerful history and natural features identify Missouri and provide the crucial theme for what has been acknowledged as one of our nation's finest and most diverse state park systems.

Mission

"To preserve and interpret the finest examples of Missouri's natural landscapes; to preserve and interpret Missouri's cultural landmarks; and to provide healthy and enjoyable outdoor recreation opportunities for all Missourians and visitors to the state."

The Beginning of the Missouri State Park System

Upon encouragement from many citizens, state legislators introduced a bill in the Missouri General Assembly in 1907 that would develop a state park system. Although the bill did not pass on the first attempt, interest nurtured and in 1914, a committee of six senators traveled four days by train, car, wagon and foot, assessing proposed sites to be developed as state parks. One of these sites was Ha Ha Tonka State Park.

Missouri's hard work to establish a state park system were some of the earliest in the country; however, without legislation authorizing funds for acquisition of state park land, the first state park purchase would have to wait.

Many other states also were beginning to feel the demand for recreational areas, and the requests to preserve outstanding natural lands at the state level were being heeded throughout the country. In 1916, the National Park Service was formed to administer national sites and it pledged guidance and aid in helping to establish state park systems.

The Beginning: Purchase of State Parks

In 1917, the Missouri Legislature recognized the call for public recreation areas and approved a law establishing a state park fund using revenue from the fish and game department. With the fund established, the fish and game department took charge of the parks.

In 1923, the state acquired the historic Arrow Rock Tavern. However, it was not until 1924 that the first state park tracts were secured. On Oct. 17, 1924, Big Spring State Park became the first Missouri state park. That park, Alley Spring State Park and Round Spring State Park later were recognized as being nationally significant and became part of the National Park Service's Ozark National Scenic Riverways.

By the end of 1925, the state park system had grown to eight areas with a total of 23,244 acres. That same year, the Legislature increased revenues to support the growing state park system. In 1928, the dedication of Meramec State Park drew more than 10,000 visitors; there were more than 400,000 visitors statewide during the summer of 1929, largely due to new and better highways in the state.

As the system grew, the public showed a big interest in state parks. In addition to enjoying the recreational areas available, many Missourians began to articulate a desire to preserve portions of their state's grandest natural landscapes as well as sites important to the history of the state and its people.

By 1932, the state had 18 state parks. Missourians showed their endorsements of the state park system not only through the rising attendance, but also through the donation of Roaring River, Van Meter and Washington state parks.

CCC - Civilian Conservation Corps

In the 1930s, the state park system matured and developed. Starting in 1933, under the direction of President Franklin Roosevelt, Congress authorized many federal public works programs to help reduce unemployment. The program that meant the most to Missouri's state park system was the Civilian Conservation Corps (CCC), an organization providing jobs for young men ages 18 to 25.

By 1934, about 4,000 men were employed to complete both conservation and construction work in national and state forests and state parks. Projects ranged from construction of dining lodges, picnic shelters, cabins and campgrounds to installation of sewer lines and other infrastructure.

The National Parks Service supervised work and the quality of the construction was exceptional, establishing a wonderful rustic standard for decades to come. The skill and pride these men took in their work is still evident in our state park system and around the nation. In fact, in 1985, most of the CCC work, including 247 buildings and 95 structures in the Missouri state park system, were included in the only nomination of its kind to the National Register of Historic Places.

State Park Board is formed

In 1937, the management of state parks was separated from the state fish and game department and was placed under the supervision of a new Missouri State Park Board.

This was done for two purposes: To find a separate source of revenue for the system without using the fish and game revenues, and to clarify and separate the operation of state parks from the management of Missouri's fish, forests and game. Twelve years after its first purchase, the state park system was recognized as a separate and distinct use of state-owned public land in the state.

Funding the expanding state park system soon became a key issue. To address this need, drafters of the 1945 state constitution included a provision establishing a mill tax, earmarking a portion for state parks. This special tax for state parks was in effect for 27 years and expired in 1972. At that point, state park officials implemented a user fee program. These fees were collected for the first few months of 1973; however, due to public opposition, the user fee was eliminated.

The system also drew from federal funding sources. The state's receipt of federal revenue sharing funds provided a better budget for state parks. Since 1965, the system has sought assistance from the federal Land and Water Conservation Fund to acquire and develop state parklands and facilities. More than half of Missouri's state parks have benefited from the fund.

Missouri Department of Natural Resources – Strength and Resilience

In the mid-1970s, with the reorganization of nearly all of state government, the Missouri Department of Natural Resources was formed and assumed the state park board's responsibilities for the administration of the state park system. Under the Department of Natural Resources, the park system has continued to expand and improve.

The department oversees nearly 138,000 acres in more than 80 areas (this includes dedicated historic sites). Although this books details only the state parks, I urge everyone to include historic sites in your travel plans.

In the 1980s, the nation experienced a recession, which led to reduced state revenues and mandatory budget cuts for state parks. At the same time, federal revenue sharing and Land and Water Conservation Funds were also shrinking. In response to this financial crisis, state park officials again proposed the user fee program. Again the idea was dropped because of legislative opposition. The funding shortage remained but in 1982, Missouri voters approved a $600 million statewide bond issue that included $55 million for major renovation and construction projects in state parks. It was the largest single building program initiated in Missouri state parks since the earlier work of the Civilian Conservation Corps.

In 1984, voters again illustrated their support by approving a dedicated sales tax to be used for state parks and soil and water conservation efforts in Missouri. Funds from the one-tenth-of-one-percent sales tax are divided equally between the two programs, both of which are administered by the Missouri Department of Natural Resources.

With a secure funding base, widespread repair and renovation of the park system is occurring, as well as the completion of development at newly acquired parks.

As the state's literature says, "The Missouri state park system is entering a new era." The history of the park system that is being written today will continue to reflect the strong traditions that have developed from years of robust public guidance. The Missouri state park system was developed for Missourians, and reflects an enduring state heritage.

Amenities and Facilities of the State Parks

Camping
Online campsite reservations
available 24 hours a day
www.mostateparks.com

Reservation Center
7 a.m. - 10 p.m. CST, seven days a week
Call toll-free: (877)ICampMO or (1-877-422-6766)

The state accepts campsite reservations in 35 state park campgrounds (many more parks will be added to the reservation system soon). A portion of campsites at these 24 parks is available for our first-come, first-served users except at Johnson's Shut-Ins State Park, which is 100 percent reservable. There is a reservation fee.

Six-Month Reservation Window

■ Make your reservation six months to two days in advance of arrival (for example, make your reservation Jan. 3 for July 3 arrival and no later than July 1 for July 3 arrival).

■ Altering the arrival date for camping stays of trout park opening at Roaring River, Montauk and Bennett Spring state parks, and Memorial Day weekend, July 3 and 4, and Labor Day weekend at all state parks will result in forfeiture of two camping days if the reservation was originally made within the first month of the six-month reservation window.

Be Ready to Make Your Reservation

Have the following information in hand before you make your reservation:

■ The name of the park where you want to camp

■ The dates you want to reserve

■ The type of campsite needed (basic, electric, electric/water, sewer/electric/water) and the site number, if known

■ The type and size of camping unit you will use

■ The number of persons in your camping party

■ Occupant's name, address and telephone number for each site reserved

■ MasterCard, Visa or Discover credit card number, debit card backed by major credit card, personal check, coupon, etc.

Methods of Payment

■ Pay by credit card, debit card backed by major credit cards, check, money order, and free camping coupons and camping gift certificates issued by the Missouri Department of Natural Resources.

■ Camping and reservation fees are due at the time the reservation is made.

- The reservation fee applies to each site reserved, whether one day or 15 days, and is non-refundable.

- Electronic payment methods are accepted as late as midnight Wednesday for a Friday evening arrival (approximately two days).

- Non-electronic payment methods are accepted up to 21 days before arrival with receipt of payment within 10 days from the date the reservation was made.

- Confirmation is made when all fees are paid.

Arrivals and Departures

- Early departures may result in forfeiture of camping fees and a transaction fee.

- Campers must arrive within the first camping day (3 p.m. to 3 p.m. the next day) or the site will be available for resale.

- On the day of departure, campers must exit their campsite by 2 p.m.

Cancellations and Changes

- Cancellations at least two days before arrival will result in a refund of all camping fees less the cancellation fee.

- Cancellations less than two days before arrival will result in a forfeiture of up to two camping days plus the cancellation fee.

- Early departures may result in forfeiture of camping fees and a transaction fee.

- Altering the arrival date for camping stays of trout park opening at Roaring River, Montauk and Bennett Spring state parks, and Memorial Day weekend, July 3 and 4, and Labor Day weekend at all state parks will result in forfeiture of two camping days if the reservation was originally made within the first month of the six-month reservation window.

Other Things to Know

- A minimum stay of two nights is required for weekends and major holidays from May 15 through Sept. 15. Some state parks may have additional minimum requirements.

▓ Five campsites are the maximum you may reserve for one arrival day. You may make reservations for an unlimited number of camping trips at one or more parks during one transaction. Each campsite and camping trip is charged a separate reservation fee.

▓ A fee is charged to change or cancel a reservation.

▓ Electric hookups are available year-round, while water and showers are usually available from April 1 through Oct. 31 in most state parks.

▓ The maximum stay is 15 days in any 30-day period.

▓ The maximum number of persons on a site is six, unless the unit is indivisible. Also, there are limits on the number of sleeping units you may place on each campsite. Check with park staff for policies.

▓ Many of our parks contain rules and policies that are specific to the individual park and its resources. Please call the individual park to inquire of specific rules and, upon your arrival, check the park's bulletin boards for additional rules.

Operations

State park campgrounds are open year-round. Table Rock State Park closes its campgrounds from December through February. Electric hookups are available year-round while water and showers are available from April 1 through Oct. 31 in most state parks. To secure a campsite, campers should be prepared to place on the campsite substantial personal property (i.e. dining fly, trailer, tent, licensed vehicle, etc.)

Pets

Pets must be on a secured leash that is no longer than 10 feet, reasonably quiet at all times, under control of the owner and never left unsupervised. Pets are not allowed in any park structures (including restrooms and showerhouses). Also, pets are restricted from swimming areas (including beaches) and waters reserved for fishing.

Special-Use Areas

Many state parks have special-use areas for use by nonprofit youth organizations. These areas are assigned on a first-come, first-served basis and may be reserved by phone. Organized youth groups have priority.

Organized Group Camps

There are 13 organized group camps in seven Missouri state parks: Crowder, Cuivre River, Knob Noster, Lake of the Ozarks, Roaring River, Mark Twain and Dr. Edmund A. Babler Memorial. Each camp includes cabins, dining lodge and kitchen facilities, restrooms and showers, and various outdoor recreation facilities. At Babler State Park, the Jacob L. Babler Outdoor Education Center has facilities designed for campers with disabilities. The camps can accommodate from 40 to 200 campers and are available from April 15 to Oct. 15. Organizations must make reservations in advance directly with the park.

Seniors and Disabled Citizens

Citizens who are 65 years of age or older or persons with disabilities are entitled to a reduced camping fee. An official document such as a driver's license certifying proof of age or disability must be presented when registering.

Parks Programs

Passport Program

A souvenir passport booklet, designed to serve as a guide to planning your Missouri state park adventure and as a journal to record your experiences, is available for purchase at most state parks and historic sites, by calling the department toll-free at (800) 334-6946 or by mailing in the order form.

Passports can be purchased at any state park or historic site, or by calling the Department of Natural Resources toll free at (800) 334-6946 (voice) or (800) 379-2419 (Telecommunications Device for the Deaf).

Junior Naturalist Program

You can become a Junior Naturalist by fulfilling several fun-filled requirements at many state parks and historic sites. As you earn your Junior Naturalist patch, you will learn more about nature, wildlife and Missouri's outdoor world.

Camper Awards

Each family member camping in five state parks during one year and not violating any park rules and regulations is awarded a certificate and patch. Families must have camper verification cards. These are available at all state parks and historic sites and must be verified by staff at each place the family camps.

Volunteers in Parks (VIP) Program

Do you like people? Are you concerned about state parks and the outdoors? Do you need to gain work experience, or want a break from your routine and want to meet new people?

The Missouri Department of Natural Resources' Division of State Parks has something for you. It's called the V.I.P. or Volunteers in Parks Program, and it's for everyone - professionals, senior citizens, housewives, students and young people. The type of work volunteers do includes the following:

Volunteer campground hosts assist park superintendents in various aspects of the daily operation of campgrounds. This work is seasonal during the summer months. They serve a minimum of four weeks except for emergencies.

Duties of volunteer campground hosts may include the following: Greet incoming campground users and make available any pamphlets, brochures or other information; instruct park users in locating vacant sites and parking their camping units; collect camping fees and issue permits; report any problems to the ranger or superintendent; keep the area presentable by picking up litter and replenishing tissue in shower and toilet buildings; and report maintenance problems to the appropriate park personnel.

Volunteer interpreters assist full-time park naturalists and site administrators in the interpretive programming for a facility. This work can be done at any time during the year.

Duties of volunteer interpreters may include the following: Assist in meeting and talking to the public about park information, points of interest, facilities, and rules and regulations; assist in developing or giving slide programs developed by full-time staff; develop in-park posters on interpretive programs and post at appropriate locations; assist in providing tours through the park or through park facilities such as trail walks, historic site tours, special demonstrations and evening programs; assist in other aspects of natural or cultural history work assignments as needed; and assist in the maintenance and care of interpretive facilities.

Aides in Missouri's state parks and historic sites assist full-time staff in the daily operations of the facility during summer and other high-use periods. Duties of park aides may include the following: Work in contact stations or going to individual campsites to collect fees and give out information to the public; assist in cleaning restrooms, latrines and buildings; assist with trash collection and cleaning of grounds; and assist in mowing and cutting weeds.

Volunteer trail workers assist park superintendents in all aspects of trail maintenance and construction. This work can be done any time during the year. Duties of volunteer trail workers are to assist in trail construction and maintenance.

Pets as Park Visitors

More and more visitors are bringing their pets to the park, which is increasing complaints about fecal waste. Waste deposits are sometimes unknowingly tracked onto carpet and floors of buildings, tents, vehicles, etc. The smell of any feces is offensive and will attract flies or other vermin to the area.

Dog waste can pose health threats to park users and other dogs, including the transmission of Parvovirus to unexposed and unvaccinated dogs. It can also carry waterborne disease organisms such as E. coli, salmonella and other gastrointestinal organisms and parasites that can cause serious health effects.

Waste deposits can impact lakes and streams used for

recreation by increasing fecal bacteria and other organisms to levels unsafe for swimming. It can diminish the water supply's ecological health through increased plant and algae growth. Waste also can increase the spread of nitrogen-loving noxious weeds at the expense of our native plants.

Here are some things to keep in mind

- Responsible pet owners will properly remove and dispose of their pet's waste in Dumpsters or trash receptacles.

- State law requires pets to be on a secured leash that is no longer than 10 feet. When meeting or passing other users, please reduce the rein to four feet.

- Pets may feel more secure and dogs will be less likely to bark if kept inside your sleeping unit when camping overnight. Barking is disturbing to other park users.

- Never leave your pet unattended in the park.

- Pets are not allowed in public swimming areas (including beaches) or in public buildings. Service animals assisting persons with disabilities are permitted in these areas.

- Wash your pet at home, not in state park showers, streams, rivers or lakes.

- Never allow your pet to dig in any area of the park or historic site.

- Don't leave your pet inside a vehicle (even with the windows slightly open), as seasonal temperatures can quickly reach dangerous levels.

- Make sure your pet has identification tags in case it gets separated from you.

- State law requires owners to report to park personnel any incidents of pet bites or attacks. Be prepared to show proof that your pet's vaccinations are current.

- Park personnel may ask pet owners to leave the park if their pet is being disruptive to other visitors or if pet owners blatantly ignore pet policies of the park.

- Leaving your pet in the comfort of your home with a caregiver could benefit both you and your pet.

CAMPSITES	SERVICES							SPEICAL AREAS							
SEEP = State Park SHS = State Historic Site	Basic	Electric	Electric/Water	Sewer/Electric/Water	Reserable	Accessible	Walk-in Sites	Maximum Amps	Firewood	Dump Station	Showers	Water Available	Laundry	Gate/After Hours Access	Organized Group Camps
Arrow Rock SHS	12	34		1	Y	3		50	Y	Y	Y	Y		Y	
Babler Memorial SP	30	43			Y	4		50	Y	Y	Y	Y		Y	Y
Sam A. Baker SP	66	118			Y	6		50	Y	Y	Y	Y	Y		
Battle of Athens SHS	14	15						30	Y			Y			
Bennet Spring SP	15	128		46	Y	10		30	Y	Y	Y	Y	Y		
Big Lake SP	18	57			Y	4		30	Y	Y	Y	Y	Y		
Crowder SP	10	31			Y	2		30	Y	Y	Y	Y	Y		Y
Cuive River SP	52	23		31	Y	6	5	30	Y	Y	Y	Y	Y		Y
Finger Lakes SP	19	16			Y	2		50	Y	Y	Y	Y		Y	
Graham Cave SP	34	18			Y			30	Y	Y	Y	Y	Y		
Ha Ha Tonka SP															
Hawn SP	19	26			Y	4	5	30	Y	Y	Y	Y	Y	Y	
Johnson's Shut-ins SP	26	23			Y	3		30	Y	Y	Y	Y	Y	Y	
Knob Noster SP	39	37			Y	4		30	Y	Y	Y	Y	Y	Y	Y
Lake of the Ozarks SP	101	88			Y	10		50	Y	Y	Y	Y	Y		Y
Lake Wappapello SP	7	71			Y	4		50	Y	Y	Y	Y	Y		
Lewis and Clark SP	7	63			Y	3		50	Y	Y	Y	Y	Y		
Long Branch SP	9	64				7	9	50	Y	Y	Y	Y			
Mastodon SHS															
Meramec SP	52	125	14	18	Y	10		50	Y	Y	Y	Y	Y		
Montauk SP	31	123			Y	8		50	Y	Y	Y	Y	Y		
Onandaga Cave SP	19		47		Y	3		50	Y	Y	Y	Y	Y	Y	

CAMPSITES	SERVICES							SPEICAL AREAS							
SEEP = State Park SHS = State Historic Site	Basic	Electric	Electric/Water	Sewer/Electric/Water	Reserable	Accessible	Walk-in Sites	Maximum Amps	Firewood	Dump Station	Showers	Water Available	Laundry	Gate/After Hours Access	Organized Group Camps
Pershing SP	12	26			Y	2		30	Y	Y	Y	Y	Y		
Pomme de Terre SP	41	193	20		Y	9		50	Y	Y	Y	Y	Y		
Prairie SP	2													Y	
Roaring River SP	48	137			Y	10		30	Y	Y	Y	Y	Y		Y
Robertsville SP	12	14			Y	2		30	Y	Y	Y	Y	Y	Y	
Rock Bridge Memorial SP															
St. Francis SP	47	63			Y	6		30	Y	Y	Y	Y	Y	Y	
St. Joe SP	43	53			Y	2		50	Y	Y	Y	Y	Y		
Stockton SP	14	60			Y	5		50	Y	Y	Y	Y	Y		
Table Rock SP	43	89		29	Y	4		50	Y	Y	Y	Y	Y	Y	
Taum Sauk Mountain SP							12					Y			
Thousand Hills SP	15	42			Y	3		50	Y	Y	Y	Y		Y	
Trail of Tears SP	35	10		7	Y	1		30	Y	Y	Y	Y	Y	Y	
Harry S. Truman SP	100	98			Y	11		50	Y	Y	Y	Y	Y	Y	
Mark Twain SP	22	75			Y	8		50	Y	Y	Y	Y	Y		Y
Van Meter SP	9	12				1		30	Y		Y	Y			
Wakonda SP	49	29			Y	4		30	Y	Y	Y	Y	Y	Y	
Wallace SP	35	42			Y	4	4	50	Y	Y	Y	Y		Y	
Washington SP	26	24			Y	3		30	Y	Y	Y	Y	Y		
Watkins Woolen Mill SP, SHS	23	75			Y	5		50	Y	Y	Y	Y	Y	Y	
Weston Bend SP	4	32			Y	2		50	Y	Y	Y	Y	Y	Y	

Lodging and Concessions

Many concession facilities such as dining lodges, motels and marinas are operated through contracts with private companies and individuals. Details about these operations are found on the individual park and site pages. For more information about concession opportunities, check ***www.mostateparks.com/concession.htm.***

Lodging and Dining

Facilities

Eight state parks have dining facilities ranging from modern restaurants to rustic lodges. Eleven state parks provide lodging facilities ranging from stone cabins to modern motels. Additional lodging options include recreational vehicles at Wakonda State Park and log camper cabins at Lake of the Ozarks State Park.

Seasons

Lodging accommodations are open from April 15 through Oct. 31, except at Bennett Spring, Montauk and Roaring River state parks, where cabins and motel rooms are open from Feb. 25 through Oct. 31. Motel rooms are available at Big Lake State Park from April 15 through the last weekend in November. To accommodate winter visitors, some housekeeping cabins and the motel at Montauk State Park are open from Nov. 1 to Feb. 24.

Lodging Reservations

Lodging is available to suit every budget. Check with the park concessionaire to learn what is available and the nightly rate. Reservations for any period between Memorial Day and Labor Day must be a minimum of two nights.

Stables

If you are interested in exploring Missouri state parks on horseback, Lake of the Ozarks State Park and Dr. Edmund A. Babler Memorial State Park offer stables where horses can be rented. Many other parks provide trails where you can bring your own horse.

Marinas

Everything you need to enjoy the water is available at marinas in Missouri state parks. At most marinas, you can rent a boat or personal watercraft, fill up on gasoline, or purchase those last-minute fishing supplies or snacks.

Canoeing

Missouri's many clear streams and rivers are perfect for a relaxing canoe trip. Several state parks offer canoe rentals and shuttles.

Cave Tours

You can explore underground Missouri with its fascinating formations in three state parks. Guided tours are available at Onondaga Cave State Park, Meramec State Park and Ozark Caverns at Lake of the Ozarks State Park.

State Park Accessibility

Facilities such as campgrounds, showerhouses, picnic areas, fishing docks and other areas comply with the Americans with Disabilities Act. New programmable aids such as audiotapes, photographs and video presentations allow visitors to have a more full experience. These aids are also available in Braille and on audiotape. For the most current information on what features are accessible, call the individual park or call the department toll free at (800) 334-6946 (voice) or (800) 379-2419 (Telecommunications Device for the Deaf).

Frequently asked questions

When do the state parks close for the winter?

The state parks are open year-round. Generally, water is turned off in most of the campgrounds Nov. 1 and turned on again April 1. Electricity is on year-round. Table Rock State Park closes its campgrounds from December through February.

Can I bring alcohol into a state park?
Alcohol is allowed at your campsite, but it is not allowed in parking lots, beach areas and off-road vehicle areas.

Which state parks offer canoe/raft rentals and shuttles?
Sam A. Baker State Park
Bennett Spring State Park
Meramec State Park
Washington State Park

Which state parks accept campground reservations?
Sam A. Baker State Park
Bennett Spring State Park
Hawn State Park
Johnson's Shut-Ins State Park
Lake of the Ozarks State Park
Meramec State Park
Montauk State Park
Roaring River State Park
Trail of Tears State Park
Harry S Truman State Park
Mark Twain State Park
Washington State Park
Watkins Woolen Mill State Park and
State Historic Site
Reservations are taken only during certain hours and cannot be made within 48 hours of your arrival. To make a reservation, please visit the Campground Reservations page.

Which state parks allow metal detecting (by permit only)?
Crowder State Park
Cuivre River State Park
Finger Lakes State Park
Lake of the Ozarks State Park
Lake Wappapello State Park
Lewis and Clark State Park
Long Branch State Park
Pershing State Park
Pomme de Terre State Park
St. Joe State Park
Stockton State Park
Trail of Tears State Park
Harry S. Truman State Park

Wakonda State Park
Wallace State Park
Watkins Woolen Mill State Park and State Historic Site
This activity is allowed only on specific sand beaches. A
permit is required and may be obtained free of charge by
writing to Missouri Department of Natural Resources,
Operations and Resource Management Program, P.O. Box
176, Jefferson City, MO 65102, or by e-mail at
moparks@mail.dnr.state.mo.us.

Which state parks allow rock climbing and rappelling (by permit only)?

Elephant Rocks State Park
Johnson's Shut-Ins State Park
Lake of the Ozarks State Park
Meramec State Park
St. Francois State Park
This activity is allowed only during certain months. A
permit is required and may be obtained by contacting the
park before your visit.

Which state parks have camping with sewer hookups?
Bennett Spring State Park

Cuivre River State Park
Meramec State Park   Table Rock State Park
Trail of Tears State Park

Which state parks have group camps?

Dr. Edmund A. Babler Memorial State Park
Crowder State Park
Cuivre River State Park
Knob Noster State Park
Lake of the Ozarks State Park
Roaring River State Park
Mark Twain State Park

Which state parks have an equestrian campground?

Sam A. Baker State Park
Cuivre River State Park

Knob Noster State Park
St. Joe State Park

Which state parks have lodging?

Sam A. Baker State Park
Bennett Spring State Park
Big Lake State Park
Lake of the Ozarks State Park*
Lake Wappapello State Park
Meramec State Park
Montauk State Park
Roaring River State Park
Stockton State Park
Thousand Hills State Park
Washington State Park
(*Camper Cabins - no running water or electricity)

Which state parks have all-terrain vehicle or motorcycle trails?

Finger Lakes State Park
St. Joe State Park

Which state parks have all-terrain bicycle trails?

Castlewood State Park
Crowder State Park
Finger Lakes State Park
Graham Cave State Park
Katy Trail State Park
Knob Noster State Park
Lake of the Ozarks State Park
Lake Wappapello State Park
Rock Bridge Memorial State Park
St. Joe State Park
Thousand Hills State Park

Which state parks have horse rentals?

Dr. Edmund A. Babler Memorial State Park
Lake of the Ozarks State Park

Which state parks have cave tours?
Lake of the Ozarks State Park
Meramec State Park
Onondaga Cave State Park

Which state parks have trout fishing?
Bennett Spring State Park
Montauk State Park
Roaring River State Park

Which state parks have swimming pools?
Dr. Edmund A. Babler Memorial State Park
Bennett Spring State Park
Big Lake State Park
Roaring River State Park
Washington State Park

Which state parks have swimming beaches?
Crowder State Park
Cuivre River State Park
Finger Lakes State Park
Lake of the Ozarks State Park
Lake Wappapello State Park
Lewis and Clark State Park
Long Branch State Park
Pomme de Terre State Park
St. Joe State Park
Stockton State Park
Thousand Hills State Park
Trail of Tears State Park
Harry S Truman State Park
Mark Twain State Park
Wakonda State Park
Wallace State Park
Watkins Woolen Mill State Park and
State Historic Site

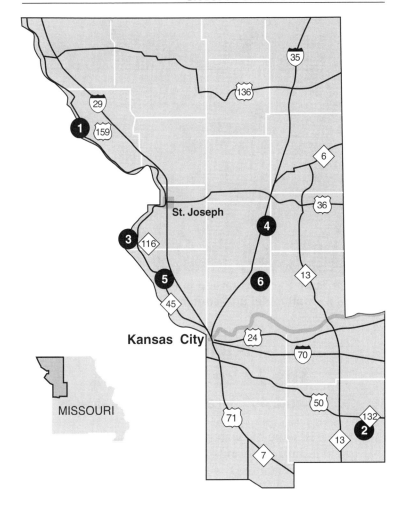

Kansas City Region

1. Big Lake State Park
2. Knob Noster State Park
3. Lewis and Clark State Park
4. Wallace State Park
5. Weston Bend State Park
6. Watkins Mill State Park and Historic Site

Big Lake State Park swimming pool. The park also features a small motel and conference area.

CHAPTER 1
Big Lake State Park
Land: 407 acres Water: Big Lake

There is some big water around Big Lake State Park and intimate wetlands that are some of the finest and most important in the state. Speaking of water, the park is also on the state's biggest oxbox lake. It is quite possibly one of the lakes Lewis and Clark described in their journals as they explored the Missouri River and lands contained in the Louisiana Purchase.

The marshlands in the park offer refuge for a wide variety of faunas including flashy yellow-headed blackbirds. A number of walks and access points allow park guests to view the wetlands up close where cottonwood tree sometimes flutter and shorebirds and waterfowl ride the winds over the lake. Growing along the banks of the lake are floodplain plants such as peach-leaf willow, black willow, bulrush, rose mallow and sandbur. The lake has fish species that include bass, catfish, crappie and carp. Wildlife such as map turtles, smooth soft-shelled turtles, wintering American bald eagles and a variety of waterfowl are commonly found.

Several times a year, park visitors are treated to spectacular migrations and other bird activity from great blue herons, pintails, teals, mallards, snow geese, cormorants and American white pelicans.

The region around the park has all kinds of lake-related developments including shopping, fishing, cottages, water sports, full-service restaurants and lots more.

Information and activities

Big Lake State Park
204 Lake Shore Drive
Craig, MO 64437
(660) 442-3770
(877) I Camp Mo: Camp Reservations
www.mostateparks.com

Directions:

From Kansas City

Big Lake State Park is about 75 miles north of Kansas City International Airport. Travel north on I-29 to Exit 79 (U.S. Hwy. 159). Proceed west on U.S. Hwy. 159 for about nine miles to Hwy. 111. Turn right onto Hwy. 111 and travel one mile to the park entrance.

From Omaha, Neb.

Big Lake State Park is about 90 miles south of Omaha. Travel south on I-29 to the Mound City exit (Exit 84). Take Hwy. 118 west to Hwy. 111. Turn left onto Hwy. 111 and proceed to the state park.

Emergency number: 911 system.

Campground: Big Lake State Park offers 18 basic and 57 electric campsites. Services include a dump station, showers, water, coin-operated laundry and reservable sites. A horseshoes court is behind the showerhouse.

Campers can see the lake, distant cabins and residential neighborhoods. Huge walnut trees shade sites 2-5 and

Big Lake State Park has eight cabins near a walnut grove. They are some of the finest cabins in the parks system.

others nearby. Site 15 and others have roofed picnic tables. There are some mowed spaces between sites in the teens. Site 8 has some extra space around it and a big maple shades the space. It's also steps away from a horseshoes court. A large number of the sites on the interior of the loop are pull-through. About the only flaw in the shady campground is the narrow park road. Big rigs will need to be a bit more cautious as they maneuver their rigs, but the good news is there are lots of pull-through sites.

Most of the sites have gravel pads, lantern hooks and ground-mounted fire rings. Sites in the 20s are on a slight rise and have plenty of midday shade. Sites in the 30s are level and near the showerhouse and laundry.

Lodge: Big Lake State Park offers motel, suite and cabin accommodations from April through November. A small store is operated at the lodge. The store sells soft drinks, coolers, some camping equipment, candy, ice cream, pizza, canned goods, charcoal, chips, laundry supplies, personal hygiene items, milk and other items.

The full-service restaurant has about a dozen tables where some excellent broasted chicken and Texan toast are served. I also tried a number of sandwiches and excellent desserts; just ask my cardiologist. Breakfast is served, also.

The 22 motel rooms have two double beds, TV, telephone, air-conditioning/heat and a private lakeside balcony. One handicap accessible room on the lower level with a queen-size bed and the aforementioned amenities is available. A maximum of three persons are allowed in that particular room and two-day stays are required.

Each suite has a kitchenette, living/dining room, basic cookware and utensils, microwave, coffeemaker, TV, sofa bed, separate bedroom with two full-size beds and a private lakeside patio.

A conference room complete with eight-foot tables and chairs is offered for meetings. Room occupancy is up to about 100 guests. It is open from the end of April to the Sunday after Thanksgiving and you can begin booking for the entire season on Jan. 2. Catering is available.

There is a small game area in the lobby. Rates and availability of lodge rooms differ during the week. Sometimes you can get rooms cheaper during the weekdays.

Cabins: The eight brown cabins with blue trim have two bedrooms with a double bed per room (linens provided), one single-size rollaway bed (linens not provided), a fireplace, air conditioning, heat, bathroom with shower, kitchen, basic cookware and utensils, toaster, coffeemaker, microwave, TV, screened porch and grill and picnic table. A maximum of six people per cabin are allowed. Each waterfront cabin also has mowed open spaces down to the lakeshore. These are some of the nicest cabins in the Missouri State Park system. Behind the cabins are a view of a walnut grove and open spaces within walking distance of the park store, pool and restaurant. Four scoop chairs and a table are in the screened porches. There are some huge trees that dot the area where the cabins lie.

Swimming: The swimming pool is near the modern two-story motel overlooking the lake. The pool is open daily from noon to 8 p.m. Memorial Day to Labor Day, weather permitting. Family and individual passes are available.

Cabins have two bedrooms, double beds, screen porches, TV's, bathrooms with shower, and fireplaces.

There is a daily fee; children under 3 are free. No oils or lotions are allowed in the pool. Sunbathers must shower before entering the water. There is an L-shaped kiddie's pool that is 18 inches deep. There is plenty of room on the pool decks for sunbathing.

Boating: A concrete boat launch is a quarter-mile north of the park entrance. There are no launch fees or motor restrictions on Big Lake. There is shoreline access near the boat launch for fishing. There is parking for about 15 boats and trailers, and the launch is about 100 yards from the last cabin.

Fishing: Fishing is permitted anywhere on the lake. Bass, catfish, crappie and bluegill are all found in Big Lake. Some of the shoreline is soft with cattails and other aquatic vegetation that hold a variety of fish species. There are plenty of shoreline access points, with many having picnic tables.

Day-use area: An open picnic shelter with electricity can be reserved for a fee. If not reserved, the shelter is available for free on a first-come, first-served basis. Shelter capacity is about 75 guests.

There are playgrounds in both the main day-use area and the campground. Many overlooks, intimate picnic sites and access points are along the lake. Some of the shoreline is soft and excellent places to view wildlife and distant views of village homes.

Insider's tips: Visit the Squaw Creek Visitor Center about 10 miles from the state park. The drive to the park is through some of the most fertile lands in the world. The park is next to the village of Big Lake and the area has all kinds of restaurants and shopping.

Notice the snake grass that looks like thousands of green pencils sprouting from the soil. Often these snake grass areas surround shady private picnic sites along the hard-surface park drive. While admiring the snake grass alcoves, watch for poison ivy that grows abundantly.

Amenities are nicely clustered. In 1989, the state purchased almost 300 acres of wetlands next to the lake. This nearly quadrupled the size of Big Lake State Park, and added a major wetland ecosystem to the park system. Big Lake State Park now contains the biggest single marsh in all of Missouri's state parks.

Knob Noster State Park has many classic park buildings, day-use amenities and other WPA-era structures.

CHAPTER 2
Knob Noster State Park
Land: 3,567 acres Water: Lakes

The scenic Clearfork Creek meanders through the center of the park and trees line its bank. Many of the trees are oaks, which produce acorns that offer food for the many turkeys that live in the area. Barred owls are often heard by campers. They are the only owls that have dark eyes.

Small lakes, a quiet campground and easy hiking trails make Knob Noster State Park a perfect family retreat. Equestrians and all-terrain bike riders will also enjoy the amenities and natural features of the unit.

Knob Noster State Park was opened 1946 and the town of Knob Noster was named in the 1850s for two hills, or knobs, that are northeast of town. "Noster" is the Latin word for "our." Today, our park has greatly healed from the farming, overgrazing and coal mining of 150 years ago. When the park was administered by the federal government, it was called Montserrat.

The restored tall prairies in the National Recreation Demonstration Area now offer food and habitat for large mammals including deer, grassland birds and insects.

Information and activities

Knob Noster State Park
873 SE 10
Knob Noster, MO 65336
(660) 563-2363
(877) I Camp Mo: Camp Reservations
www.mostateparks.com

Directions:

From the Kansas City Area

Knob Noster State Park is about 50 miles from the junction of U.S. Hwy. 50 and Hwy. 291 at Lee's Summit; the trip will take about one hour. Travel east on U.S. Hwy. 50 to the Hwy. 23/Knob Noster exit. Turn right/south onto Hwy. 23 and continue for about one mile before turning right at the main park entrance.

From Columbia

Knob Noster State Park is about 90 miles from Columbia; the trip will take 1.5 hours. Travel west on I-70 to Exit 78/U.S. Hwy. 65. Take U.S. Hwy. 65 south to U.S. Hwy. 50 in Sedalia; turn right/west onto U.S. Hwy. 50. Continue about 20 miles to the Hwy. 23/Knob Noster exit. Turn left/south onto Hwy. 23 and continue for about one mile before turning right at the main park entrance.

From Springfield

Knob Noster State Park is about 140 miles from Springfield; the trip will take about 2.5 hours. Travel north on U.S. Hwy. 65 to Sedalia. Turn left/west onto U.S. Hwy. 50 and continue about 20 miles to the Hwy. 23/Knob Noster exit. Turn left/south onto Hwy. 23 and continue for about one mile before turning right at the main park entrance.

Emergency numbers: 911- system; sheriff (660) 747-5511.
Campground: A heavy wood gate welcomes visitors to the meandering campground. The mostly wooded campground has a showerhouse that has a pay phone and laundry. Sites

The campground is mostly wooded and features a showerhouse, amphitheater and peace and quiet.

4-9 are near the showerhouse. Tent and RV campers use many of these sites. Site 18 is near a vault toilet and the Discovery Trailhead. Sites in the 20s are compact and get afternoon sunshine. Small oaks of about 12 inches in diameter offer shade throughout much of the campground. Sites in the 30s are on a rise and near a restroom and showerhouse. The amphitheater is near this area of the campground. Sites 31 and 33 are double sites that are great for two families who want to camp together.

Oaks shade most of the sites in the 30s. Sites on the outside of the loop are backed up against a wooded area. Site 48 has more sunshine than those in the low 40s and 30s. Site 52 is on a curve and sunny. Sites 57 and 58 are the most private and probably the best if tent camping. Both are tucked into the woods and set back from the road. Other sites that are large are in the low 60s. These sites are on a curve and backed up against the woods. These are also great sites for motor homes that need a little extra space for backing up.

Sites in the 60s and low 70s are sunny during the late morning and early evening. A basketball court is near the campground.

Equestrian campground: The horse camp is up a winding road and sites are shady. A small paddock and hitching posts are near camping sites that are equipped with picnic tables and fire rings. A vault toilet, frost-freeze hydrant and watering trough are also at the campground. Site E6 is an especially nice area under an oak with plenty of shade and a grassy area for your horse. There is plenty of room to maneuver your horse trailers.

Visitors center: Around the center are labeled trees. The brown clapboard building has offices and brochures, plus interpretive displays.

Hiking: The North Loop (2 miles) begins at the campground near the showerhouse. The trails leads hikers past a prairie management area before meandering to a moist bottomland. Wildlife sightings might include the Eastern bluebird, pileated woodpecker, turkeys and deer. Connector trails can also be taken. The Buteo Trail (1 miles) circles the lake and allows easy access to anglers. Freshwater jellyfish inhabit Buteo Lake. Some of this trail is on the park road.

The Hawk Nest Trail (1.75 miles) is in the open woodlands that are dominated by oak and hickory. Hawk Nest Trail shares parts of other trails. The Clearfork Trail (.5-mile) loops through a woodland management area.

The park has a seven-mile multi-use trail known as the McAdooTrail and is used by mountain bike riders too. The trail is 1.6 miles from the visitor center. The Opossum Trail (1.5 miles) has an incline and passes three small lakes and a dense forest.

Fishing: There are consumption guidelines for eating the fish taken in Lake Buteo. The floating vegetation in front of the dam gives up panfish during the evening. The shoreline access for families is excellent on the scenic little lake. Anglers may also slip a canoe into the retreat-like lake for better access; electric motors are allowed.

Nature: Park naturalists offer a number of interpretive programs that include bird study, mammal manias, natural hikes, evening programs, stealth flyers of Missouri, the art of nature, common wildflower and others. Tall grasslands are along the North Loop Trail where sensitive brier, black-eyed Susan and blazing star bloom. Wild turkeys, raccoon, deer and red fox live along the forest edges and grasslands.

A savanna (Clearfork Savanna Area) is an area that combines open park-like forest with prairie grasses and wildflowers. During pre-settlement times, Missouri was about one-third savanna. Today, controlled burns and selective timber removal are used to reduce encroachment of woody species and to stimulate native grass and plant growth. Seeding and transplanting also encourage the growth of prairie plants.

Wildflowers in the park include Dutchman's breeches, wild ginger, bloodroot, spring beauty, trillium and others.

Day-use areas: A Works Progress Administration (WPA) picnic shelter has plenty of space and is near the special-use campground. There is shoreline access to the lake, and picnic tables are scattered around the campground. A cove by Buteo Lake is one of the nicest places in the park.

Insider's tips: Knob Noster is a clean state park. Some of the WPA-built walls and small bridges are scenic. The park road is flat and an easy walk between amenities. Notice the land management that is happening within the park's boundaries. Lake Buteo has a great walking trail and fishing spots. Bristle Ridge Winery is between Warrensburg and Knob Noster. The stealth bomber calls the nearby Whiteman Air Force Base home. The park is within 30 miles of Katy Trail State park, and the State Fair Grounds in Sedalia.

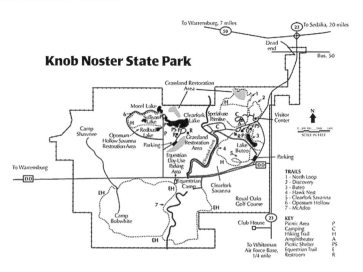

Knob Noster State Park

The park has 70 campsites. Nearby Lewis and Clark Village has a population of 142.

CHAPTER 3
Lewis and Clark State Park
Land: 189 acres   Water: Lewis and Clark Lake

"The object of our mission is to explore the Missouri River and such principal streams of it as by its coarse and communication with the waters of Pacific Ocean, may offer the most direct and practical communication across the continent for the purpose of commerce."
— **President Thomas Jefferson**

Lewis and Clark's expedition lasted 26 months. They spent 103 days in Missouri camping at 70 sites along the Missouri and Mississippi rivers. A readerboard at the park features photographs and details about the Louisiana Purchase, examples of hand-written journals and other information about the historic adventure.

Meriwether Lewis and William Clark, along with their expedition crew of more than 40 people, set out May 14,

1804, on their journey from the confluence of the Missouri and Mississippi rivers to discover what lie west.

The team followed the Missouri River to the northern Rocky Mountains, across the Continental Divide to the Pacific Ocean and back again. They kept detailed journals of their findings, including landscapes, flora, animals and native people. On their return, these journals provided settlers with knowledge of what awaited them and a thirst to explore the land themselves.

Lewis and Clark told of a wilderness containing dense forests, prairie openings and abundant wildlife such as whitetailed deer, beavers and buffalo. Today, this area is known as Missouri.

The team kept incredible notes and the Missouri River, the explorers' highway, was a featured topic of their writings. At the time, the river meandered freely across the landscape. In places, its course formed an almost complete loop and then cut across the neck of the loop to shorten itself. As the ends of the loop silted with sediment, an oxbow lake was formed. The journal entry for July 4, 1804 described such a lake. Lewis and Clark "saw great numbers of Goslings today which were nearly grown, the before mentioned lake is clear and contain great quantities of fish and Gees & Goslings. The great quantity of those fowl in this Lake induced me to Call it Gosling Lake." The lake that Clark described in that journal entry is in Buchanan County and is known today as Lewis and Clark Lake.

Lewis and Clark State Park is one of the smallest units in the system.

Information and activities

Lewis and Clark State Park
801 Lake Crest Blvd.
Rushville, MO 64484
(816) 579-5564
(877) I Camp Mo: Camp Reservations
www.mostateparks.com

Directions:

From St. Joseph

Lewis and Clark State Park is 18 miles from St. Joseph.

The trip will take 20 minutes. Take U.S. Hwy. 59 south to Hwy. 45. Go south on Hwy. 45 to Hwy. 138. Travel west on Hwy. 138 until you reach the state park.

From Kansas City

Lewis and Clark State Park is 58 miles from downtown Kansas City. The trip will take 1 hour, 15 minutes. Take I-29 north to Hwy. 92 (Platte City). Go west on Hwy. 92 through Platte City to Hwy. 45. Travel north on Hwy. 45 to Hwy. 138. Take Hwy. 138 west until you reach the state park.

Emergency numbers: Ambulance, (913) 367-2131; sheriff, 911.

Campground: Many of the 70 campsites have unique triangular-shaped shed-like structures that offer protection from the wind and a great place for the picnic table. The campground is flat and more sunny than shady. It also has broad mowed spaces and is available most summer weekends. These expansive mowed areas are great for walking and field games.

Site 1 is open and sunny with plenty of room around it. It is also near the mustard-colored showerhouse. A newspaper vending machine and laundry are at the showerhouse. Sites in the teens are all the same size and many are pull-through sites. Sites in the 20s have 12- to 14-inch trees that offer shade. Next to site 30 is a water bib.

Across from site 32 is a newer play structure with sand. A big maple tree shades site 40 and across from site 39 is a small swing set for kids. Sites in the high 30s have plenty of room around them, more room than most state park campground sites. They also get great midday shade. From some of the sites you can see residential houses. Sites in the high 60s are against a fence and the backyards of local residents. There is plenty of room to maneuver your big RV in virtually all areas of the campground. Grab a map and identify all of the pull-through sites. They are easy in and easy out.

Site 49 is near a water bib and vault toilet. Site 59 is a pullthrough, shaded by maples and near a farm field. Site 60 is also a pull-through and shaded by maples, but it does

The 365-acre oxbow lake is scenic and popular with paddlers and anglers.

receive some midday sun. Sites 61 and 62 are pull-through sites near the residential area.

Boating: Low water levels have reduced boating to canoes or car-top models. The tiny ramp is often closed due to low water levels.

Fishing: The park lies on the southeast corner of 365-acre Lewis and Clark Lake, commonly called Sugar Lake, which offers opportunities for fishing. The shallow areas of the lake make fertile grounds for bass, bluegill, channel catfish, carp, buffalo and other game and some nongame fish. The lake is also popular for canoeing, boating and water skiing.

Nature: Sugar Lake is an oxbow lake. Such geographic features are defined as "abandoned floodplain meanders," in this case the Missouri River. Without continual drainage, nature eventually fills lakes with silt. One hundred years ago the lake meandered over a wide valley and created vast wetlands. Constant riverbed erosion during flooding deepened the main channel, gradually isolating bends or oxbows. Eventually the oxbow lost all its flood-level contact with the river. Flood control in recent times has continued to isolate the lake.

Beach: The basic beach has coarse sand and is about 50 feet wide. It is lightly used, but there are picnic tables, parking, shade and pedestal grills.

Day-use areas: A playground is near the mustard-colored park office.

On shore, visitors can watch the many waterfowl that still

visit the park. Along with the "goslings" seen by Lewis and Clark, great blue herons, snowy egrets and many types of ducks make regular appearances. Nestled in the shade on the shoreline are numerous picnic tables with grills, making the park an excellent place to enjoy a picnic lunch. The Civilian Conservation Corps-built open picnic shelter, with electricity and a playground nearby, can be reserved for larger gatherings by calling the park office.

Insider's tips: The Lewis and Clark village has a population of 142 and is at the entrance to the campground. Because you can see from one end of the campground to the other, it is a safe-feeling area. The park operates a wood lot that sells firewood. One of the best views is from the CCC-built picnic shelter. This is one of the most mowed parks in the system.

Large cottonwoods and sycamore trees shade part of the campground.

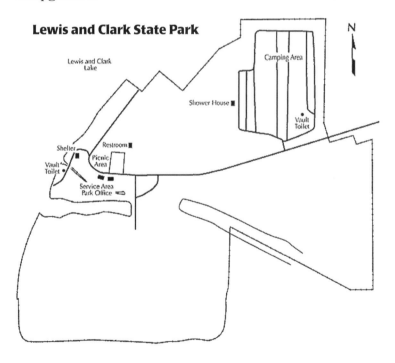

Lewis and Clark State Park

Wallace State Park was the second park opened by the state of Missouri. It has a peaceful, family-oriented campground.

CHAPTER 4
Wallace State Park
Land: 501 acres Water: Lake Allaman, ponds

According to the brochure, "The feature attraction at Wallace State Park is peace and quiet." I agree, and so will you.

Wallace State Park is a lovely oasis of natural lands preserved amid fertile farmlands that roll off to the horizon. The park is less than an hour from Kansas City and offers forested hills and more than a mile of Deer Creek valley. The unit is actually along the glaciated plains of northwest Missouri, but you might think you are in the Ozarks.

The hillsides in the park are cloaked with white, black and red oaks that shade a variety of habitats and offer a lovely canopy to walk beneath. Other tree types include hickory, black walnut and redbud. All of this diversity equals an interesting natural history and a chance to see wildlife while camping in a terrific area and quiet, clean park.

The park was purchased from the Wallace family in 1932 and became one of the first outdoor recreation areas in northwest Missouri. Before this time, the Mormons, led by Joseph Smith, briefly settled in the area before being chased west.

The Trice-Dedman Memorial Wood is owned by the Nature Conservancy about 20 miles southwest of the park. The area has some of the finest examples of hardwoods in the state. It's worth a day trip to see these sentinels.

Information and activities

Wallace State Park
10621 N.E. Highway 121
Cameron, MO 64429
(816) 632-3745
(877) I Camp Mo: Camp Reservations
www.mostateparks.com

When you visit the office, notice how the Wallace State Park sign is made in the shape of the state of Missouri.

Directions:

From Kansas City

Wallace State Park is about 50 miles from the Kansas/Missouri line. Travel north on I-35 to Exit 48. Make a right turn off the exit ramp onto Hwy. 69. Turn left at Hwy. 121 and continue into the state park. The park is about two miles from I-35.

From Des Moines, Iowa

Wallace State Park is 68 miles from the Iowa/Missouri line. Travel south on I-35 to Exit 48. Make a left turn off the exit ramp onto Hwy. 69. Turn left at Hwy. 121 and continue into the state park. The park is about two miles from I-35.

From St. Joseph

Wallace State Park is 36 miles from St. Joseph. Travel east on Hwy. 36 to I-35. Proceed south on I-35 to Exit 48. Make a left turn off the exit ramp onto Hwy. 69. Turn left at Hwy. 121 and continue into the state park. The park is about two miles from I-35.

Emergency number: 911 system.

Campground: The park's peaceful, family-oriented campgrounds include both basic and electric campsites - a variety of which are reservable. The campgrounds also offer modern restrooms, hot showers and a trailer dump station. Playground equipment is near Campground No. 2 and the travel camp. Walk-in campsites are available for those seeking more seclusion.

The drive to the campgrounds is often through a tunnel of trees along the rolling park roadway.

Campground No.1 is on a hilltop and sites are rustic and private. Often a wall of vegetation separates the sites. Some sites in this area have small fences outlining the site. Tent camping is best for this campground. Sites on the outside of the loop are against the woods. Site 12 is one of the more secluded sites in this tract. A number of the sites have roofed picnic tables. Sites 15 and 16 are also private at the end of the loop. The Lake Trail wanders between sites 16 and 17. Site 17 allows you to pitch your tent on a level spot with a view of a densely wooded ravine. A vault toilet is near site 23.

Site 25 is notched out of the woods, while site 27 is a larger site for multiple tents and across from the hose bib. Site 29 is especially private. The walk-in sites 33-36 require a short hike to your tent camping site. Site 35 is 750 feet from the parking place; site 36 is an 850-foot walk. A cement-block showerhouse and playground are near the parking area. Two-wheel carts are available for walk-in campers to haul their stuff to their sites.

A separate laundry with an outside sink serves campers in Campground No. 2. A horseshoe court, play equipment and an amphitheater are near the entrance to the campground. Site 41 is near the play equipment and generally speaking this area is more manicured than Campground No. 1. It also has less shade and privacy.

Site 44 is private and a short trailhead is near site 46. Sites on the interior of the loop are open and airy, while sites on the outside of the loop are near the natural areas. Site 48 is a tent-only site. Sites in the 50s are on a rise and are mostly shaded. Site 52 is a pull-through and an ash tree

Camping is a favorite activitiy at the park. So is swimming, hiking and picnics in the shelters that are scattered around the park.

shades site 54. Site 59 is also a pull-through and site 60 is sunny and open. Site 62 is a pull-through and close to the showerhouse.

Campground No. 3 is a small loop. Sites in this loop are about 50 percent shaded. Several huge oaks shade the small loop. Sites in the 70s are more open and about 70 percent sun. Sites 83 and 85 are pull-through sites, flat, level and big enough for the largest RVs. Private shady sites are 76, 78 and 80. Behind site 70 is a small playground. Site 70 has a little additional space for a family to use. Sites in the 70s on the outside of the loop and are against the natural areas. Site 75 is near the toilets. Site 79 is a terrific site, and near site 80 is the Skunk Hollow Trail. The lake and day-use area are about a half-mile from this part of the campground. A number of sites have roofed picnic tables.

A group camp is operated for organized groups of 40 to 50.

Youth groups can reserve the park's special-use area. It includes three areas for camping, all of which have a vault toilet, water spigot and fire ring. Each camping area can accommodate groups of 40 to 50. For more information or to make a reservation, please call the park office at (816)

632-3745.

Hiking: Deer Run Trail (3.5 miles) has several streams that run flush after rain. This area was probably a fjord on the Mormon trail. The streams are hard to cross at times. The trail starts at the southwest corner of the lake and takes you by a couple of small ponds, past labeled trees, over a wooden bridge and near wildlife - if you are quiet! The bridge is about two miles down the trail and a bench is three miles out.

Old Quarry Trail (1.25 miles) is a triangular route past Osage orange trees, through woods and fields and is generally easy and flat walking. An old limestone quarry is along the trail, but little is known about it. You may park outside the special-use area to access the trail.

Nature: Osage orange trees grow here. So do bladdernut trees. Spring wildflowers include trout lilies, May apples, touch-me-nots and Dutchman's breeches. Yellow ladies slipper, shooing star, prairie rose, wild geranium, purple trillium, spiderwort and others are also found in the park.

Five-lined skink, Eastern American toad, Southern leopard frog and Northern fence lizard are also found. The park publishes a bird checklist that details seasons and abundance of species.

Beach: The small beach is outlined by a split-rail fence and is about 40 yard wide. A picnic shelter is nearby. About 25 cars can park at the intimate beach that has a small playground and vault toilet. The picnic shelter at the beach can be rented. A dozen picnic tables are under the shelter. The views from the beach are of a hilly shoreline, dam and lots of Canadian geese that paddle around the cove.

Day-use areas: Volleyball and horseshoe equipment is available for checkout at the park office. The volleyball court is near the enclosed shelter and there are horseshoe pits at the campground amphitheater and both picnic shelters.

An amphitheater features a variety of nature programs including films, walks, crafts, games and talks. Nature programs are usually offered on Saturdays from Memorial Day to Labor Day. These programs are free and open to the public. Non-campers are invited to join the fun. Program schedules are normally posted in the park each week.

Insider's tips: You can hike along an old Mormon trail next to limestone shelves. Wallace State Park was the second park opened after Mark Twain State Park north of the Missouri River. The picnic shelter near the lake is scenic. The canopy of trees overhead makes for interesting evening walks along the park roads or paths.

There are lot of shoreline fishing access points at the park. The recycling containers are themselves recycled. They are made from old fuel oil tanks. Campground No. 1 is closest to the lake.

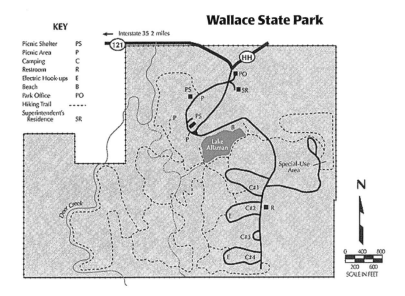

Wallace State Park

KEY

Picnic Shelter	PS
Picnic Area	P
Camping	C
Restroom	R
Electric Hook-ups	E
Beach	B
Park Office	PO
Hiking Trail	-----
Superintendent's Residence	SR

Interstate 35 2 miles

Lake Allaman

Special-Use Area

Deer Creek

N

0   400   800
200   600
SCALE IN FEET

Weston Bend State Park is a popular destination for educational day trips, camping and private picnic areas.

CHAPTER 5
Weston Bend State Park
Land: 1,133 acres Water: Missouri River

Flags flap in the breeze over the park's contact station as you drive up to the hilly park that is minutes from Kansas City and along the Missouri River. "Old Muddy" continues to be a gateway for trade and commerce, including some tobacco farming that is interpreted at the park. The park displays an old tobacco barn and reader boards that tell the story of local tobacco farming.

Weston Bend has a three-mile hard-surface trail that winds up and down the loess (pronounced "luss") Hills that dominate the terrain. The trail crosses the creek twice and the trailhead is a short walk from the campground, rest rooms and contact station.

The most recent native Americans to this area arrived about 1 A.D. Explorers and traders from France and Spain traveled the Missouri River, penetrating into this area about 1600. They probably traded with the Kansas and

Missourian Indians, but by 1798 the Missourians were so ravaged by warfare that they abandoned the area. On July 2, 1804, Lewis and Clark reached what is now the Winston vicinity. They recorded in their journal evidence of an old "Kansa" village. Two years later on their return, they encountered fur traders traveling on the Missouri River.

Weston was a tobacco town and the jumping-off point of the Oregon Trail. Steamboats also used the Missouri River to transport hemp and tobacco during the middle 1800s.

Information and activities

Weston Bend State Park
16600 Hwy. 45 N.
Weston, MO 64098
(816) 640-5443
(877) I Camp Mo: Camping Reservations
www.mostateparks.com

Directions: One mile south of Weston on Hwy 45 in Platte County.

From Kansas City/St. Joseph

Take I-29 to Exit 20 (Weston/Leavenworth and Atchison, Kan.). Take Hwy. 273 toward Weston. At the intersection of Hwy. 273 and Hwy. 45, turn south/left. The state park entrance is one-half mile on the right/west side.

Emergency number: 911 system.

Campground: The showerhouse has stainless steel sinks, showers, pay phones and a coin-operated laundry. Site 1 is Y-shaped and site 3 and others in this area are near the showerhouse in the rolling campground. Site 4 is generally shady, but does get some midday sunshine. Sites 5-11 are open and sunny with hard-surface pads. Site 11 is a pull-through. Sites in the teens are relatively open and popular with larger RVs. The park road is wide and forgiving.

Sites in the low 20s are sunny, with site 25 against a wooded area. Site 26 is an ideal tent site that is under a canopy of trees and more secluded than most. It is also near a vault toilet with a corrugated steel roof. Up the hill are the sites in the high 20s, where you are greeted by several mature trees. Site 27 is flat and perfect for a medium-size RV. Site 28 is a pull-through and there is room for an additional tent under one of the big trees that shade the site. Sites 30 and 32 are against a wooded area and are also great for tent camping. All of the sites in the 30s are about 50 percent shady. Sites 35 and 36 are sunny, wide and great for two families who want to camp next to each other. Site 37 gets plenty of midday sun. Sites 27 - 37 offer 50 amp electric service.

A pet walking area is across from the showerhouse. It would be great if other parks developed a pet walking area like Weston Bend. The campground has a good mix of cozy, secluded tent sites and places for the big rigs.

Tobacco barn: The old tobacco barn is near the park office. A corner of the barn is open to viewing and you can look up and see the filtered light pouring through the clapboards and imagine what life was like for the tobacco farmer 150 years ago.

Tobacco is deeply rooted in the history of the New World. Christopher Columbus found native humans smoking before the close of the 15th century. During this time, people also ate tobacco.

Smoking was the preferred use by native Americans, usually as part of a ceremonial rite. These natives also sniffed and chewed the plant. All of these habits Europeans quickly adopted. Once tried, the use of tobacco spread rapidly and better-tasting varieties were developed from South American species. These crops were first planted in 1612 in Virginia. For many early American towns, tobacco was a salvation that spread westward.

Puritans called tobacco "devil weed" and lobbied for its demise. American Indians were the first to use snuff in the late 18th century, and the French elevated the practice to high fashion. During the 16th century, chew was commonplace in the United States. Europeans labeled the country, "Land of the moving jaw." An English visitor cautiously suggested that the spittoon replace the eagle as the American symbol.

Chewing tobacco was "cased" or soaked in a sauce of alcohol, molasses and licorice. These formulas were often

The old tobacco barn has intrepretive signs. Puritans called tobacco the "devil weed."

"secret" and carefully guarded by their manufacturers. This natural taste was sweetened, which stimulated the salivary glands. One brand's colorful advertisement claimed you could "get one thousand spits to the chew." Near the end of the Civil War, a new product called "burley" tobacco became popular. Its leaves soaked up flavors and thrived in the Midwest. Within a decade, manufacturers were locked in a competitive struggle with their burley western rivals.

Missouri was the nation's leading producer of chew (or plug) tobacco and was the scene of a frenzy of competition among plug makers. Hundreds of brands appeared with names like "Battle Axe," "Wiggletail Twist," "Honeydew Hardpan" and "Mule Ear." Tobacco chewers spat frequently at cuspidors, spittoons, fireplaces, stove grates and sandboxes that were placed near doorways.

Hiking: The hard-surface trail is a three-mile-long loop that winds up and down the loess hills, which dominate Weston Bend State Park. The trail crosses a creek twice and intersects with Harpst Valley at the yellow bench, and the west ridge section of Harpst Trail at the white bench. Stenciled on the trail are mile markers to assist walkers wishing to increase their distance and time. Hikers may walk in either direction. Bicyclists must keep to the right.

Campground Trail is a one-half-mile loop between the campground and the office. It offers hikers a glimpse of the warehouses at the distillery. This trail also surrounds a favorite bedding spot for some of the wildlife of the park.

North Ridge Trail is a two-mile trail (one up/one down) that follows the circa 1900 roadbed that once led from the farm (where you park to access the trail) to the barn and eventually Weston. The trail now takes you to the top of the loess bluffs offering a panoramic view of the Weston bend in the Missouri River. A French Canadian named Pensineau operated his circa 1830s trading house in this area.

The Weston Bluffs Trail is a three-mile hiking and biking trail that formerly was a gravel road. The trail runs adjacent to the river from Weston to Beverly. This trail is a cooperative effort between Platte County Parks and Recreation, the City of Weston and the Department of Natural Resources.

Missouri River Trail is a one-half-mile trail that takes hikers directly to the edge of the Missouri River.

Bear Creek Trail is a one-half-mile trail that takes hikers to what was the pre-1858 channel of the Missouri River. Sloughing of the bank changes the view and direction this trail meanders as it follows the creek to the Missouri River.

Those following the Lewis and Clark Trail (July 1804), will have the opportunity to gain first-hand knowledge of the "mud, muck, mire and mosquitoes" that the Corps of Discovery experienced as you walk along Bear Creek Trail.

Harpst Trail consists of two distinct routes: Harpst Valley and the West Ridge section.

Harpst Valley (1 mile) begins on the ridge to the left of the overlook path. The trail follows along the loess Missouri River bluffs until it reaches the manmade pass that once connected the internationally famous Harpst Orchards (circa 1900) to a farm between the bluffs and the Missouri River. The valley once housed the orchards' large warehouse. Newspaper articles of the period note that peaches grown here were exported to English royalty.

The West Ridge loop (2.5 miles) continues straight (south) past Harpst Valley and wanders through the forested bluff, paralleling the remnants of an old road that once led to a homestead. Once hikers begin their descent, they enter the Bee Creek bottoms. In the late 1850s, Potawatomis were encamped here during a forced relocation. Hikers will find maples and wild raspberries along the trail.

Nature: The pothole-like wetlands are great places for birding and wildlife observation.

Day-use areas: The park features lots of secluded picnicking sites. A former tobacco-drying shed was converted to a picnic shelter. Some picnic tables are also scattered under walnut and other species of trees. Another tobacco barn has been converted to an enclosed shelter near Bee Creek on the south end of the park.

The Missouri River overlook has parking for about 10 cars where a hard-surface walkway takes you to a vista that Lewis and Clark might have experienced. The wide views include the brown river, thick woods, steep hills and low bluffs.

Insider's tips: There are some steep inclines and the campground is hilly. Tobacco production in Missouri is now about three million pounds, or 13th in production in the United States. Sometimes you might see a train running along the Missouri River from the overlook. The park is very quiet during the week.

Visit historic Weston (population 1,600) and the Lewis and Clark Festival. Did you know that for many years Missouri was the largest state in the Union? Loess is fine-grained soil. Some of the state's best fall color is found at Weston Bend State Park.

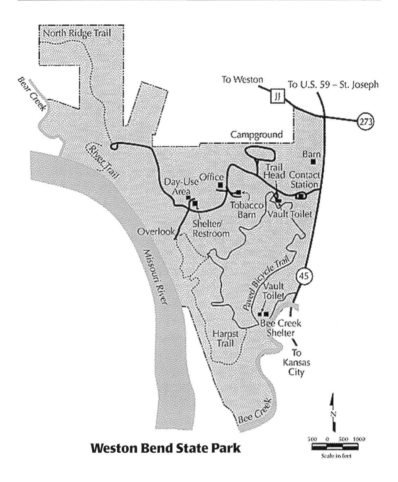

Weston Bend State Park

MISSOURI
State Parks

CHAPTER 6

Watkins Woolen Mill State Park and State Historic Site

Land: 1,442 acres Water: Williams Creek Lake

The park is both a terrific natural area with fishing and camping, trails and swimming and a place of fascinating historic significance. Visitors may tour a huge 1800s mill, museum, Watkins House and other amenities.

Waltus L. Watkins, like most farmers of his day, practiced diversified farming and built diverse businesses. He raised shorthorn cattle, mules, horses, swine, sheep and poultry, grew various grain crops, and planted extensive orchards. He also marketed the services of his mills, kiln and blacksmith shop to people in the region. When the woolen industry reached Missouri in the 1850s, Watkins decided to take advantage of his early training in Kentucky textile mills and in 1860 constructed the Watkins Woolen Mill. Park visitors will learn a lot about Watkins' work and historic business endeavors via the museum and tours of the mill and other sites.

The million-dollar visitor center is accessible and includes restrooms, a souvenir sales counter and a beverage vending machine. In addition, the museum includes climate-controlled storage facilities for the historic site's archives and artifact collections, and a conservation and exhibit work area. There is a small fee to visit and for various tours.

Guided tours are available of the large Watkins Woolen Mill and the Watkins family home. The mill is a National Historic Landmark and is the only 19th-century textile mill in the country with its original machinery intact. The visitor center offers an introduction to the Watkins family and their many business ventures.

During the summer (May through August), the historic site's Living History Farm Program offers visitors a glimpse into the life of a family in the 1870s. Costumed staff and volunteers give demonstrations on cooking, gardening and other period activities.

From April 16 through Oct. 15, the visitor center is open from 9:30 a.m. to 5 p.m. Monday through Saturday and 10:30 a.m. to 6 p.m. on Sunday. From Oct. 16 through April 15, the visitor center is open from 9:30 a.m. to 4:30 p.m. Monday through Saturday and 10:30 a.m. to 4:30 p.m. on Sunday.

Guided tours start on the hour. Visitors must be with a tour guide to enter the woolen mill and house.

Information and activities

**Watkins Woolen Mill State Park and State Historic Site
26600 Park Road North
Lawson, MO 64062
(816) 580-3387
Camping reservations: (877) I Camp Mo**
www.mostateparks.com

Directions:

From Kansas City

From I-70, take Exit 8 north to I-435 northbound. Travel on I-435 north for 11 miles until it merges into northbound I-35. Continue north on I-35 for 15 miles, exiting at Kearney

(Exit 26). Turn right onto eastbound Hwy. 92 and continue east for five miles, then turn left (north) onto Route RA. The park entrance is on the right off of Route RA.

From St. Joseph

Take U.S. Hwy. 36 east for 27 miles to Cameron. From there, take I-35 south for 28 miles, exiting at Kearney (Exit 26). Turn left onto eastbound Hwy. 92 and continue east for five miles, then turn left (north) onto Route RA. The park entrance is on the right off of Route RA.

Watkins Woolen Mill: In 1870, there were more than 2,400 small woolen mills in America. They operated in every state. Today, Watkins Mill is the only one remaining with its original machinery still in place.

The mill was constructed of bricks made at the site and timbers cut from Watkins' land. The mill contains more than 50 major textile machines, which were shipped by railroad from the east. The steam engine and the 30-foot riverboat boiler that powered it were shipped by steamboat from St. Louis. The mill opened in 1860.

During the Civil War, Watkins sold lots of woolen cloth, but raids by bushwhackers in 1864 forced him to temporarily close the factory and the grist mill.

More than 40 mill workers processed 40,000 to 60,000 pounds of wool into fabrics, blankets, shawls, knitting yarns and batting each year. In the mid-1880s, the woolen industry began to decline in the state. The Watkins family cut back on production and eventually closed the mill in 1898. Unlike the hundreds of other woolen mills closing throughout North America, the Watkins mill was not scrapped out or converted to serve a different business.

The grist mill was built in 1849 and was moved inside the factory building sometime in the 1860s. An Oliver Evans-type mill with two sets of French buhr stones, it produced flour and corn meal sold in stores, and also did custom grain grinding for local farmers until 1905.

Watkins House: Watkins started his farm in 1839 and built a small two-room log cabin for his young family. In 1850, he began construction of a large brick home. It took four years to complete the 2.5-story Classic Revival home. The house has a parlor, the family reading room, a dining room, eight bedrooms, an inside winter kitchen and four food storage rooms in the basement, as well as an outside summer kitchen. The basement also housed the farm dairy, where butter and cheese were produced.

The big house was a busy place. Waltus and Mary Ann Watkins raised nine children and two foster children while operating several businesses. His mother and one of his sisters lived with them, and seven or eight of the farm and mill hands boarded with the family. Visiting friends and relatives were a constant part of the household as well. The family routinely fed 20 people and up to 50 hungry workers during planting and harvesting.

Heirloom gardens: The park grows vegetables, fruit, herbs and flowers that were available before 1880. Planted in a combination of raised beds and open plots of vegetables surrounded by herb and flower borders, the garden is based on descriptions of the Watkins garden and gardening practices in use in Clay County during the 1870s.

Many of the world's food plants are disappearing, including vegetables, grains and fruit varieties. Some 70 percent of the world's major food plants have already been lost and this is a small effort to education us about heirloom types of edible plants.

Because we demand high yields and uniform plant production today, the genetic base of the world's food plants has been reduced in the name of progress. This has created reliable crops but has left agriculture dependent on a few, closely related varieties of each crop. When a blight or disease gets into one of these crops, it can spread rapidly, causing widespread crop failure. One of the best known is the blight-induced failure of the Irish potato crop in the 1840s. The result was the Great Famine, during which almost two million people starved to death.

Camping: Watkins has 96 campsites, 74 with electric hookups. Each site has a graveled parking pad, picnic table, grill and lantern hook. Parking pads vary in length from 38 feet to 80 feet, with the electric sites having the longer pads.

Five sites, three electric and two basic, are accessible for campers with disabilities. Four of these campsites are reservable.

Two showerhouses, a coin-operated laundry and a sanitary dumping station are available for registered campers. These facilities, along with the water, are not available during the off-season.

A woodlot is open in the evening for campers to purchase wood. During the off-season, the fee collector will sell wood upon request.

Campsites 35 to 97 are closed November through March.

A primitive camping area is available for organized youth groups. The area is divided into five sections, each with a picnic table and fire ring. The area has a vault toilet but no water. There is direct access to the bike trail. Groups interested in reserving a campsite in the special-use area should call (816) 580-3387.

Fishing: Catfish, bass, crappie and sunfish are abundant in Williams Creek Lake. Boat motors used on the 100-acre lake are restricted to 10 horsepower or less, and there is a small launch at the lake. An accessible fishing dock is near the western end of the dam. A permit must be obtained at the office for night fishing.

Rare farm livestock exhibit: Commercial breeders raise a limited variety of livestock that work best for market demands and are easy to raise. Modern breeds are bred to be uniform and to produce large, consistent offspring, but they are often more expensive to feed, house and care for than rare breeds are.

As older breed lines decline, many good characteristics are being lost forever. Many of these characteristics, such as parasite resistance, would benefit today's commercial herds and flocks. Pure flocks of minor breeds are necessary to preserve a source of desirable traits and to maintain hybrid vigor in more popular breeds. They also provide products that fulfill the needs of small markets, such as hand weavers or health advocates who want low-fat meat. The park maintains a small flock with the help of the American Minor Breeds Association.

Beach: The sandy beach is at the north end of the lake close to the picnic areas. The beach is open 10 a.m. to sunset, Memorial Day weekend to Labor Day. A change house is at the beach.

Trails: The 3.8-mile hard-surface bicycling and walking trail traces the shoreline of the 100-acre lake. The circular trail is accessed at several points along the west side of the lake, and from the northern picnic area.

The 3.5-mile horse trail is accessed from Endsley or Baxter roads on the east side of the park. Horse trailer parking is at the trailhead near the special-use area on Endsley Road. Horses are restricted to the horse trail and may not be ridden in other areas of the facility. Bicycles are not permitted on the horse trail.

Day-use areas: The park has three picnic areas, with tables and grills. Additional picnic tables and grills are along the bike trail near the beach and the shelter house. The north picnic area connects directly to the bike trail. An open shelter is available and may be reserved by calling (816) 580-3387.

Insider's tips: Mt. Vernon Church, built in 1871, may be reserved for weddings. The church has been restored and includes the original pews and pulpit. For information on reserving the church and associated fees, contact the office at (816) 580-338. The history is fun, but the most popular part of the park is the bike path.

Watkins Woolen Mill State Park and Historic site

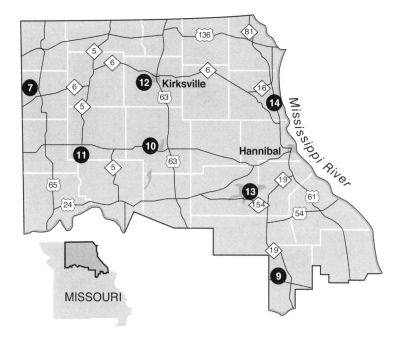

Northeast Region

7. Crowder State Park
8. Cuivre River State Park
9. Graham Cave State Park
10. Long Branch State Park
11. Pershing State Park
12. Thousand Hills State Park
13. Mark Twain State Park
14. Wakonda State Park

Crowder State Park beach.

CHAPTER 7

Crowder State Park
Land: 1,912 acres   Water: Crowder Lake, 18 acres; Thompson River

Although surrounded by lush, flat farm fields, the park is rolling with occasional steep valleys and it is loaded with an interesting history. Crowder State Park is a commemorative park dedicated to the memory of Maj. Gen. Enoch H. Crowder, one of several American military leaders who were raised in the hills of northern Missouri.

Enoch was born in poverty before the Civil War in Grundy County five miles west of Trenton, and is best remembered as the "father of the selective service," known today as the military draft. As judge advocate general, Crowder wrote the Selective Service Act of 1917 along with other legislation during his 50 years of public service. He also was a stern military man who helped control and capture Geronimo's Apaches in the 1880s. He also was indirectly involved in the arrest and death of Sitting Bull a few years later.

General Crowder didn't stop with these exploits. He was the chief military officer in the Philippines. Crowder College and Crowder Hall on the campus of the University of Missouri are named for the brash General. Enoch was a West Point graduate and had a law degree from the University of Missouri. He was also a professor of military tactics. He died in 1932.

Crowder was the first in his West Point class to reach the rank of general, and during World War I, he was the United States' first ambassador to Cuba.

Information and activities

Crowder State Park
76 N.W. Hwy. 128
Trenton, MO 64683
(660) 359-6473(877) I Camp Mo: Camp Reservations
www.mostateparks.com

Directions: Four miles west of Trenton on Hwy 146 in Grundy County.

From Kansas City

Take I-35 north about 57 miles to Exit 61. Travel east on Hwy. 69/6. Turn north/left onto Hwy. 146, about two miles west of Trenton. Follow Hwy. 146 about one mile, then turn right onto Hwy. 128 to enter the state park.

From St. Joseph

Take Hwy. 6 east to Hwy. 146, about two miles west of Trenton. Turn north/left onto Hwy. 146 and continue for one mile to Hwy. 128. Hwy. 128 will take you into the state park.

From Kirksville

Take Hwy. 6 west through the town of Trenton. About two miles west of Trenton, turn north/right onto Hwy. 146 (the first blacktop road) and continue for one mile to Hwy. 128. Hwy. 128 will take you into the state park.

From Des Moines, Iowa

Take I-35 south to Exit 84 for Route H. Travel east on Route H to Hwy. 146. Turn right/south onto Hwy. 146, which takes a sharp left at Gilman City shortly after the

No motors are allowed on Crowder Lake. It's a very peaceful lake that has good fishing and shoreline access.

intersection with Route H. Continue on Hwy. 146 until reaching Hwy. 128. Turn left/north onto Hwy. 128 to enter the state park.

From Marshall/Princeton

From either location, take U.S. Hwy. 65 to Trenton. Turn west onto Hwy. 6. About two miles west of Trenton, turn right/north onto Hwy. 146 and continue for one mile to Hwy. 128. Hwy. 128 will take you into the state park..

Emergency numbers: Ambulance, (660) 359-4357; sheriff, (660) 359-2828; 911.

Campground: Day-use Shelter No. 3 is near the entrance to the campground and shaded by a giant oak. A tiny bridge over a boulder-strewn creek greets campground visitors. Towering sycamores and oaks also greet campers in the gently rolling campground that has 42 sites with 32 of them offering electrical hookups. The campground is about 75 percent shady.

A newer showerhouse is at the beginning of the concentric loops that make up the campground. Sites often are available, even on summer weekends. Check out the tube-like skylights in the rest rooms. The modern building is clean and attractive.

Site 3 is near a hose bib and evergreens offer shade for sites in this part of the loop. Site 9 is a small pull-through. All of the sites in loop 1-11 are close to the showerhouse. Site 12 is a pull-through and shaded by cedars. Site 13 is sunny part of the day and ideal for a large RV rig. Site 18 is a pull-through and ideal for a medium-sized RV rig. It is also next to a small grassy area that's perfect for a family with small children. Electric site 19 is probably the best tent site in the park.

The other loop offers pull-throughs at sites 18, 19, 20, 31, 34 and 42. Site 26 is good for a big RV unit. Site 33 has a wonderful cedar and privacy because it is notched out of the dense woods. Site 37 is a great site for a medium-sized RV rig. Sites 28 and 29 are close to each other but on different elevations. Site 32 is sunny and across from pull-through site 31 and near the playground equipment. Site 42 is near the vault toilet.

Camp Grand River is a group camping area available to nonprofit organizations. It has six sleeping cabins, a dining lodge with kitchen, a recreation hall and outdoor recreational facilities, including a play court and swimming beach. Organizations that want to book the area must apply 11 months before the first day of camp. For application information, please call (660) 359-6473.

Beach: The small sand beach is outlined by some yellow and white floating tubes. The views of the beach are classic. A dam and wooded shoreline are in the distance. There is an outdoor shower at the tan-colored changing house at the beach on Lake Crowder. Two benches are above the beach for parents to rest while the kids swim and play near the water. The River Forks Trail (2 miles) is accessible and tracks along the lake and east near to the confluence of the Thompson and Weldon rivers.

Fishing: Crowder Lake offers great fishing opportunities. The small lake offers channel catfish, largemouth bass, crappie and bluegill during park hours. No motors are allowed on the lake. A number of cozy coves are accessible for shoreline fishing. In fact, lake access is good in many locations. Many anglers fish from the low earthen dam. It's

The campground has 42 sites, showerhouse, playground and shelters.

a great place to fly fish from because there is plenty of room for back casting. Try some poppers in the spring for panfish. There are also some overhangs and weed beds that pan fishermen should try. Local anglers report that live bait in the evening is the best technique in the small lake.

Hiking: Hikers and all-terrain bikers can explore nearly 15 miles of trails. The Red Bud Trail is not open to bike riders. Trails can be muddy after it rains.

The Thompson River Trail has a steep climb, while Tall Oaks Trail (4 miles) is the most difficult in the park. It's also fun! Most of the Tall Oaks Trail is on a single track, with one mile on an old roadbed that passes a hay field, tall oaks (of course!) and along a streambed. At the southern end of the trail are some tight turns if you are riding a mountain bike. The trail ends at the lake. Look for lightning damaged and twisted trees along this popular trail.

The River Forks Trail (2.5 miles) starts at the beach and is a wide dirt path lined with maples, walnuts and other hardwoods. The trees offer a towering canopy over the trail that offers river views, a tiny stream and Kentucky coffee trees about a half-mile out.

Day-use area: An enclosed shelter overlooking Crowder Lake is perfect for large family gatherings, reunions or receptions. Shelter occupancy is about 60 guests. The shelter is fully furnished and equipped with a restroom, sink, stove, refrigerator, heater and fireplace. The shelter is available April through October and reservations can be made up to nine months in advance.

Shelter No. 2 is on a knoll above the lake.

Insider's tips: A fenced tennis court is part of the day-use area. Even the playground has a lake view. Coffee trees and ostrich ferns grow at Crowder State Park. The park has a newer showerhouse and modern playground. It also has some great sycamore trees and small creeks that run flush after rains. Green frogs are commonly heard at night. They sound like you are running your thumb over the teeth of a comb.

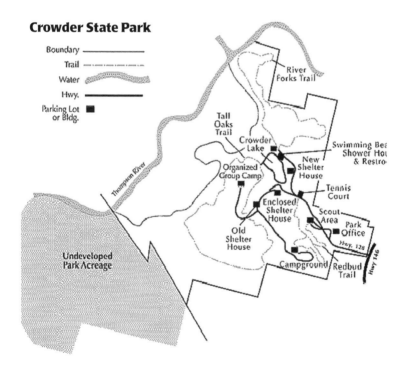

Crowder State Park

Boundary
Trail
Water
Hwy.
Parking Lot or Bldg.

River Forks Trail

Tall Oaks Trail

Crowder Lake

Swimming Bea Shower Hou & Restro

Organized Group Camp

New Shelter House

Tennis Court

Thompson River

Enclosed Shelter House

Scout Area

Park Office

Old Shelter House

Hwy. 128

Hwy. 146

Undeveloped Park Acreage

Campground

Redbud Trail

Cuivre River State Park Visitor Center.

CHAPTER 8
Cuivre River State Park
Land: 6,394 acres   Water: Big Sugar Creek

A tunnel of trees, buckled landscape and arched stone bridges are along the way to a 60-mile stretch of uplifted bedrock known as Lincoln Hills. The striking topography has rich limestone glades, upland sinkhole ponds and glacial erratics. This area somehow missed the leveling effect of the last glacier, leaving flora and fauna that are normally found in the smooth plains of Missouri.

The gravel-bottomed clear Big Sugar Creek, a tributary of the Cuirve (pronounced "quiver") River, carves through the valley of limestone that was once an ancient seabed and home to millions of animals of the Mississippian-age. The bedrock formed more than 300 million years ago offers numerous scenic outlooks.

A special feature of the park is the two wild areas that are being carefully protected. The Big Sugar Creek Wild Area is 1,675 acres where the creek sculpted the rugged area over the eons. The creek carved limestone into jagged forested watersheds. Bluffs along portions of the creek are sharp and a number of limestone glades are on the blufftops. These glades are dry and almost desert-like.

Also in the wild areas are sinkholes and springs. This karst topography is the result of water that has percolated through the underlying limestone bedrock, dissolving and carrying away subterranean rock. This karst topography is common in southern Missouri, but also seen here at Cuivre River State Park. Due to all of this diversity, the park has 760 species of plants (650 are native). At least 150 species of birds have been identified, 54 types of fish, 18 amphibians, 27 reptiles and 28 mammal species.

Information and activities

Cuivre River became a state park in 1946.
Cuivre River State Park
678 Hwy. 147
Troy, MO 63379
(636) 528-7247
(877) I Camp Mo; Camping Reservations
www.mostateparks.com

Directions: 3 miles east of Troy on Hwy. 47 in Lincoln County.

From St. Louis

Travel west on I-70 or U.S. Hwy. 40 to Exit 210/Wentzville. Take U.S. Hwy. 61 north for 14 miles to Troy. Travel east on Hwy. 47 for 2.8 miles to Hwy. 147, which is the main entrance to the state park.

From Jefferson City

Travel east on I-70 to Exit 210/Wentzville. Take U.S. Hwy. 61 north for 14 miles to Troy. Travel east on Hwy. 47 for 2.8 miles to Hwy. 147, which is the main entrance to the state park.

From Springfield/Rolla

Travel east on I-44 to Exit 276/St. Louis. Take I-270 north for 6.6 miles to U.S. Hwy. 40. Travel west on U.S. Hwy. 40 to Exit 210/Wentzville. Take U.S. Hwy. 61 for 14 miles to Troy, then go east on Hwy. 47 for 2.8 miles to Hwy. 147, which is the main entrance to the state park.

Emergency numbers: 911 system. Ambulance, (636) 528-8488; sheriff, (636) 528-5846.

Visitors center/park office: The brown clapboard building has a shake roof and a broad porch with a flag that flaps in a whisper of wind. A sizable bulletin board outside the twin doors of the center has plenty of information about the park.

Inside are animal mounts that include a turkey, whitetail deer and small birds. There also are fossil displays, interpretive signs, diorama and a pool table-size relief map of the park.

Camping: The park's three organized group camps are large and popular. Generations of eastern Missouri school children have stayed here and learned about the area's natural history.

Red and bright-yellow play equipment is near the campground entrance. It has four swings and is near the campground host.

The campground is about 75 percent shade. A tent-only special-use camp is also in the neatly maintained tract with a gray bathhouse. A water bib is near site 7 and convenient to the bathhouse. Site 8 looks down a wooded valley and it's a pull-through. Site 10 is ideal for a small pop-up camper and all of the sites have ground-mounted fire rings and picnic tables. Site 11 is a pull-through. Sites on the inside of this oblong loop are less shaded and best used by small- to medium-size rigs. Site 14 at the end of this small loop is private and shaded by a cedar and elm. It gets midday sun and has a mature sumac on the site. Site 15 also gets midday sunshine and is perfect for a medium-size RV unit. Site 19 is a pull-through and near the vault toilet house. Sites 23 and 24 are pop-up sites. Extra parking is near site 38.

Site 41 is a nice tent site against the woods. It's also a pull-through and a small RV unit could use the pad. Sites in the 50s are best for pop-up campers. All of these sites are well shaded and hose bibs are at regular intervals. Sites in the high 40s have a great view of a wooded valley and side slopes. Some of the sites have stones around the fire rings.

Shoreline angling at its best. Try your luck near the boat ramp.

Maples also grace the area around sites in the high 40s. I like this area. Several trees offer places where tents can be carefully pitched.

Sites in the high 20s and 30s are often big, near the vault toilet and private. This tiny loop has a distant water view and plenty of woods surrounding them. Sites 30 and 31 are family sites. Sites 33 and 34 are close to the vault toilets and shady. Sites in the 60s are near the bathhouse and pay phone.

Full hookup sites (sites 69-100) are near the firewood lot and the old white water tower. These sites are more open, with cedars offering some shade. The pads are gravel and motor homes and bigger trailers tend to stay in this section. All of the sites are the same size and a vault toilet is near sites 89 and 95. The Blazing Star Trail (2 miles) is accessible at the end of the popular RV loop. Near this trailhead is a small grassy open space for field games.

Hiking: Trailheads have parking and there are about 38 miles of trails on nine routes. Trails are from one to eight miles in length. The Lakeside Trail is the easiest and starts from the beach or boat ramp and is a cool trail along the lakeshore. Turkey Hollow Trail (1 mile) is also easy. On the Cuivre River Trail (7 miles) you'll proceed along the Goedde Creek and ascend the Frenchmen's Bluff. Several trails are shared with equestrians.

The 6-mile Long Spring Trail has a couple of rugged areas that pass moist seeps and rocky ledges. RV campers should try the Mossy Hill Trail (1 mile) that starts in the campground.

Beach: The scenic beach is on Beach Loop Road. That shouldn't be a surprise. The small 40-yard-wide beach is at the end of the lake with brown coarse sand. The nearest phone is at the campground entrance. Vault toilets and parking for about 40 cars are outlined by a split-rail fence. The view from the beach is outstanding and features large trees, rolling hillside and sparkling waters. A yellow rope marks off the designated swimming area.

Fishing: Pole and line fishing only are allowed. Shoreline angling near the boat ramp and through the park is safe and has easy access. Panfish and largemouth bass are taken from the lake.

Boating: The small two-lane boat ramp has parking for about a dozen cars. A vault toilet is at the ramp. Electric motors only are allowed.

Nature: As mentioned, the Cuivre River has a unique set of flora and fauna due to the way the land was formed. Some of the wildlife here is rarely seen in the northern plains of Missouri. Ozark-like species include certain salamanders. Part of the natural areas have been protected, fostered and developed since the Missouri Wild Area System was established in 1978. It was modeled after the National Wilderness Preservation System that has been a boon for backpackers, environmental education, science and the ultimate safekeeping of the nation's remaining wild areas.

Most of the wild areas possess many of the characteristics of the Ozarks, including clear running streams and seeps. Forests on the side slopes are white oak canopy where deer, turkey are often seen or heard.

Day-use areas: Shady picnic tables, including some within a half-mile of the visitor center, are scattered around the park. The Civilian Conservation Corps constructed many of the pleasing timber and stone buildings in the 1930s. The mowed open spaces along the park road offer four places to picnic.

Insider's tips: Some of the turnouts have a single private picnic table with great views. There are steep grades, and amenities are spread out over the big park. Watch for old CCC-era stone walls scattered throughout the park. Interestingly shaped trees (mostly oaks) dot the property and outline vistas and deep ravines.

The park has lots of Jack-in-the pulpits along the low hillsides and between the cascading rocks. In 1997 the Missouri state parks were voted the fourth best system in the United States by the National Sporting Goods Association.

The Cuivre River is one of the more wooded parks in the system. The park also has some upland grassy areas. Many of these grasslands are under restoration.The park is also spread out, so bring your bikes. Consider it a quiet retreat, yet the park is fairly close to St. Louis. The campground is a long way from the beach and there are a lot of deer in this unit. In the 1930s a skeleton and pot chards were found on the property. Archaeologists believe people lived in the area 12,000 years ago.

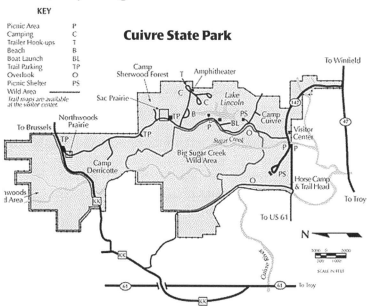

KEY

Picnic Area	P
Camping	C
Trailer Hook-ups	T
Beach	B
Boat Launch	BL
Trail Parking	TP
Overlook	O
Picnic Shelter	PS
Wild Area	

Trail maps are available at the visitor center.

Cuivre State Park

Graham Cave is about 120-feet wide and extends 100-feet into the hill.

CHAPTER 9
Graham Cave State Park
Land: 359 acres   Water: Loutre River

Tucked in the side slopes above the Loutre River is Graham Cave State Park. It features a sandstone cave that contains evidence that past cultures hunted in the area. Once used for shelter (and a pig house), Graham Cave became historically significant when archaeologists discovered how long ago human occupation had occurred. The rainbow-shaped cave seems to wink at you when you approach it from the grassy knoll, and information reader boards are at the entrance detailing archaeological techniques and important discoveries. You'll see the archaeological stakes and grids system that scientists used to carefully record artifacts they excavated.

Notice the smoke that has discolored the cave roof. Staff says that if you stood on top of the cave before the trees grew up, you could see the Graham house in the distance and Picnic Rock. The viewing of the cave is self-guided.

Missouri has about 5,000 caves. Most were formed when soft rock weathered away, leaving more resistant layers of sandstone. Graham Cave is shallow and virtually on the surface. Plus, the short hike to it is terrific. The cave was the first site in the United States to be designated a National Historic Landmark.

Information and activities

Graham Cave State Park
217 Highway TT
Montgomery City, MO 63361
(573) 564-3476
(877) I Camp Mo; Camping Reservations
www.mostateparks.com

Directions:

From St. Charles

Graham Cave State Park is 54 miles west of St. Charles. Allow one hour for the trip. Travel west on I-70 to Exit 170 (Danville/Montgomery City). Turn right, then turn immediately left onto Hwy. TT (North Outer Road). Continue on Hwy. TT for two miles; it ends in the state park.

From Kansas City

Graham Cave State Park is 162 miles east of Kansas City. Allow three hours for the trip. Travel east on I-70 to Exit 170 (Danville/Montgomery City). Turn left, then make another immediate left onto Hwy. TT (North Outer Road). Continue on Hwy. TT for two miles; it ends in the state park.

From Jefferson City

Graham Cave State Park is 61 miles northeast of Jefferson City. Allow 1 hour 15 minutes for the trip. Travel north on U.S. Hwy. 54 to Kingdom City. Take I-70 east to Exit 170 (Danville/Montgomery City). Turn left, then make another immediate left onto Hwy. TT (North Outer Road). Continue on Hwy. TT for two miles; it ends in the state park.

From Hannibal

Graham Cave State Park is about 110 miles southwest of Hannibal. Allow two hours for the trip. Travel south on U.S. Hwy. 61 south to Wentzville. Take I-70 west to Exit 170 (Danville/Montgomery City). Turn right, then turn immediately left onto Hwy. TT (North Outer Road).

Continue on Hwy. TT for two miles; it ends in the state park.

Emergency numbers: 911 system; hospital, (573) 456-2191.

Visitor Contact Station: Three glass display cases represent the various geological features of the park, the cave and the first Missourian who made stone tools and lived in the area more than 10,000 years ago. There is also information about plant species in the park's dry glades. A small set of red and yellow play equipment is near the lower parking area.

Campground: There are 18 electric sites (36-53) and 34 basic sites (1-34) at the small, hilly campground. The first eight sites are terrific pop-up camper sites. Sites 1-11 are not very private. Use caution when selecting your site; some are a bit uneven. Sites on the outside of the loop are against the woods. Sites in the high teens are near the vault toilet. The modern showerhouse is a brown rough-sawn clapboard building that is near the woodlot. There is a split log bench outside the hot shower stalls. All campsites are wooded and all are paved.

Twisted oak trees are scattered around the campground. Sites in the 30s are best for smaller RV units or tents. Sites in the 40s are shady and have pleasing views of the wooded hills. Sites in the mid-40s are private and highly recommended. A small play lot is across from the Showerhouse. Some of the sites in the high 20s are tight and close together, but they are against a natural area.

Cave: Graham Cave is named for the original settler who owned the cave. In 1816, Robert Graham purchased the moist lands along the Loutre River from Daniel Boone's son, Daniel Morgan Boone. In 1847, he purchased the cave property. The cave and its environs stayed in the family until they were transferred to the state in 1964.

A foot-tall stone wall outlines open spaces near the cave, and an interpretive display details facts about the area and the archaeological digs. Flashlights are not necessary to view the cave and trailheads are nearby.

Graham Cave was created at the point of contact between Jefferson City dolomite and St. Peter sandstone. Water

Boardwalks and trails allow visitors an intimate opportunity to view the caves and natural history.

flowing through the sandstone, along with wind and freezing, carved a relatively large but shallow cave. The cave originally extended about 100 feet into the hill, but an accumulation of natural debris over the years filled the lower part of the cave with about seven feet of deposits. An arch-like entrance, 120 feet wide and 16 feet high, provides easy access to shelter.

As you follow the 1,000-foot trail to Graham Cave, you'll hike along the edge of the Graham Cave Glades Natural Area, which is part of the Missouri Natural Area System. The glades possess much of the same character as when humans first inhabited the tract. Surrounding the valley are picturesque sandstone ledges often covered with lichen, moss and ferns. Above the ledges are open rocky glades that contain unique plants such as prickly pear, rushfoil, rose verbena and hairy lip fern. Animals that live on the desert-like glade include lichen grasshopper and fence lizards.

D.F. Graham, son of the original owner, housed his hogs in the cavern for a time, and also became interested in archaeology and ancient artifacts that he found in the cave. After his death, his son Benjamin offered his father's collection of artifacts to the University of Missouri, which spawned archaeological interest in the 1930s.

His daughter and her husband enlarged the shelter for his livestock and were persuaded to stop until they could conduct thoughtful excavations.

From 1949 to 1955, the University of Missouri and the Missouri Archaeological Society dug in the cave, with excellent results. Artifacts found in Graham Cave, associated with charcoal dated by the radiocarbon method, provided important evidence about man's adaptation to the environment at the end of the Ice Age. Archaeological findings revealed different periods in man's use of the cave, dating back 10,000 years ago.

Archaeologists uncovered artifacts that gave clues to the lifestyle of the ancient Dalton and Archaic period Native Americans who first inhabited the cave. They used a grid system as depicted at the cave to catalog and carefully record their finds. Archaeologists dig, but they don't destroy.

Artifacts revealed that these early Native Americans depended mainly on hunting and fishing for food, using spears as weapons. They occupied the cave seasonally and apparently believed in the supernatural. A ring of rocks that encircle a large stone, believed to be a council ring, was found in the cave and suggests that they held ceremonies. Pottery chards found in the cave suggest that it was also occupied by a more recent culture of Native Americans.

Nature: The Graham Glades Natural Area is an 82-acre portion of Graham Cave State Park about two miles west of Danville. Access is by trail from the Graham Cave parking area. It was designated March 22, 1989.

The natural area has sandstone and limestone glades, dry sandstone forest and dry sandstone cliffs in the Missouri River section of the Ozark Border Natural Division. Also included in the area is a small headwaters valley surrounded by cliffs and rocky hills formed in St. Peters sandstone. The proximity of some of the sandstone and limestone glades allows limestone glade species to occur alongside sandstone glade species.

Boating: The narrow single-lane ramp can handle smaller craft like canoes and car-top boats. There is parking for 10 cars and it is surrounded by woods.

Fishing: Catfish and bluegill are taken from the slow-moving river. There is no designated fishing area in the park.

Hiking: Hiking in the park is continuing to develop and the trails can be challenging. All-terrain biking is offered on the Loutre River Trail and some of the trails are rocky. The park is a quiet place to enjoy nature. There are two small waterfalls along the point-to-point Indian Glade Trail (1 mile) that connects the campground to the cave. Traffic on the short 1,000-foot Graham Cave Trail can be heavy on the weekends. The short trail is beautiful and flanks a hill and over a boardwalk.   Graham Cave Trail also has a wet-season waterfall.

The Loutre River Trail (1.5 mile) may be extended in the future but currently offers mossy rocks, stream crossings, and views of the river shallows and past the campground.

Day-use areas: The unit has a number of picnic areas and one rental shelter, playground equipment and other amenities. Day-use areas are located in lush bottomland and rugged hillsides.

Insider's tips: Interpretive signs point out cave discoveries. Park roads are rolling, scenic and excellent for walking or bike riding. The hilly roads offer views and a number of rock outcroppings.

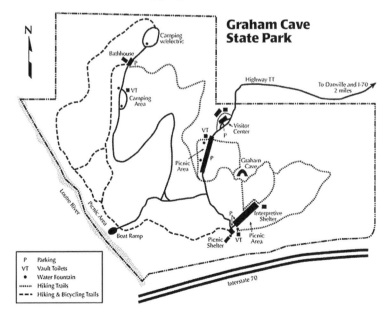

Graham Cave State Park

Many visitors say the Long Branch State Park beach is the finest state park beach in the state.

CHAPTER 10
Long Branch State Park
Land: 1,828 acres   Water:
2,429 acres Long Branch Lake

The mix of habitats and long views of the lake make Long Branch State Park a favorite destination for water sports enthusiasts, campers, boaters and anglers. The rolling meadows and farmlands frame the park that offers lake access, a remnant prairie and a variety of flora and fauna. The park has three boat ramps, quiet coves and an excellent reputation for bass fishing.

In the early 1800s, settlers from North Carolina and Kentucky followed Daniel Boone from the Appalachian hills and valleys to northern Missouri near the vicinity of the park. Some continued westward while many settled in Randolph, Macon and Adair counties because the lush landscape reminded them of home. The woods provided lumber for homes and barns while the bottomlands were fertile for crops.

The earliest inhabitants lived in the area about 12,000 years ago while the last of the native Americans, the Sauk and Fax tribes, left the region in the 1830s. During that time, European settlers were starting to clear the land and raise hogs, hemp and tobacco. The area was also near the Bee Trace trade route. The Bee Trace was known for honeybee hives, the only sweetener of the time. Settlers often chopped down hollow trees that had honeybee hives and harvested the sweet stuff. A few years later, sweeteners were made from sorghum cane that became widely distributed and popular with settlers. Bee trees became scarce and few exist today.

The Long Branch dam is a 3,800-foot-long earthen structure that holds back 2,429 acres of water that drains more than 109 square miles. A nearby U.S. Army Corps of Engineers Visitor Center provides information about the lake and environs. The dam was completed in 1980.

Information and activities

Long Branch State Park
28615 Visitor Center Road
Macon, MO 63552
(660) 773-5529
(877) I Camp Mo: Camping Reservations
www.mostateparks.com

Directions:

From St. Louis

Take I-70 west about 125 miles to Columbia, and turn north on U.S. Hwy. 63. Go about 60 miles to Macon, and turn west onto U.S. Hwy. 36. Travel about two miles to the Long Branch Lake and State Park exit. Turn north and go one block. Turn left onto Visitor Center Road; you will pass by the Corps of Engineers' visitor center and cross the Long Branch Lake Dam. Visitor Center Road ends in Long Branch State Park.

From Kansas City

Take I-70 east 126 miles to Columbia, and turn north on

U.S. Hwy. 63. Go about 60 miles to Macon, and turn west onto U.S. Hwy. 36. Travel about two miles to the Long Branch Lake and State Park exit. Turn north and go one block. Turn left onto Visitor Center Road; you will pass by the Corps of Engineers' visitor center and cross the Long Branch Lake Dam. Visitor Center Road ends in Long Branch State Park.

From Columbia

Take U.S. Hwy. 63 north about 60 miles to Macon, and turn west onto U.S. Hwy. 36. Travel about two miles to the Long Branch Lake and State Park exit. Turn north and go one block. Turn left onto Visitor Center Road; you will pass by the Corps of Engineers' visitor center and cross the Long Branch Lake Dam. Visitor Center Road ends in Long Branch State Park.

From Springfield

Take I-44 east about 110 miles to Rolla and turn north onto U.S. Hwy. 63. Travel 152 miles to Macon, and turn west onto U.S. Hwy. 36. Go about two miles to the Long Branch Lake and State Park exit. Turn north and go one block. Turn left on Visitor Center Road; you will pass by the Corps of Engineers' visitor center and cross the Long Branch Lake Dam. Visitor Center Road ends in Long Branch State Park.

Emergency numbers: 911 system; hospital, (660) 385-3151.
Campground: Long Branch State Park offers 83 basic and electric campsites and a special-use camping area along a flat hill. About 64 sites have electrical hookups. Services include a dump station, showers and water. There also are nine walk-in basic campsites.

Site 1 is great for a pop-up camper with midday sunshine. Sites 1-10 are near the showerhouse and larger enough for big RVs. The gray brick showerhouse has a soft drink machine, phone and an A-frame reader board. Site 10 is sunny. Site 12 is near a new playground with four swings and a tube slide that is on a knoll next to the showerhouse. The views from the showerhouse are of grasslands and silo roofs. There are also views of the lake from different

There are three boat ramps and courtesy docks at the park.

vantage points in the wandering campground.

Sites in the teens are shady. Sites in the 20s are on a slightly narrower park road. Site 26 is an ideal pop-up site. Sites in the 20s are private with lots of vegetation offering screening between the sites. Site 29 is a pull-through with a limited view of the water. Site 30 is private and ideal for a pop-up camper. Site 31 has a side yard and an obscured view of the lake. Site 33 is equally nice and has access to the water with a side yard. As you climb the hill to sites in the 30s, you find site 34 near the vault toilet and hose bib. Sites in the high 30s are great for any size RV.

Site 39 is wide open and sunny, while site 40 has an exquisite oak that shades it. Site 41 is for campers with disabilities and near a flush toilet. Site 42 has some oaks. Twelve- to 14-inch diameter trees separate many of the sites in this area. Sites in the high 40s have a distant lake view. Site 46 has its pad toward the back of the site. Sites in the low 50s have good water views. All of these sites can accommodate larger RVs. Sites 47 - 64 are basic campsites.

The nine walk-in tent camping sites have parking spots at the trailhead where there is a hose bib. Sites 54 and 56 are walk-ins that aren't far from the parking area. The walk to the tent sites is under a canopy of 8- to 10-inch diameter

It's a great great beach. Clean sand, open spaces and great swimming.

trees. The walk-in sites have wonderful water views and are highly recommended.

Site 63 is cozy and at the entrance to a small loop with a flush toilet and small mowed open space. Site 66 is shady at the back of the site and near a hose bib. Site 67 is one of the most private sites in the loop with lots of distance between it and neighboring site 68. Site 67 is also under a canopy of trees. Site 69 is in full sun. Sites in the 70s are open and sunny within easy walking distance to playground and vault toilet. Site 74 has a hint of shade. Sites in the 80s are best for medium and smaller RVs or tents. Site 79 is one of the best in the campground with water views and access to the water. Site 80 is also a terrific camping site that has extra room for parking a small boat and trailer. A hose bib is next to sites 83 and 75.

Site 73 is open, sunny and near the playground. It also has a small mowed area next door. Sites in the low 70s are open and backed against a natural area. Many of them have some grassy space between.

The special-use area is designated for camping and other

outdoor activities for organized nonprofit youth groups.

Store: The small store above the marina sells ice, fuel, fishing tackle, oil, charcoal, soft drinks, T-shirts, foil, paper towels, candy, milk, lunch meat, ice cream and chips, and you can rent boats there.

Hiking: The park has two popular recreation trails.

The Lake View Trail is a 1.5-mile trail with a compacted rock surface that leads to a point and offers scenic views of the lake.

The Little Chariton Prairie Trail is 2.7 miles long and winds through the native tall grass prairie. It provides nice views of the lake, along with good examples of flora and fauna.

Fishing: Long Branch Lake has excellent bass fishing, and for catfish, walleye and crappie as well. The lake's 24 miles of shoreline have many small coves with diverse habitats and structure. A partially covered accessible fishing dock is near the beach. The length limits for bass are 15 inches or longer and for walleye 18 inches or longer.

There's no lake map but just about every cove has standing timber, many gravel points and underwater structures. Staff at the C-Store are knowledgeable about fishing the lake.

A fish cleaning station with running water and garbage cans is near the convenience store and boat ramp. A picnic shelter looks down upon the boat launch and anglers. A fishing pier is near the beach.

Nature: The 640-acre Bee Trace area is between the two arms of the reservoir and offers wildlife observation. "Trace" is the original meaning of a beaten trail. Prescribed fires keep the area prairie-like.

Boating: There are three boat launching ramps at different points on Long Branch Lake. All of the ramps have hard-surfaces. There are no launch fees or horsepower restrictions for boats on the lake. The ramp near the park store has three lanes and five minute courtesy docks.

Swimming: A clean sand beach is near the campground, complete with sand volleyball net. The beach is open from sunrise to sunset year-round. There is no lifeguard on duty so swimming is at your own risk. A wood-sided changing house is near the beach and many picnic tables are throughout the day-use area. This is one of the nicest beaches in the state park system. The beach is about 125 yards wide and has floating red balls that outline the swimming area. The view from the beach is of the distant dam and the roof of the marina that can moor about 30 boats.

Day-use areas: Picnic sites, scattered under trees and along the lake, offer a quiet spot for lunch and a scenic view. The park has two open picnic shelters that can be reserved for $30 per day by contacting the park office at (660) 773-5229. If not reserved, the shelters are available on a first-come, first-served basis at no charge. Both shelters are equipped with electricity, picnic tables, an outdoor grill and restroom facilities nearby. The south shelter has newer plastic playground equipment, volleyball court and a vault toilet. The North Shelter overlooks the beach.

Insider's tips: The U.S. Army Corps of Engineers Visitor Center has dioramas, displays and artifacts about the lake and region. The center details the dam-building process. The dam has a clay core and the visitor center offers great detail how the dam was constructed. Also at the center are a large aquarium tank, archaeological artifacts, samples of stones and minerals, how native Americans made projectile points, native American pottery, farm implements, coal mining, wildlife feeders, safe recreation, common snake quiz board, bobcat mount and views of the dam. From the visitor station, you drive over the dam to the state park. There are nice views from the top of the dam.

The beach, picnic shelter and C-Store are close to each other. The campground typically has vacancies during the week, but fills on holiday weekends and most summer weekends. The area is generally flat with broad grassy areas. The campground has a good mix of private and open sites, sun, shade and tent sites. Bald eagles nest in the area and hunt the shallows of the lake. The lake also has some mud flats that are great for shorebird watching. You can walk across the dam.

Long Branch State Park

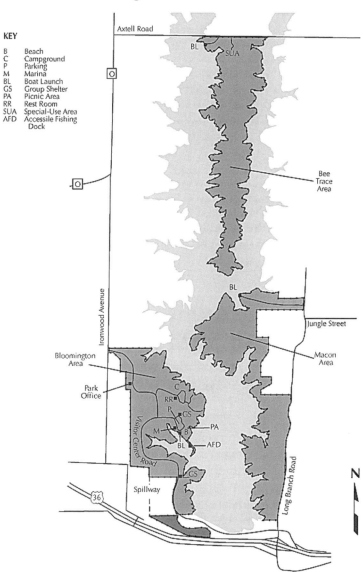

KEY

B	Beach
C	Campground
P	Parking
M	Marina
BL	Boat Launch
GS	Group Shelter
PA	Picnic Area
RR	Rest Room
SUA	Special-Use Area
AFD	Accessile Fishing Dock

Axtell Road

BL

SUA

Bee
Trace
Area

BL

Jungle Street

Ironwood Avenue

Bloomington
Area

Macon
Area

Park
Office

C

RR

P

GS

M

B

PA

BL

AFD

Visitor Center Road

GS

Long Branch Road

Spillway

36

N

Pershing State Park opened in the 1930s.

CHAPTER 11
Pershing State Park
Land: 3,565 acres
Water: Four small lakes, Locust Creek

Pershing State Park has many scenic picnic areas, breezy uplands above a creek, vast wetlands and a shady, comfortable campground. It also contains thousands of acres of lakes, sloughs, upland forests and bottomland hardwoods that can be found virtually nowhere else.

Sprawling wetlands are part of the unchanneled Locust Creek that can be reached by a long boardwalk. Pershing has the largest remaining wet prairie in the state.

General John J. Pershing hunted the virgin woods and wandered the countryside around his nearby home and became America's top-ranking military officer. The park is a fitting memorial to the spirit of the general, especially since his boyhood adventures shaped his spirit and military character. Much more about the history of the World War I hero is available at the Pershing Boyhood Home State Historic site in Laclede.

Locust Creek, which actually is a small river, traces through the middle of the park to where it joins the Grand River. Unlike many creeks that have been channelized, Locust Creek still meanders lazily across floodplains and bottomlands forming lakes, small ponds and sloughs. Waving grasses and untouched wetlands are protected by the state and are the home to abundant waterfowl, shorebirds and all types of fauna and flora. The natural beauty of the park is hard to duplicate and the natural history is a precious resource that the state is doing a wonderful job of preserving.

The park was acquired in 1937.

Information and activities

Pershing State Park
29277 Highway 130
Laclede, MO 64651
(660) 963-2299
(877) I Camp Mo: Camp Reservations
www.mostateparks.com

Directions: Pershing State Park is in Linn County, 18 miles east of Chillicothe or 7 miles west of Brookfield on U.S. Hwy. 36. The main facilities are two miles south on Hwy. 130. The park is about two hours from the Kansas City area and four hours from the St. Louis area.

Emergency numbers: 911 system; sheriff, (660) 258-3385; ambulance, (660) 258-2261. There is a phone at the campground.

Campground: The cement block showerhouse, like the rest of the park, is neat and clean. A phone is next to the reader board at the showerhouse that also has a laundry. The showerhouse area is well lit that makes it bright for evening use.

Sites 1-7 are excellent for large RVs and folks who like to be out in the open. Site 8 is a bit uneven, so check it out before you reserve this site. Across from site 9 is a hose bib. Site 10 is shaded by towering oaks and is great for a medium-sized RV. Sites 12-14 are shaded and site 13 is a pull-through with midday sun. Site 15 is shady and near the vault toilet. Site 17 can accommodate larger rigs, as can most sites in this area of the campground.

Sites in the low 20s are near the showerhouse and great for tent camping. They are sunny most of the day. Site 21 is shaded by a large oak tree. A hose bib is next to site 23. These sites are along the park road, so check them out before you choose a place to set up. Medium to large RVs could also use these sites. Sites in the higher 20s are even better for RVs and sunny with a scattering of large trees offering dappled shade. These sites are easy in and out. From these sites you climb a knoll into a shady area in the low 30s. Site 30 is near the vault toilet and not far from the showerhouse. All of the sites in the 30s are nicely shaded and popular along this tight loop with gravel pads.

Twelve- to 20-inch trees shade most of the generally flat campsites. Site 23 allows campers to park about 30 yards off the park road. All of these sites are across from the savanna where prairie restoration is ongoing. A tan and green amphitheater with three rows of benches is in this area of the campground.

Hiking: Aside from the trails, one of which is an award-winner, the park has plenty of places to walk along the park roads or mowed open spaces.

The Riparian Trail (6.4 miles) tracks the west bank of Locust Creek from the iron bridge in Pershing State Park to northeast portion of the Fountain Grove Conservation Area. The first seven-tenths of a mile is on the wide boardwalk; then the trail branches off and follows the natural levee along the creek bed..

The trail is a study of the various lands along the stream. In fact, "riparian" refers to land alongside rivers and streams. The trail follows a prairie stream that is associated with lakes and wetlands under a tall canopy of bottomland trees that remain much as the first settlers would have found them. The trail is not a loop.

The Lake Trail (.5-mile) takes only 15 minutes to

Pershing State Park has award-winning trails.

complete and it takes you around a small lake where green herons can sometimes be seen wading and stalking minnows. Largemouth bass are seen in the shallows of the lake where nearby sumac plant lines the trail. The trail has small wooden bridges.

Fishing: You may take six largemouth bass of less than 15 inches. Locust Creek has some hot spots and channel catfishing is considered good.

Beach: The small beach is surrounded by mowed areas and within walking distance of the shelters. Sycamores also shade the 30-yard-wide beach. The water is weedy on both sides of the sandy beach. Views from the beach are of gently rolling day-use areas. There is parking for about 20 cars at the swimming area.

Day-use areas: Several picnic sites, an enclosed picnic shelter with kitchen facilities and an open shelter with water and electricity are available in the park. The enclosed shelter requires a reservation. The open shelter is available on a first-come, first-served basis or may be reserved in advance for a fee. Both shelters have playground equipment and suit large family gatherings or special outings well. Please call the park office at (660) 963-2299 for more information or reservations.

Nature: More than 100 species of birds have been identified in the park.

When along the Riparian Trail look for bulrush, a wetland plant that takes its oxygen through the stalks instead of the roots. The wetland prairie is two miles long and one mile wide. It has an observation tower.

Much of the fertile land in northern Missouri has converted to farmland. The wetland is the only large surviving example of northern Missouri natural marshes. In this remnant of an almost lost landscape, the Department of Natural Resources is working hard to restore and maintain as much of the natural forces that shaped the wetlands as possible. The primary forces are flood cycles and fire. Locust Creek wetlands also provide us a chance to explore the vanishing landscape. The boardwalk allows visitors to reach the heart of the wetland and information boards along the walk explain the complex natural flood cycles that are need to nourish and maintain a healthy wetland. Reader boards also provide information about bottomlands, shrub swamps, natural lakes, wet prairie savanna and upland prairies.

Imagine ice more than 3,000 feet thick covering the northern half of Missouri. As these glaciers melted, many south-flowing rivers were created which wandered through this part of the state. Between these river upland prairies, park-like savannas, wide valleys of marshes, wet prairies, hardwood forests and sloughs dominated the landscape. Fire, weather, floods and grazing animals all had a part in shaping the landscape.

Locust Creek is the main artery to bring water to the park and its quality is important. The high quality of the water was observed by explorer Edwin James in 1820: "The waters are transparent, except in time of high flood." To see the creek at its best, observe it from the iron bridge on the Locust Creek Trail.

Plants of the wetlands and levee include river birch, cottonwood, cat briar, rough leaf dogwood, red mulberry and golden glow. These plants love the fast-draining sandy soils of the river levees. Other plants in the Mesic-type forest include pin oaks, silver maples, swamp white oak, stinging nettles and burr oak. Wildflowers include smartweed, pale greed orchids, swamp milkweed and clumps of ostrich ferns.

Pershing State Park is one of only two areas in the state where the Massasagua rattlesnake inhabits. Other reptiles and amphibians include the gray tree frog, small mouth salamanders, soft-shell turtle and Graham's crayfish snake.

Spring brings a wide variety of birds to the park including warblers, wood thrushes, bitterns, common snipe, woodcock, pileated woodpeckers and at least three types of owls. Bald eagles sometimes are seen in winter.

Insider's tips: The park has a bird checklist from the 1989 breeding bird count. There are some excellent design features at the park including the vault toilets with angular roof lines. The park can be peaceful on weekdays all summer long. Plan a trip to General Pershing's boyhood home in Laclede. It's a rural Gothic building that's on the National Historic Landmark list and reflects the ramrod-straight nature of its namesake.

The wetland's boardwalk won the Renaissance Award from the state acknowledging excellence in state parks. Annual flooding can make some of the park inaccessible during the spring. In a region of endless row crops, the park is a rare chance to see quality forests and old-growth bottomland tracts.

Locust Creek Covered Bridge isn't far from the park. Get directions from the park office. It is about three miles west of Laclede on Highway 36.

Did you know that litter remains for many years? A glass bottle stays for 1,000 years, aluminum cans for 500 years, plastic six-pack holders for 100 years and cigarette butts for five years.

A small archery range is near the park office, and interpretive signs are some of the finest in the state park system. Monarch butterflies are often seen in large numbers during their fall migration.

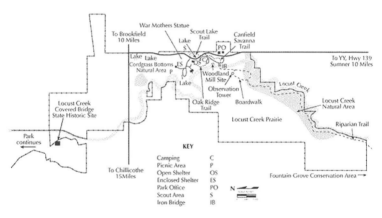

Pershing State Park

Thousand Hills State Park has excellent cultural and natural history learning opportunities.

CHAPTER 12

Thousand Hills State Park
Land: 3,079 acres   Water: Forest Lake, 573 acres

L egend says more than a thousand hills and rugged inclines gather in the patchwork of woodlands and grassy meadows that surround the sparkling clean park. The neighboring lake and its 17 miles of shoreline make this unit a popular destination for fishing, water skiing, paddle boating, canoeing, camping and boating.

Most of the original facilities were built at the park during the middle 1950s and in 1964. Later, the dining lodge was added. The facilities were carefully crafted in an effort to protect the rolling expanses of prairie that once covered more than half of the state. The park's hills support a mosaic of tall grass prairies, grassy openings, hot savannas, mixed hardwoods and remnants of natural communities.

Despite the rugged area's beauty, many settlers bypassed the belts of hills for western prairies. But some settlers did stay including a large landowner and young doctor named

George Mark Laughlin. Other settlers tapped into the coal reserves and clay deposits. Settlers also raised prize hogs and cattle along the fringes of the hills and on the rich prairies.

Dr. Laughlin's heirs donated the land for the reservoir that dammed Big Creek, and the entire tract was given to the state in 1953.

The state's development of the area brought outdoor recreation to this part of the state.

Information and activities

Thousand Hills State Park
20431 State Highway 157
Kirksville, MO 63501
(660) 665-6995
(660) 665-7119 Cabin Reservations
(877)-I Camp Mo
www.mostateparks.com

Directions:

From Jefferson City

Thousand Hills State Park is about 2.5 hours from Jefferson City. Travel north on U.S. Hwy. 63 to Kirksville. Follow U.S. Hwy. 63 (Baltimore Street) through Kirksville. At the north end of town, turn left/west onto Hwy. 6 and continue for about three miles to Hwy. 157. Turn left/south onto Hwy. 157 and continue about two miles to the park entrance.

From St. Louis

Thousand Hills State Park is five hours from St. Louis. Travel west on I-70 to Columbia. Take U.S. Hwy. 63 north to Kirksville. Follow U.S. Hwy. 63 (Baltimore Street) through Kirksville. At the north end of town, turn left/west onto Hwy. 6 and continue for about three miles to Hwy. 157. Turn left/south onto Hwy. 157 and continue about two miles to the park entrance.

From Kansas City

Thousand Hills State Park is close to five hours from Kansas City. Travel north on I-35 to Exit 54 near Cameron. Take U.S. Hwy. 36 east to Macon. Turn left/north onto U.S.

A concession stand and showers are also at the sandy beach.

Hwy. 63 and continue to Kirksville. Follow U.S. Hwy. 63 (Baltimore Street) through Kirksville. At the north end of town, turn left/west onto Hwy. 6 and continue for about three miles to Hwy. 157. Turn left/south onto Hwy. 157 and continue about two miles to the park entrance.

Emergency numbers: Northeast Regional Medical Center, (660) 785-1000; ambulance and police are on the 911 system. The sheriff is (660) 665-4644.

Campgrounds: Thousand Hills State Park offers two campgrounds. Campground 1 features basic and electric campsites, modern restrooms, showers, water and a dump station. Campground 2 has electric campsites, modern restrooms, showers, water and a dump station. Both campgrounds have reservable campsites.

Campground No. 1: For shade, try sites 1 and 2. The amphitheater is near site 2 and has a reader board that details weekend naturalist programs. Many of the campground picnic tables are on wooden deck-like spaces. Site 8 is great for a medium-sized RV. Site 13 is near an open space and a short walk from the vault toilet. All of the campsites in this section are hard-surfaced and level. Sites

12 and 47 are pull-through near the showerhouse. A timber-style playground is also in this area. Sites in the high teens are sunny. Site 29 is a pull-through that is open. Sites in the low 20s are divided by mowed spaces, and there is a toilet near sites 23 and 44. Site 41 is sunny. Site 24 is an excellent tent camping site. Many of the sites in the 20s are particularly good for pop-up campers or tents. Sites in the 30s have a view of the woods. Site 33 has a distant view of the lake and rolling hills. Many of the sites in this area have a wooden platform where the picnic tables rests. Site 35 is near a hose bib.

Sites in the high 40s have midday sun and are big enough for medium to large RVs. The park road is wide in this area. The showerhouse is near this area and complete with stainless steel fixtures, pay phone and laundry facilities. Sites 47 and 15 are pull-through near the modern showerhouse.

Campground No. 2: This campground is just past the park office. Sites in the 50s are about three-quarters shady, and a timber-style playground and toilet are near the entrance. Sites in the 50s have gravel pads and tent campers often use the area. Site 55 is a grassy pull-through site. The Petroglyph Trail head is near this camping site. Site 56 is next to the trail and against the woods. If you like to be under big trees, try sites 57 and 58.

Cabins: Thousand Hills State Park features seven duplex cabins overlooking Forest Lake. The cabins are open March through November. All cabins are air conditioned and heated. Linens and towels are provided and each unit has a bath with shower, patio, picnic table, barbecue grill and color TV. Kitchen amenities include service for eight people, an apartment size stove, refrigerator and microwave. The brick cabins have great views, lake access, split-rail fences and flower pots. There is also room to moor a small boat near your cabin.

Restaurant: Nightly specials and happy hours are featured at the modern restaurant next to the marina. Reservation can be made. A boat ramp is next to the dining lodge. The restaurant has an excellent lake view.

Petroglyph: The petroglyphs and protective shelter are

above the beach. A shelter with a huge skylight and walkway protects the rock carvings. Prehistoric man left examples of his rock carving in many locations in the state. The petroglyphs were chipped, pecked and ground into the exposed sections of sandstone along Big Creek more than 1,500 years ago. Many of the symbols represent animals that had a special place in the group's rituals. Some of the carvings might have had a place in fertility rites.

Carved shapes include deer, turkeys, split-tail birds, raptors, opossums, symbols, footprints and others. Human figures, stars and footprints are the easiest pictures to pick out on the flat sandstone. About 25 birds are represented in the carvings, with many representing eagles and swallows. Deer have antlers and some of the images have long tails that might represent raccoons or opossums. At least two snakes, lizards and turtles are also carefully carved into the stone.

Little is known about the purpose of the petroglyphs. They are not a form of writing and cannot be deciphered. The figures were probably produced as part of an individual or group ritual, or maybe an element of Indian medicine. The symbols might have been designed to influence events in the natural world in which they lived and relied on for existence. The animal carvings suggest they may have been done as part of a hunting ritual. By depicting images of the quarry, perhaps the artist thought he could capture or control its spirit, thereby increasing the chances of a successful hunt.

Some of the carvings might have depicted bad experiences or dreams. This was a special part of Indians' spiritual life. The images might also have been memory devices illustrating tales and legends of the native people to tell future generations. From the deck of the building that protects the carvings are views of rolling wooded hillsides and the lake.

Hiking: Thousand Hills Trail traces both Big Creek Conservation Area and Thousand Hills State Park, and passes through one of the few remaining aspen stands in the state. The western portion of the trail follows the shoreline of Forest Lake and offers good opportunities for viewing waterfowl and other wildlife. The trail is five miles

A three-lane launching ramp is near the lodge.

long and is signed in a clockwise direction with red arrows. It is open to foot and bicycle traffic only; no equestrian or all-terrain vehicle (ATV) use is allowed.

Red Bud, Oak and Hickory Trails are developed sections of the park near the marina and dining lodge. There are also three smaller trails. Craig's Cove Loop, the shortest of the three trails, is a three-mile loop on the West Side of Forest Lake. This trail good for beginning bike riders.

The Mountain Biking/Hiking Trail is a six-mile connector trail linking Craig's Cove Loop to Thousand Hills Trail. It follows the south end of Forest Lake and is considered to be the most difficult of the three mountain biking/hiking trails.

A primitive campsite is offered along this section of trail. Campers must register at the park office.

Fishing: Thousand Hills State Park has excellent fishing on the 573-acre Forest Lake, which is stocked with crappie, largemouth bass, walleye and channel catfish, among others. A fish cleaning station is near the marina store.

Marina store: At the marina, you can rent all types of boats including paddleboats, canoes, fishing boats and pontoons. The marina also rents dock slips on a daily, weekly, monthly or annual basis, and has a variety of ski and boating accessories for rent.

At the park store, located in the marina, you will find grocery items, all your picnic necessities, bait, firewood, ice, bottled water, hot dogs, sandwiches, charcoal, chips, live bait, gasoline and permits for fishing and boating.

Boating: The three-lane paved launch is near the dining lodge. A city permit is required on all private boats. Outboard motors more than 90 horsepower are not allowed on Forest Lake. Annual permits are available. Boats can be stored at the marina and most are colorful pontoons. Jon boats, paddleboats, fishing boats and canoes can be rented.

Swimming: The sandy beach at Thousand Hills State Park is open May 31 to Sept. 1 from noon to 6 p.m. weekdays, and from noon to 7 p.m. on weekends. There is a fee. Lifeguards are on duty. Dressing rooms and showers are also provided. A concession bar is open at the beach during these times offering soda, chips, water and candy. A sand volleyball court and floating diving platform are at the beach. Above the beach is a timber-style picnic shelter complete with a large pedestal grill, parking and toilets.

The beach may be closed when the weather is inclement. Please check the boathouse for possible closing information or call the park office at (660) 665-6995. The sand is highly groomed and the views from the beach are of wooded hills.

Nature: The park naturalist offers interpretive programs during the spring, summer and fall. Programs include nature walks, games and informative discussions on topics including the area's natural landscape and wildlife. Also, an interpretive shelter displays the park's petroglyphs or rock carvings believed to have been left behind by the area's inhabitants more than 1,500 years ago.

Bats are one of the few predators that feed at night and can often be seen at dusk flying like little jet fighters chasing airborne insects. The bats do a great job of keeping insect populations low. Bats have specialized teeth in order to eat small insects. They are not rodents; they are the only flying mammals. Less than one-half of one percent of bats carry rabies, and very few bats are big enough to make a puncture bite on a human. There are 14 species of bats in

Missouri and three are on the endangered species list.

Naturalist pontoon rides are popular opportunities to learn about the natural history of the area. Learn to tell the temperature by counting the chirps of a cricket. Count the number of chirps in 14 seconds, add 40 and result is the temperature where the cricket is located.

Bluestem grass is found in the park and once covered a large portion of Missouri. The grass blooms between early August and mid-September.

Day-use areas: More than 60 picnic sites are at Thousand Hills State Park, including four open shelters and one enclosed shelter. The shelters provide a great place for large family gatherings or special outings and can be reserved in advance for a fee.

The enclosed shelter can be reserved for $50 per day and has an occupancy limit of 75 people. The shelter includes two grills, 12 tables, benches, a stove, refrigerator, electricity and a restroom facility with water on location.

Point Shelter, an open shelter that accommodates up to 69 guests, includes two grills, a children's playground, electricity and water They can be reserved for a fee.

The remaining three open shelters, Shelter 2, Dead Man's Curve Shelter and the beach shelter, also can be reserved for a fee. They accommodate between 36 and 48 guests and include outdoor grills. If not reserved, all open shelters are open to park visitors at no charge on a first-come, first-served basis.

Additional children's playground facilities are at campgrounds 1 and 2, as well as at the main day-use picnic area.

Insider's tips: A number of interpretive reader boards are scattered thoughout the park that detail the natural history of common animals and astronomy.

Fireflies are often seen at the park, where some blink quickly and other blink short signals and then leave their little lights out for a long time before blinking again. Fireflies blink more on warm moist nights than when the moon is out. Fireflies are actually soft-bodied beetles and therefore are cold-blooded, so warm nights make their flashing machine blink faster usually from June through

August. The light of the firefly differs from most other lights you are going to see. It actually comes from a chemical reaction of luciferian - cold light. We still don't completely understand how fireflies make cold light.

One boat trailer may be parked on a campsite. The small park office has about a dozen native animal mounts on display. The park has lots of wild turkeys. Wild turkey chicks are called "poults." Free coffee is offered Monday to Saturday at the boathouse marina from 8 a.m to 9 a.m. There is also a breakfast buffet on Sundays (for a fee).

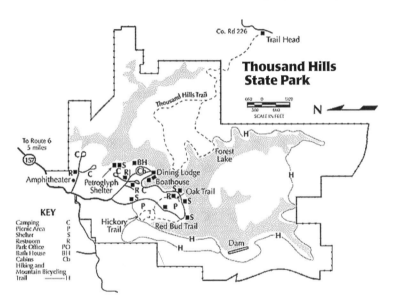

Mark Twain Birthplace Historical Park. The center has a 17-minute slide show, Twain's boyhood cabin and exhibits.

CHAPTER 13
Mark Twain State Park
Land: 2,775 acres
Water: Mark Twain Lake, 18,000 acres

Mark Twain State Park is obviously named for Missouri's best-known author and humorist, whose birth name was Samuel L. Clemens. Established in the 1920s, the tract is the third oldest state park in Missouri and the first north of the Missouri River. It also has the feel and ecology of lands found much further south.

The 2,775-acre park is in the Salt River Hills, an area created when the Salt River system carved through the glaciated plains in northeast Missouri. Here, the terrain is reminiscent of southern parts of the state with limestone bluffs overlooking woodlands of oak, hickory and maple. Bordering the park is the 18,000-acre Mark Twain Lake, featuring power boating, fishing and swimming.

The unit, which has Ozark-like topography and flora, has a wooded campground with basic and electric campsites.

The park offers many day-use areas, two four-lane boat ramps and six miles of hiking trails with broad views of the lake. Mark Twain Birthplace State Historic Site is adjacent to the park; it contains the author's cabin and detailed accounts of Samuel Clemens' life and times.

The park changed dramatically when the Clarence Cannon Dam was built across the Salt River making Mark Twain Lake. Construction of the dam began in 1966 and was completed in 1983. In addition to the power generation, the 18,000-acre lake provides flood control for the Salt River valley as well as recreational opportunities. The parkland that once overlooked the fertile Salt River now overlooks the lake.

Information and activities

Mark Twain State Park
20057 State Park Office Road
Stoutsville, MO 65283
(573) 565-3440
Camping reservations and camper cabins:
(877) I Camp Mo
www.mostateparks.com

Emergency numbers: 911 system; Sheriff, (660) 337-5175; water patrol, (573) 571-3333; ambulance, (660) 327-4252.
Directions:

From St. Louis

Mark Twain State Park is about a two-hour drive from Chesterfield. Go west on I-70 to the Montgomery City/Hermann exit and take Hwy. 19 north to the town of Perry. At Perry, turn west on Hwy. 154. Stay on Hwy. 154 for about six miles after leaving Perry. Turn north on Hwy. 107. In a half-mile, take the first paved road to the left to enter the campground. The park office is another two miles north on Hwy. 107 near the junction of Route U. Turn east on Route U and follow the signs to the park office.

From Columbia

Mark Twain State Park is about a 1.5-hour drive from I-70 in Columbia. From Columbia, go north on U.S. Hwy. 63 to Moberly. At Moberly turn east on US Hwy. 24. Continue east on U.S. Hwy. 24 until about five miles east of the town of Paris to Route U. Take Route U east 10 miles to Hwy. 107. The park office is east of Hwy. 107 on Route U - follow the signs. To get to the campground, turn south on Hwy. 107, cross the bridge and take the second paved road to the right - about two miles.

From Hannibal

Mark Twain State Park is about 35 minutes or 30 miles southwest of Hannibal. Take U.S. Hwy. 36 west from Hannibal to Monroe City. At Monroe City, turn west on U.S. Hwy. 24. Go west Hwy. 24 for about 10 miles to Hwy. 107 and turn south. In about six miles, you will come to Route U. Turn left on Route U if you wish to go to the park office and follow the signs. To get to the campground, continue south on Hwy. 107, cross the bridge and take the second paved road to the right - about two miles.

Campground: The park has 97 campsites (22 basic and 75 electric sites) available some for advance reservation. The lakeside campground has modern showers and laundry facilities. A courtesy boat ramp and fish-cleaning station are in the campground for campers' use.

Also in the park is Camp Colborn, a group camp that features a dining lodge, kitchen, sleeping cabins and outdoor play court. Camp Colborn is available by reservation only.

Sites 1-26 (Badger) are wooded and many sites are carved into the woods. Sites 5 and 7 get morning sun and are across from a hose bib. Sites in the teens are great for larger RV units, and most of the sites in this loop are separated by vegetation. Site 17 has some additional space behind it. Site 20 has full sun all day. Sites in the low 20s are shady. Sites 23, 25 and 26 offer a small grassy area next to them for additional room.

Campground roads are smooth and great for evening walking or inline skating.

At the entrance to sites 27-57 (Coyote) are the showerhouse and amphitheater. Sites in the high 20s get midday sun. Site 30 is shaded by a couple of oaks and maples, and other sites in the 30s are great for larger RVs.

Some of these sites are a bit larger than others in the loop. Sites in the 40s have a through-the-trees view of the water and have space behind the site for a second tent. Site 45 is an especially nice site at the end of the curve. Many of these sites have room to park a small fishing boat. Site 51 is neatly mowed and one site away from the hose bib. Sites in the 50s are gravel and flat. Site 54 has a trail next to it that connects to the other camping area. Site 55 has plenty of midday sun, and sites in the 50s can accommodate fifth-wheel rigs.

Sites 58-103 (Puma) are gently rolling. Sites in the 60s are more compact and best for popup campers. The showerhouse is near site 70. Sites in the 70s and 80s have views of the water though the trees. Site 84 is sunny. More vegetation that most other sites in the loop surrounds sites in the high 80s. Sites in the 90s are sunny and near the showerhouse. A big rig would be great on site 96. For a sunny spot, check out site 99.

Cabins: Many outdoor lovers who don't want a rustic camping experience now have a new lodging option in camper cabins. The wooded setting and lake views provide the perfect getaway for a quiet weekend or a weeklong vacation.

Six log cabins are in the Puma Campground. The log cabins provide accommodations for up to four adults and two children. These accommodations include a queen-size bed, full-size futon and a carpeted loft for sleeping bags.

Cabins have electricity, heating and air conditioning but do not include water, restrooms or refrigeration. All cabins have a dining table, ceiling fan and microwave/toaster oven. Exterior amenities include a porch bench, picnic table, pedestal grill and campfire grill. Drinking water is nearby. A modern central restroom and showerhouse, within walking distance of the cabins, is available during the camping on season (April 1 to Oct. 31). During the off-season, a vault toilet is open and water is available at the park office.

Bring gear such as lanterns, cooking and eating utensils, and water containers. Guests must bring their own linens and sleeping bags.

The 18,000-acre features lots of underwater stucture that hold fish. Many narrow bays and coves, too.

Hiking: Six miles of trails meander between Buzzard's Roost and the campground. Hikers will find many opportunities to see woodland wildlife and plant life, as well as scenic views of Mark Twain Lake. The Buzzard's Roost overlook provides a popular view of the lake from a towering limestone bluff.

Boating: The park has two four-lane concrete boat ramps. One is off of Route U one-half mile west of the junction of Hwy. 107 and Route U. This ramp has a view of flooded timber and a bridge in the distance. The second ramp is off of Hwy. 107 about two miles north of the same junction. Both offer access to Mark Twain Lake, and there is no charge for using these ramps. A single-lane boat ramp is in the campground for use by registered campers. The average depth of the lake is 29 feet and there are 285 miles of shoreline.

Fishing: The 18,000-acre man-made lake offers excellent fishing for crappie, catfish, largemouth bass, bluegill, carp, walleye and perch. The popular lake has secluded coves and underwater structures that hold fish much of the year. Shoreline fishing is offered in the park and around the lake at such places as Warren G. See Spillway and Bluffview

Recreation Area. Ramps have plenty of room for bass boats to maneuver.

If you don't have a boat, don't worry. You can fish from shore on the four-acre Tom Sawyer Lake, near the junction of Hwy. 107 and Route U, for bluegill, largemouth bass and catfish. Fishing at Tom Sawyer Lake is available from sunrise to sunset year-round. Ice fishing is not permitted on Tom Sawyer Lake.

Large- and smallmouth bass have a daily limit of six. A fishing cleaning station is near the Puma Campground. Buzzard's Roost Bait and Supply offers live bait and local fishing tips. They advise that bass move, but around the J post anglers often do well.

Beach: The beach is about 100 yards wide with brown sand and a retaining wall with nearby hard-surface parking. The beach has broad views of flooded timber that was created at the time of the reservoir.

Nature: A seasonal naturalist is a regular part of the park staff from Memorial Day to mid-August each summer. Please contact the park office at (573) 565-3440 for program information. Birders should try the mud flats in the refuge.

Mark Twain Birthplace State Historic Site: One of America's unique and best-loved personalities, Samuel Clemens — later known as Mark Twain — was born about one-fourth mile north of this historic site in a rented cabin in the small town of Florida. The cabin is preserved inside the museum at Mark Twain Birthplace State Historic Site. The two-room cabin was moved to the park about 30 years ago.

Details of Samuel Langhorne Clemens' remarkable life are interpreted through exhibits and audio-visual programs at the museum. Along with the two-room cabin in which he was born, the museum features first editions of Mark Twain's works, a handwritten manuscript of "The Adventures of Tom Sawyer," and furnishings from his Hartford, Conn., home. A public reading room is available for personal study and research. Visitors may see these exhibits and the birthplace year-round (except New Year's Day, Thanksgiving and Christmas). A nominal admission fee is charged.

Inside the cabin are dishware, candles, cradle, chest and

other furnishings. Eight people lived in the tiny cabin when Twain was born. The museum houses interesting artifacts including the marbles Twain used as a youngster, a musket, tools, carriage, the writing desk from the second floor of his Hartford, Conn., home, other tables and furnishings and a 17-minute slide show. The most impressive part of the museum for me was the old wheel from a Mississippi River steamboat pilothouse. You can spin the wheel and imagine what it was like to navigate the huge Missouri River.

America's best-loved writer, Mark Twain.

"Shebang" was one of the many words Twain coined.

Day-use areas: There are two picnic areas at Mark Twain State Park:

Buzzard's Roost has about 30 picnic sites and distant views of the lake. The Hwy. 107 Picnic Area has six picnic sites and is near the boat ramp off of Hwy. 107. All picnic sites are available on a first-come, first-served basis.

There are two shelter houses at Buzzard's Roost Picnic Area. The open shelter built by the Civilian Conservation Corps holds between 40 and 45 people and was built in 1941. It is available by reservation (rental fee), or if not reserved, is available at no charge to users on a first-come, first-served basis. The building has picnic tables, electrical outlets, a water hydrant and an outdoor cooking grill.

The Huck Hall enclosed shelter is offered by reservation only. The building accommodates up to 100 people and rents for a small fee. The big shelter has folding tables and chairs, two modern restrooms, a small kitchen with a refrigerator and stove, and two outdoor cooking grills.

The park has a playground in the Buzzard's Roost Picnic Area that was built in 2002.

Insider' tips: A favorite spot for all park visitors is the overlook at Buzzard's Roost Picnic Area. The overlook offers a panoramic view of Mark Twain Lake and is one of the most photographed locations on the lake. The all-African American Civilian Conservation Corps Company 1743 did much of the wonderful work from 1939-1942.

There are 450,000 cubic yards of concrete in the dam. The many coves and bays offer great views of productive fishing areas. Bring your bass boat to explore the many underwater structures, submerged timber and points.

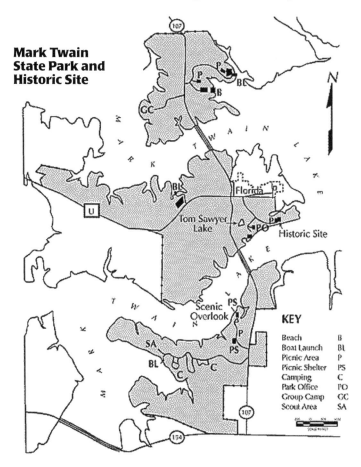

Mark Twain State Park and Historic Site

Florida

Tom Sawyer Lake

Historic Site

Scenic Overlook

KEY

Beach	B
Boat Launch	BL
Picnic Area	P
Picnic Shelter	PS
Camping	C
Park Office	PO
Group Camp	GC
Scout Area	SA

Wakonda State Park has eight miles of nature trails, beach, small craft boating and camping.

CHAPTER 14
Wakonda State Park
Land: 1,053 acres Water: Wakonda Lake

The rolling landscape, which is now rich farmlands, was formed during the Pleistocene Period by the southward thrust of giant ice sheets and then by their retreat. Huge mounded gravel deposits are the primary legacy. Today, silos and agricultural crops frame the popular park and its 79 campsites, terrific swimming beach, quarries that are now lakes and great fishing.

Beginning in 1930, about 16 million tons of gravel were excavated and used for highway construction in the state. After most of the gravel deposits were exhausted, the state highway commission deeded 273 acres to the Missouri State Park Board in 1960.

The new park was named "Wakonda," a word taken from

the Osage and Missouri Indian languages meaning something "consecrated." In 1992, the Missouri Department of Natural Resources acquired an additional 777 acres from Central Stone Co. The natural and manmade features of the park have blended together to create a variety of recreational activities. The park has six lakes.

A white flagpole and modern office with exhibits are at the entrance to the clean park. A reader board and soft drink machine are outside of the office.

Information and activities

Wakonda State Park
32836 State Park Road
La Grange, MO 63448
(573) 655-2280
Camping and Recreational Vehicle Reservations: (877) I Camp Mo
www.mostateparks.com

Directions:

From Macon

Wakonda State Park is about 78 miles or 1 hour 40 minutes from Macon. Take U.S. Hwy. 63 north to U.S. Hwy. 36 east. Continue on U.S. Hwy. 36 for about 26 miles to U.S. Hwy. 61/24. On U.S. Hwy. 61, the park is on the right.

From St. Louis

Wakonda State Park is about 142 miles or 2 hours 50 minutes from St. Louis. Take U.S. Hwy. 40/64 north. Continue on U.S. Hwy. 40 as it changes to U.S. Hwy. 40/61 and then to U.S. Hwy. 61 for about 130 miles. The park is on the right.

From Columbia

Wakonda State Park is about 117 miles or 2 hours 30 minutes from Columbia. Take U.S. Hwy. 63 north for about 31 miles to U.S. Hwy. 24. Go east on U.S. Hwy. 24 about 74 miles to U.S. Hwy. 61. On U.S. Hwy. 61, the park is on the right.

Emergency numbers: 911 system; hospital, (217) 223-1200.

Campground: The park has 79 campsites, with site 1

shaded by a beech tree where a large RV can be easily parked. Many sites have water views and are complete with ground-mounted fire rings and tables. Site 3 is on a knoll and site 4 is wide open and sunny. Site 7 has a view of a meadow and a bluebird nesting box. Site 8 is near the hose bib. Many sites in the teens and 20s are pull-through and have easy access to the lake.

The clapboard-sided showerhouse is near the wood lot and laundry. The scenic 20-acre Boulder Lake is adjacent to the campground.

Sites in the 30s are best for pop-up campers and other small rigs. Site 42 is on the water and has access to the shoreline. Sites in the middle 40s are separated only by the park road from the lakeshore. Although the sites in the 40s are near the water, they are not very private. Many of the sites in the 50s are also near the lake. The pull-through sites are popular with campers with large RVs.

Behind site 61 are the playground with four swings and a sand volleyball court. Many sites in the 60s are against natural areas. Site 62 is one of the more private sites in the campground. Site 72 is great for a large rig and near the hose bib. Other sites in the 70s are best for small- to medium-size RV rigs. Site 78 is also fairly private, but small. Site 79 is large and private on one side.

Recreational trailer rental: Try before you buy is good advice. At Wakonda State Park, you can rent a recreational trailer without the hassle of towing and packing. The 35-foot trailers are equipped with a kitchen, including cookware (place settings for six), linens, towels are available for a fee and the unit sleeps four adults. Families with kids can exceed the maximum occupancy. The trailers are about one mile from the park office and they do not have showers, but you may use the campground showerhouse. There are minimum stays and reservations are necessary. No pets are allowed. A volleyball court is nearby.

Trailer No. 2 is sunny, while No. 4 is shaded by a few trees. The area is generally open. The view and access to the water are the main sales points for renting a recreational trailer. The most private trailer is No. 10.

The trailers are rented from April 15 until the end of

The park has 79 camping sites.

October and there is room next to the trailers to park a boat trailer. Due to the good shoreline access, you can fish from behind your trailer.

Hiking: The park has four hiking trails meandering along eight miles of native sand prairies, lakes and nearby wildlife. The trails are for foot and bikes. The trails are flat and easy walking.

Campground Trail (.3-mile) takes you from the campground to the trailheads at the main parking lot. Be on the lookout during the growing season for prairie and forest animals and plants, including rare tiger beetles and not-so-rare poison ivy. Both are native to the sand prairie and dry woodland habitat.

Jasper Lake Trail (2.1 miles) encircles Jasper Lake and a wetland complex, as well as connects to Agate Lake Trail. Here you may see good fishing opportunities, waterfowl and signs of various wetland animals, including beavers, muskrats and raccoons.

Agate Lake Trail (3.5 miles) encircles the park's largest manmade lake, and connects to both of the other hiking trails. Look for waterfowl, evidence of prairie restoration (such as controlled burning) and signs of the extensive gravel dredging operation before it became a park. Parts of this trail may be closed during the waterfowl migration.

Peninsula Trail (one mile) is a loop trail, taking hikers through the sand prairie itself. Look for all manner of insect and bird life during summer; watch overhead for migrating waterfowl in spring and fall. This sparse grassland is as important to small prairie songbirds as the wetlands are to migrating waterfowl.

Swimming: Natural brown sand from the quarries helped to create the Missouri state park system's largest natural sand swimming beach along Wakonda Lake. The 20,000-square-foot beach offers plenty of room to lounge in the sun or get in a game of sand volleyball. A snack bar is near the beach. No lifeguard is on duty.

The beach is on a point between a couple of coves and has a volleyball court, benches, plenty of parking and a view of the wooded shoreline.

The beach is open from Memorial Day weekend through Labor Day weekend from 10 a.m. to 8 p.m. There are a showerhouse and restrooms at the beach. The snack bar is open Memorial Day weekend until mid-August and on holiday weekends and has ice cream, hot dogs, soft drinks, chicken snacks, hamburgers, fries and chips. Eight fiberglass tables are next to the concession.

Boating: Gasoline motors may not exceed 10 horsepower. Paddleboats and canoes are rented by the hour and day at the concession stand and lakes. The boat launch on the 78-acre lake has hard-surface parking and a single lane. A fishing cleaning station is at the boat launch. A solar-powered toilet is also at the launch. Other lakes also have small launches. Agate Lake has a boat rental, finger dock and launch. The Jasper Lake Trailhead is also at Agate Lake.

Fishing: Largemouth bass are protected when they are 12 to 15 inches. You may take six daily. Ice fishing is considered good to excellent at the park. The clear water, however, requires a delicate technique when the water turns hard.

Nature: Bird watchers will find thousands of waterfowl species that live on the lakes, including Canada geese, snow geese, mallards, lesser scaups, northern shovelers, great blue herons, snowy egrets and many species of ducks and gulls. Agate Lake is closed to boating between Oct. 15 and Dec. 31 and again Feb. 15 through March 31 for the annual waterfowl migrations. Wakonda State Park is becoming one of the best places to observe waterfowl in northeast Missouri. Small prairies along sandy traces contain some rare plants.

Sand-loving plants such as sandgrass, sand dropseed and prairie sunflower flourish, along with rare plants including sand primrose, dotted beebalm and winged pigweed. Hiking and bicycling trails provide access to view the sand prairie, lakes and waterfowl. Bird and wildlife checklists are available online.

Day-use areas: Timber frame play apparatus and picnic tables are tucked into many places along the park roads.

Insider's tips: The park has a bullfrog season by hand, hand net gig, longbow or hook and line. Many of the mounds you see at the park are spoils from the gravel mining days. Check out the innovative bluebird nesting box at the park office that uses a plastic bucket as part of the design.

The park roads are smooth, wide and rolling, and some have wonderful lake overlooks. Many of the day-use picnic tables are set on wooden platforms.

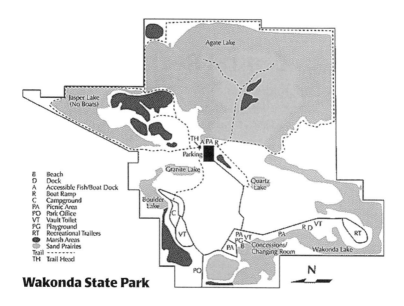

Wakonda State Park

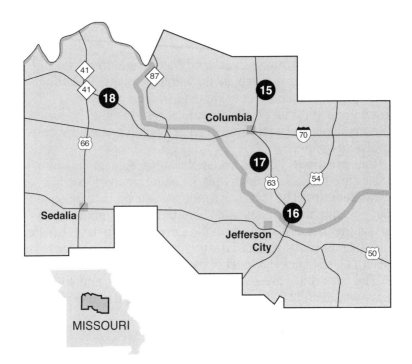

Central Region

15. Finger Lakes State Park
16. Katy Trail State Park
17. Rock Bridge Memorial State Park
18. Van Meter State Park

On a busy weekend more than 250 riders converge on Finger Lakes State Park.

CHAPTER 15

Finger Lakes State Park
Land: 1,128 acres   Water: small lakes

Several decades have passed since the Peabody Coal Co.'s shovels stopped scraping the rich coal of Boone County. This strip mining left a virtual wasteland that is slowly being reclaimed and used for slightly unconventional recreational purposes. Between 1964 and 1967, about 1.2 million tons of coal were removed, leaving water-filled ponds and huge piles of earth.

Missouri ranks in the top 10 states with coal reserves, and this asset continues to power the state's towns and industry. The Peabody Coal Co. donated much of the land that dirt bike riders use today. A federal grant was secured to help finance the reclamation of the lands. Today, the area has 70 miles of off-road motorcycle and all-terrain vehicle trails. The rugged and steep hills challenge the skills of all riders. This steepness and washouts are a bit of a challenge for off-road bicyclists, however.

The big motorcross track, complete with humps and

bumps, travels through a 10-acre area and was designed by professional riders. The big track hosts lots of special events. Part of the course runs past a grandstand that fills up on race days. Like all motorized sports, off-road biking is also increasingly popular on the trails.

If you aren't a dirt bike or all-terrain vehicle rider, there is some traditional outdoor recreation, like fishing in the many finger-shaped lakes, canoeing, swimming and even scuba diving. There are nearly a dozen small lakes, many of them connected, left from the mining days. The linkage of lakes runs for more than 1.5 miles along the eastern side of the property. A beach is also in this area.

Information and activities

Finger Lakes State Park
1505 E. Peabody Road
Columbia, MO 65202-9484
573-443-5315
(877) I Camp Mo: Camp Reservations
www.mostateparks.com

Directions: 10 miles north of Columbia, off U.S. Hwy. 63 in Boone County.

From Kansas City

Travel east on I-70 to Exit 128A/U.S. Hwy. 63 North. Take U.S. Hwy. 63 north for 10 miles, then turn right onto East Peabody Road. Continue for 1.5 miles and turn left at the park sign.

From St. Louis

Travel west on I-70 to Exit 128A/U.S. Hwy. 63 North. Take U.S. Hwy. 63 north for 10 miles, then turn right onto East Peabody Road. Continue for 1.5 miles and turn left at the park sign.

From Jefferson City

Travel north on U.S. Hwy. 63 through Columbia. Turn right onto East Peabody Road and continue for 1.5 miles. Turn left at the park sign.

Emergency numbers: 911 system; ambulance, (573) 882-6128; hospital, (573) 882-0891.

Motorcross track tower.

Campground: About half of the campsites have electrical hookups and some are first come, first served. The unit has modern showers and restroom facilities. ORV are prohibited from riding in the campground. Site 10 is on a rise. Sites in loop 1-10 are backed up against trees and shrubs. The campground has overflow parking for small trailers and other vehicles.

Sites in the high teens are open and best for large RVs. Across from site 19 is the play equipment that has four swings and a tube slide. The showerhouse has a telephone, park maps and lists of motels. Firewood is sold from 8 a.m. to 5 p.m. at the park office. Site 26 and 27 is near the showerhouse but open. Site 31 is best for smaller RV units. Many of the sites in the 30s are shady. Site 36 is one of the better sites with sunshine and room around it. It's also near the showerhouse. Electric site 1 - 17 and basic site 18 - 36.

Off-road riding: On a busy weekend, more than 250 riders convene on the rugged terrain. The staging area has lots of trash barrels, loading ramps and is large enough for long trailers filled with off-road machines. There are also vault toilets at the gravel staging spot. Riders must have a permit from the park office and there is no riding on paved roads or parking lots. Don't forget your helmet.

Fishing: Shoreline access is difficult in some places and easy in other areas of the park. There is a limit on black bass. You can use up to three poles and lines. Anglers tend to work the overhangs, shadows and stickups. Some weed beds are along the shore where bass are taken. All black bass up to 15 inches, striped bass and hybrid striped bass less than 20 inches long must be returned to the water unharmed immediately after being caught.

Boating: Canoes and small boats have a single-lane launch from which to operate along the water corridor. Electric motors only are allowed.

Beach: The sandy beach is on the eastern side of the park on one of the many lakes that are remnants of coal mining activities. A changing house with vault toilets is at the beach. Orange floats define the swimming area. Views from the beach are of tree-lined shores and tracts of the old mined landscape. There also are an outdoor shower and drinking fountain.

Insider's tips: A bird list from the park's master plan is available upon request. Finger Lakes is one of two parks that cater to off-road riders. The other is St. Joe State Park and is 90 miles south on U.S. 32. The park has lots of woodchucks.

Before the state began reclamation, the tract looked like the face of the moon. Trails are constantly being developed at the park. It's a fun place to ride.

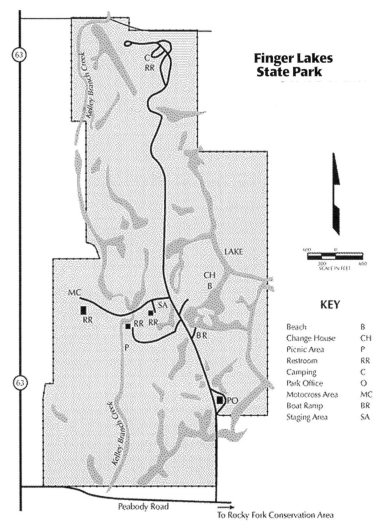

Finger Lakes State Park

KEY

Beach	B
Change House	CH
Picnic Area	P
Restroom	RR
Camping	C
Park Office	O
Motocross Area	MC
Boat Ramp	BR
Staging Area	SA

Katy Trail
State Park

Map continued on
page 101 ▶

CHAPTER 16
Katy Trail State Park
Land: 2,936 acres
www.katytrailstatepark.com

Every Missouri state park has unique features, but none are as unusual as Katy Trail State Park, which stretches more than 200 miles across the state. It's mostly 100 feet wide and great for walking and bicycling past great scenery, small towns and a broad menu of cultural sites.

Katy Trail State Park is built on the former corridor of the Missouri-Kansas-Texas (MKT) Railroad (better known as the Katy). When the railroad stopped operation on its route from Machens, in St. Charles County, to Sedalia, in Pettis County, in 1986, it afforded an opportunity to create an extraordinary recreational opportunity — a long-distance hiking and bicycling trail that would run across a huge part of the state.

No other park can offer visitors such a diversity of both cultural and natural resources to be studied and enjoyed.

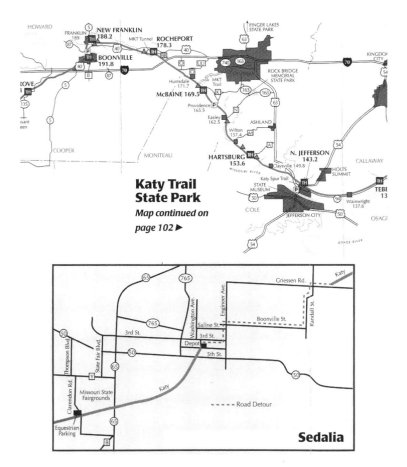

Katy Trail
State Park

Map continued on
page 102 ▶

Sedalia

The opportunity for the Missouri Department of Natural
Resources to acquire the right-of-way was made possible by
the National Trails System Act, which provides that railroad
corridors no longer needed for active rail service can be
banked for future transportation needs and used on an
interim basis for recreational trails. Because of a generous
donation by the late Edward D. "Ted" Jones, the
department was able to secure the right-of-way and
construct the trail. In 1991, the Union Pacific Railroad
donated to the state an additional 33 miles of rail corridor
from Sedalia to east of Clinton. Additional purchases and
donations were added. Today, Katy Trail State Park is open

Katy Trail State Park

Map continued on page 103 ▶

for 225 miles from St. Charles to Clinton and is operated by the Department of Natural Resources as part of the state park system.

Information and activities

Katy Trail State Park
320 First Street
Boonville, MO 65233
(660) 882-8196
www.katytrailstatepark.com

Emergency numbers:
Henry County (660) 885-5587
Pettis County (660) 827-0052
Cooper County (660) 882-2771
Howard County (660) 248-2477
Boone County (573) 442-6131
Cole County (573) 634-9160
Callaway County (573) 642-7291
Montgomery County (573) 564-3378
Warren County (636) 456-7088
St. Charles County (636) 949-0809

Trail history: Most of the trail traces the Missouri River, so hikers and bicyclists often find themselves with the river on one side and towering bluffs on the other.

Katy Trail travels through diverse landscapes and

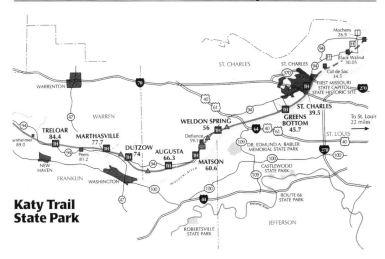

**Katy Trail
State Park**

topography including dense forests, wetlands, deep valleys, remnant prairies, open pastureland and gently rolling farm fields.

There are many types of habitats and wildlife is plentiful, especially songbirds. Chickadees, nuthatches, robins, orioles and many types of woodpeckers are common along the trail. Red-tailed hawks and turkey vultures are often seen soaring above the trail, and bald eagles are common in the winter. Because of its location along the Missouri River flyway, migrating birds and waterfowl are seen frequently. In addition, watch for great blue herons, sandpipers, Canada geese and belted kingfishers.

Katy Trail State Park also travels through a slice of rural history as it meanders through the small towns that once thrived along the railroad corridor. From the area known as "Missouri's Rhineland" that portrays the heritage of the German migrants to the historic town of Rocheport that dates from before the Civil War, these towns reflect the rich heritage of Missouri. These communities make great places to stop and explore during a ride on the trail.

Although the scenery often changes, the trail remains fairly level as it meanders through the countryside. Trailheads, which provide parking areas and other amenities, are located periodically along the trail. Many communities also offer services to trail users.

Mile markers: The trail is marked every mile with a signpost that corresponds to the traditional railroad mileage system. To determine the distance traveled, subtract the mile post number at the trailhead from the mile post number on the trail, or vice versa. Mile post number 27 is on the east end of the trail, at Machens in St. Charles County, and post number 265 is on the west end near Clinton in Henry County.

Shuttle services: The following businesses offer a shuttle service for hikers and bicyclists that use the Katy Trail:

Creason Bike Rentals and Shuttle Service (573) 694-2027

Katy Trail Shuttle Service (636) 497-5812

Insider's tips: Donation boxes are at trailheads all along Katy Trail State Park. If you enjoy the Katy Trail and wish to make a donation, your contributions will be used for maintenance, repair and interpretation. Check on trail conditions at this Web site:

www.mostateparks.com/katytrail/conditions.htm.

Several special events are also scheduled annual along the linear corridor. There is no camping along the trail except at private campgrounds and a few communities. The most scenic areas of the trail are in the Rocheport to Jefferson City area, Portland to Treloar, and Augusta to St. Charles — especially those areas along the river below the river bluffs.

The natural bridge is 125 feet long.

CHAPTER 17
Rock Bridge Memorial State Park
Land: 2,273 acres   Water: Rock Bridge Creek

Rock Bridge Memorial State Park is teeming with natural phenomena rarely seen in such a concentrated area. The park has 15 miles of trails, several caves, wild cave tours, an orienteering course, all-terrain biking, springs, boardwalks, forested hills, sinkholes, a spectacular chasm and a massive limestone bridge that is topped by trees. The 63-foot-high arch gives the park its name. The rock bridge is about 125 feet long and can be explored by natural light.

Cave tours are exciting. Trained park staff offer tours into Devil's Icebox Cave that require boats to access. The first half-mile of the cave is filled with water. The cave maintains a constant temperature of 56 degrees. Ask the staff about entering Connor's Cave and more about the seasonal tours of Devil's Icebox Cave.

Admittance to Devil's Icebox Cave is allowed from April

15 to May 16 and August 1 to October 8 and only on park led tours to preserve a quiet time for endangered gray bats to raise their offspring and for endangered Indiana Bats to hibernate.

In 1924, Ben and William Yates were first to explore the cave and to prepare a crude map.

About 150 years ago, the park also featured a whiskey distillery that made "McConathy's Rye." Like today's spirits, the whiskey makers of that era touted the clear waters that comprise it. In 1922, the park was operated as an amusement park that sold floss candy, shot fireworks and operated merry-go-round rides. The state took over the property in 1967.

Rock Bridge is one of the state's most fascinating state parks.

Information and activities

Rock Bridge Memorial State Park
5901 S. Highway 163
Columbia, MO 65203
(573) 449-7402
www.mostateparks.com

Directions:

From St. Louis/Kansas City

Rock Bridge Memorial State Park is about 130 miles from Kansas City and St. Louis and should take 2.5 hours. From either location, take I-70 to Columbia, Exit 126 (Providence Road/Downtown). Go south through Columbia on Providence Road/Hwy. 163 about seven miles.

From Jefferson City/Rolla

Rock Bridge Memorial State Park is about 40 minutes from Jefferson City and 1.5 hours from Rolla. From either location, take U.S. Hwy. 63 north. About six miles north of Ashland, turn left onto Hwy. 163 (toward Pierpont). Travel three miles, passing the Shooting Star and Karst trailheads, to a four-way stop. Turn right, staying on Hwy. 163. The Devil's Icebox and Rock Bridge entrance are one mile ahead on the left. The park office and main entrance are another mile ahead, also on the left.

From Macon/Kirksville

From either location, take U.S. Hwy. 63 south through Columbia to the Route AC/Grindstone Parkway exit. Turn right at the top of the exit and go about three miles to Hwy. 163/Providence Road; turn left onto Providence Road. At the first traffic light after the road narrows to two lanes, turn left, staying on Hwy. 163. Travel one mile; the park office and main park entrance are on the right. The Devil's Icebox and Rock Bridge entrance are an additional mile and also on the right.

Emergency number: 911 system.

Devil's Icebox Cave: An interpretive reader board is at the head of the half-mile trail to the double sinkhole cave. A busy stream rushes along under the 150 feet of boardwalk as you approach the gaping cave. The cool walk has a number of twisting stairs. Inside the cave, you'll find solidified limestone formations sometimes known as soda straws, curtains, stalactites and stalagmites. The cave has about seven miles of its interior mapped. Guided wild cave tours are given seasonally.

Millions of years ago, the interior of the cave was formed by water percolating through the soil, dissolving the limestone rock. The bluff face and rock bridge are actually the remains of a big cave and ultimately the remnants of an ancient sea. When the cave collapsed, portions of the roof remained, forming the natural bridge. If you look closely at the face of the bluff, you'll see traces of the tiny sea animals that settled to the bottom of the ocean and eventually formed the rock that overlays huge parts of the state.

People have inhabited the area since the 1830s. The stream was dammed and used by early settlers to power a gristmill. The mill was later used to make paper - the first such operation west of the Mississippi River. A whiskey distillery was in place by 1827. It ran until 1866 and then operated intermittently until 1907.

Hiking/biking: The park has more than 15 miles of biking and hiking trails over mostly easy topography. The Spring Brook Trail (2.5 miles) is hilly; so is the Sinkhole Trail (1.5 miles). The High Ridge Trail (2.3 miles) tracks through mostly open country.

Nature: A number of interpretive programs are offered including the natural history of bats, creatures of the night, history hikes, fall colors, seasonal cave tours and others.

The park is in an area known as "karst" topography. The rugged lands were formed by water carving through 300 million-year-old Burlington limestone. The water dissolved rock and formed sinkholes, caves, underground streams, seeps, rivulets and springs.

Gray bats are about 3.5 inches long and weigh about 10 grams, which is little more than the weight of a quarter. They are the only bats in Missouri that live in caves all year. People are the biggest danger to gray bats. Manmade lakes have flooded many caves, and people can disturb hibernating bats in the winter.

Common wildflowers at the park include columbine, wooly blue violet, spring beauty, wild sweet William, Jack-in-the-pulpit, yellow star grass, golden Alexander, trout lilies, Dutchman's breeches, bloodroot, bird's foot violet, wild ginger and a number of morel mushrooms.

One of the entrances to Sinkhole Trail is at the entrance to the Devil's Icebox Boardwalk Trail.

Watch for belted kingfishers diving for minnows along the stream. Marble and dark-sided salamanders can often be seen from the boardwalk. Migrant warblers are seen in most parts of the park, and during the summer look for waterthrush, Wood Thrush, Acadian Flycatchers and resident woodpeckers.

The 750-acre Gans Creek Wild Area is a mixed area of forests and overgrown pastures. Vireos are common there. Also, scout the sinkhole ponds in the park for sedge wrens. Migrant sparrows are common in grasslands. A birding checklist is available at the park office, produced in cooperation with the Columbia Audubon Society. It's an excellent checklist that details information by season.

Small streams bisect the Gans Creek. Most of the creek is solid bedrock, but some stretches have jumbled boulders, sand and smooth gravel bars. On some of the bluffs, small glades open up and grasses and wildflowers flourish. The Coyote Bluff and Shooting Star trails offer some terrific vistas. Equestrians may ride in the Gans Creek Wild Area from June 1 to October 31, weather permitting. Riders should call the Trail Condition Hotline (573) 442-2249.

Day-use areas: The picnic area near the maintenance barns has playground equipment, tables and grills. The park has a number of picnic tables with grills and limited open spaces.

Insider's tips: The park has excellent staff naturalists. Indiana bats hibernate in the park. There are two species of endangered bats that live at the unit. Take an up-close look at the rock walls along the boardwalk. You will see a universe of colorful lichens, mosses and plants. At one time, two whiskey distilleries operated in the tract. So did a post office, blacksmith shops and general store.

Missouri has about 17,000 flowering plant species.

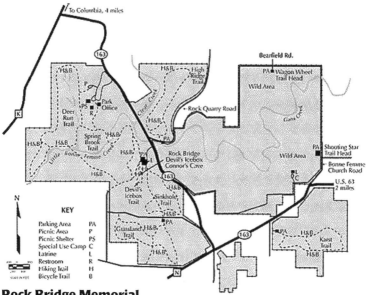

Rock Bridge Memorial State Park

For hundreds of years Native Americans hunted the scenic Van Meter park area.

CHAPTER 18

Van Meter State Park

Land: 983 acres   Water: Lake Wooldridge, 18 acres

Missouri and its main river were named after a tribe of Native Americans, known by the French explorers as the "Oumessourit" or Missouri Indians, who once occupied the state park land. Today, the park features a broad menu of outdoor recreation and opportunities to learn the cultural history of area native Americans.

For hundreds of years, Native Americans hunted the marshes, prairies, deep ravines and narrow ridges, known as the Pinnacles. In 1673, French explorers Jacques Marquette and Louis Jolliet created a map that identified the Missouri Indian village at the Great Bend of the Missouri River.

Van Meter State Park has remnants of an early Native American village site. A hand-dug earthwork, known as the Old Fort, and several burial mounds lie within park boundaries.

The 300-acre Oumessourit Natural Area features a fresh-water marsh, fens, and bottomland and upland forests, which are situated on rugged ridges, known as "loess" hills and deep ravines with remnants of old-growth forests.

The topography of the region is generally flat. The rich agricultural lands are plentiful and often dotted with red barns, full silos and farm machinery. Picnic sites and two picnic shelters are nestled under lofty trees in many places throughout the park.

Information and activities

Van Meter State Park
Route 1, Box 47
Miami, MO 65344
(660) 886-7537
www.mostateparks.com

Directions:

From Kansas City/Columbia

Van Meter State Park is about 100 miles from Kansas City and 75 miles from Columbia. From I-70, take Exit 78/U.S. Hwy. 65. Turn north onto U.S. Hwy. 65 and continue to Marshall. Travel north on Hwy. 41, then west on Hwy. 122, which leads into the state park.

From Moberly

Travel west on U.S. Hwy. 24 to Hwy. 41; turn left/south and continue to Hwy. 122. Hwy. 122 leads into the state park.

Emergency numbers: County sheriff, (660) 886-5511; ambulance, (660) 886-3315.

Campground: About half of the sites have electrical hookups. There are a number of mowed open spaces near the campground that are ideal for field games. Site 3 receives midday sunshine. Sites on the interior of the loop are open with 8- to 10-inch diameter trees offering shade. Site 4 is super with a view of the expansive agricultural lands and marsh through the trees. The area is shady and flat. All of the sites have ground-mounted fire rings, lantern hangers and picnic tables. Site 4 is open while site 5 is a

The Civilian Conservation Corps built shelters and other amenities at the park.

pull-through and has a notched-out area that is perfect for a tent setup. Site 7 is backed up against the woods and has a filtered view of the fertile farmlands and flat horizon. Site 9 is great for a tent or small unit on this pull-through pad. Most of the sites have gravel camping pads.

Site 11 is shady and grassy. Site 13 is near the water bib and a wonderful selection for a larger RV. Sites on the inside of the loop are suited for larger RVs. Site 14 is open, sunny and easy in and easy out for big RVs. All of the sites are level. Site 15 has some shade trees. Other sites in the high teens are next to natural areas. The woodlot and a hose bib are near sites 19 and 20. Sites 20 and 21 are shaded by walnut trees and have some shady grassy areas nearby. Near this area is a stone and timber frame shelter with two chimneys, picnic tables and plenty of grills.

The clapboard showerhouse has flush toilets. Some of the sites are private; others are less so. A few sites have places behind the pad where a tent would fit perfectly.

Visitors center: The arched and vaulted visitors center houses a variety of natural and cultural history displays and information. One of the insect displays has examples of katydid, stag beetle, Fisher's spider, walking stick and more. There are also color photographs of a whitetail deer fawn, raccoon, opossum, rabbit and others common mammals to the park. There are 650 species of birds in North America and about 20 billion live in this region.

Historical hand tools and artifacts are also displayed at the center. The glacier that covered the area from 2.5 million years ago until 600,000 years ago is described. The glacier was 150 feet high when it covered this area. Van Meter was also home to the Missouri Indians when Father Jacques Marquette explored the area in 1673. Father Marquette called the native people "Oumessourti." This name could also be loosely translated as "people of the dugout canoe." The Missouri Indians were not newcomers to the area. While the Osage and Illinois were pushed westward after European settlers moved into the area, the Missouri Indians lived in the region for centuries.

The Missouri were prairie dwellers and lived in large rush mat-covered houses with 15 to 25 people per household. These longhouses were well-spaced in villages of up to 5,000 people at the time of the first European contact. They grew corn, beans and squash along the bottomlands. In June, they hunted bison and harvested their crops in late summer.

The "Old Fort" is an irregular, double-ditched earthwork in the park and was built by the Oneota, ancestors of the Missouri Indians. Archaeologists as recent as 1972 uncovered artifacts when they continued their investigations at the fort. The earth fort is comprised of 3,990 feet of ditches, 2,660 feet of embankment and 3,120 feet of slopes. The fort covers 6.2 acres. I can't image hand-digging these massive trenches and ditches.

A number of artifacts are displayed at the visitors center including scrapers, drills, pottery chards, pipes, projectile points, knives, hammers, antler flakes and sharpening tools. Inside the small auditorium is a touch table filled with nature objects, bison hide and other tactile items. An eight-minute slide show about the park is also available to view. It takes about 20 minutes to read and see all of the exhibits in the visitors center.

Mounds: The gentle burial mounds, built from 1,100 to

1,600 years ago, are usually constructed to honor important people. Sometimes people were buried in old mounds instead of building new ones. Archaeologists believe the people who built the mounds lived on the rugged ridge within the park's perimeter. Some of the mounds in the park have not been studied. Today, they are neatly mowed and shaded by towering walnut trees.

The Indian Village is large and encompasses about 300 acres of the upper edges of the ridge. It appears likely that the entire region was occupied at one time. In the 1700s, the Missouri Indians were devastated by smallpox. By 1758, there were only about 500 Missouri Indians alive. The last full-blood Missourian died in 1908.

The interesting burial mounds are 1.3 miles from the visitors center. Missouri River Overlook Trail and Loess Hills Trail encircle the lake and is two-miles long.

Fishing: The lake and its trails (Lake View Trail, .7-mile) are scenic and the action is good for panfish. The rolling roadway to the lake is great for evening walks. Canoes and electric motors only are allowed. You may take four catfish daily. Try the shoreline cover with stickups. In general, the lake isn't heavily fished.

Day-use area: Civilian Conservation Corps-built shelters and picnic tables await family reunions and other uses. Swimming in the lake is prohibited.

Insider's tips: The Civilian Conservation Corps built two shelters that are still in use today. Van Meter is a very quiet park and away from main highways and populated areas. Be sure to walk out on the earthen dam. It has a subtle view of Lake Woolridge.

Often, the park's campground does not fill up on holiday weekends. A small gift shop is in the visitors center. There is lots of Lewis and Clark information at the gift shop. Don't miss the stand of black walnut trees and other specimens, including hickory and sassafras. The park roads are excellent for walking or bike riding. In many places, there is a full canopy of tree limbs overhead.

The tall star-shaped blue flowers are called bellflower, a plant that likes borders of woods and stream bottomlands. There is also the shrub wahoo that has four-lobed seedpods that turn red in the fall. Native Americans found many uses for the plant, including medicine for sores, eye lotion and stiff wood for arrows.

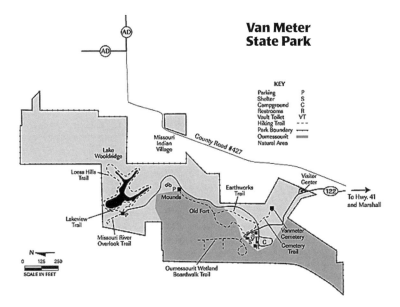

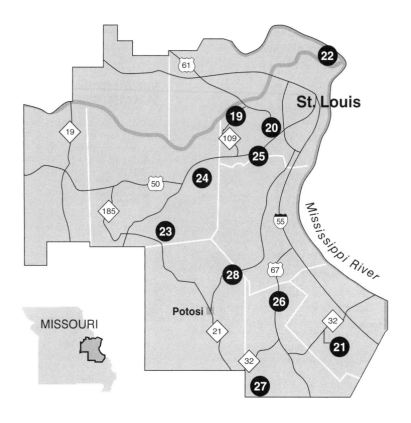

St. Louis Region

19. Dr. Edmund A. Babler Memorial State Park
20. Castlewood State Park
21. Hawn State Park
22. Edward "Ted" and Pat Jones-Confluence
Point State Park
23. Meramec State Park
24. Robertsville State Park
25. Route 66 State Park
26. St. Francois State Park
27. St. Joe State Park
28. Washington State Park

Dr. Edmund A. Babler Memorial State Park has 17 miles of rolling hiking trails, an excellent visitor's center with gift shop and classrooms, swimming and equestrian trails.

CHAPTER 19
Dr. Edmund A. Babler Memorial State Park
Land: 2,441 acres

A tree-lined entrance and massive stone gateway welcome campers, hikers and nature lovers. Overlooking this gently rolling park is a huge bronze statue of namesake Dr. Edmund A. Babler, a well-known surgeon whose brothers gifted the initial property to the state. The statue was dedicated in 1938. Babler died at 54 from pneumonia in 1930.

The inscription on the towering monument says, "Nothing is more estimable than a physician who having studied nature from his youth knows the properties of the human body and the diseases which assault it, the remedies which benefit it, exercises art with caution and pays equal attention to the rich and the poor." Also inscribed on the monument is the dedication that reads, *"He that careth for the sick and the wounded watcheth not alone. There are three in the darkness together and the third is the Lord."*

The sprawling four-square-mile park has a high point of 770 feet above sea level and rests in a transition zone between the rugged Ozarks to the south and the glacial plains to the north. Thick deposits of loess soil support towering forests and nearby agricultural land.

Although the park is an inspiring natural treasure and offers diverse ecosystems, it's also only minutes from modern services, restaurants and shopping. When walking among the 100-year-old white oaks and sugar maples in Cochran Woods at the middle of the park, you can study nature not far from the urban pleasures and resources.

Ridges that drain to the Missouri River offer timeless character.

Information and activities

Dr. Edmund A. Babler Memorial State Park
800 Guy Park Drive
Wildwood, MO 63005
(877) I Camp Mo Camping Reservations
(636) 458-3813
www.mostateparks.com

Directions:

From Eureka

From I-44, take Exit 264 onto Hwy. 109. Travel north eight miles to Route BA. Turn left and continue two miles; the park entrance is on the left.

From St. Louis

From I-270, turn west onto U.S. Hwy. 40/64 and travel for 9.5 miles to the Long Road exit. Turn left onto Long Road and travel one mile to Wild Horse Creek Road. Turn right onto Wild Horse Creek Road and continue three miles to the Hwy. 109 stop sign. Turn left and travel less than one mile to Route BA; turn right and continue for 1.5 miles to the park entrance. It takes only 20 minutes from St. Louis.

From St. Charles County

Travel east on U.S. Hwy. 40 to Chesterfield Airport Road (just after crossing the Missouri River bridge). Continue for two miles to Long Road and turn right. Travel one mile to Wild Horse Creek Road, turn right and continue to the Hwy. 109 stop sign. Turn left and travel less than one mile to Route BA; turn right and continue 1.5 miles to the park entrance.

Emergency number: 911 system

Visitor's Center: The shake-roofed and stone visitor's center has parking for 30 cars and overlooks a wooded valley. The center is open 8:30 a.m. - 4 p.m. daily. The small but well-stocked gift center sells postcards, T-shirts, books and patches. The main lobby features mounts of a wood duck, barn owl and white-tailed deer. An observation deck runs along the back of the classroom looking upon the valley and thick understory.

The classroom has six rows of red chairs and seating for about 60 people. The popular hall has audio-visual equipment, a small presentation stage and mounts of a bobcat and turkey near the front of the room.

The visitor's center has a three-dimensional model of the park and information about the Lewis and Clark expedition in the lobby. It also houses some terrific natural history dioramas and an interpretive display.

Campground: The rolling campground has 43 electrical sites and 30 basic sites. The campground is comprised of four linear lanes; the north (sites 1-11 and 52-75) and south (sites 12-30) sections are shaded and mostly reservable.

Campsites have hard-surface pads, metal-leg tables and fire rings. Most of the sites in the campground have lantern posts at the rear of the pads. If you like sun, consider site 10, which is near the shower house, dumpster and firewood shed. The gray block shower building is usually surrounded by large RV units on sunny sites. Inside the teal-colored shower house are three showers on each side. On a low rise are sites in the 30s and access to the bike path and special-use camping area.

The campground is rolling with some wooded ravines and private sites.

Sites in the teens are backed up against a wooded area on L-shaped pads. Site 21 is sunny and next to a 100-by-100-foot mowed area for field games. Sites 22 and 23 are also mostly sunny and at the end of the loop. Site 27 has a single tree and lots of sun.

According to staff, there is usually a mix of large RV units, tents and pop-ups on the weekends. Sites 1-10 are wooded, against a natural area and near the campground host. Site 50 is probably the most private site in the park. Sites in the 40s are separated by medium caliper trees and backed up against a wooded area for additional privacy. Sites 43-46 are on a hill and are some of the best sites in the campground. Site 44 is tucked into the woods and private. Sites 52-75 are reservable.

Sites in the 50s look upon a wooded ravine and there's a water bib next to site 57. Sites in the 60s are the shadiest in the campground and great for medium and small pop-up campers. Sites 67 and 68 are at the end of the loop on a low crest with a valley view. A water bib is near site 66. Sites in the 70s are heavily wooded and littered with leaves from the overhead canopy. Restrooms are across from site 72. If you need extra space for kids, consider site 75, which has a small grass area adjacent to it. The grassy area would be

MISSOURI DEPARTMENT OF NATURAL RESOURCES
DIVISION OF STATE PARKS

Meramec State Park

Receipt No.: 110-57
Date: 7/8/2009 1:14
Operator Id: 18608
Customer:

Item	Description	Qty	Price	Total
275958	Registration	1	$76.00	$76.00
			Sub-Total	$76.00
			Discount	$0.00
			Tax	$0.00
			Total	$76.00

PAYMENT INFORMATION

Payment Type:
Method: Paid
Credit Card:

Details:
EDWARD ALAN MCCOBB

Total Paid: $76.00
Change Due: $0.00

EDWARD

Firewood if purchased cannot be taken outside of park boundary
Bring receipt for validation. Reservation/Permit fees are non-refundable

THANK YOU FOR SUPPORTING MISSOURI STATE PARKS
www.mostateparks.com
General Information 800.334.6946   Reservations 877.422.6766

great for playing catch or flying a plastic disc.

Hiking: The park's five trails offer about 17 miles for hikers. Starting in March, you will see many common ferns and spring wildflowers. Common ferns are bracken, broad beech, Christmas, hairy-lip, great, sensitive and fragile fern. It's interesting to note that ferns have spores, not traditional seeds like most plants. Common trees are white and red oak, sycamore, sugar maple, ironwood, elm, flowering dogwood, red bud willow, red cedar, honey locust, Ohio buckeye, ash, sassafras and hickory.

The Guy Park trailhead has hard-surface parking for 75 cars and a nearby play apparatus outlined by landscape timbers. A CCC-era shelter is also in the area.

The Dogwood (two miles) and Woodbine (1.75 miles) trails are here. There are trail maps at the small kiosk. The Dogwood Trail (marked in green arrows) is a moderate hike with a 300-foot elevation change along some dry ridges and a wooded valley. It shares some of the Equestrian Trail and is especially interesting along the moist bottomlands, then up breezy ridges where you find a bubbling spring under a 20-foot ledge near the day-use area.

The easy Woodbine Trail (marked in blue arrows) shares part of the hard-surface bike trail up the hill and along a runoff creek past moist soils that host a variety of spring and summer wildflowers. The ridgeline is scenic, especially in autumn, and is also near a grove of sweet gum trees and a CCC-era stone building.

The Hawthorn Trail (1.25 miles) passes a narrow ridge along a single-lane dirt path that bisects two distinct habitats. The hot and dry southwest side of the spine-like ridge has sparse flora where underlying rock sometimes cracks the surface soil. On the northeastern slope, the plant life thickens and the soil layer is deeper, hosting paw paws and hardy shrubs. At the turnaround is a sizable rock outcropping that overlooks Wild Horse Creek Road.

The mossy two-mile Virginia Day Memorial Nature Trail (marked with red arrows) starts near the visitor's center and is named for a longtime park volunteer. The gentle loop traces the ridge and hollow between the visitor's center and

The park has 11-miles of equestrian trails.

the camping area. I love this loop. It has some easy climbs and descends through cedar groves and dry washes that run flush after rainstorms. Also along the trail are white oak, sugar maple, basswood, dogwood and redbud.

Biking: The bike trail is at the south end of the park. There is no access to the Katy Trail State Park from Babler. The park has seven miles of hard-surface roads that offer great walking and biking.

Equestrian trail: A gravel parking lot is available for horsemen and women to use 11 miles of rolling trails. A picnic table is also at the staging area. This trailhead is one mile from the main park entrance on the south side of the winding park road.

Nature: Babler Memorial State Park offers teacher-training workshops designed for teachers K-12. Some workshops concentrate on Project Wild to enhance student performance on the map. Project Wild is an interdisciplinary conservation and environmental education program emphasizing wildlife using hands-on activities to help students make informed decisions about our environment. Other programs include Scouting the Daniel Boone Home, Tree Treasures and use of Project Wild's 150 activities for classrooms.

The Jacob L. Babler Outdoor Education Center, operated by the Rockwood School District, at Babler State Park features a 2,400-square-foot recreation hall, eight cabins, pool, fishing, archery range, campfire areas and large activity fields for area school children. The facility is also ideal for group meetings, retreats, family reunions and overnight stays by groups. The entire camp is accessible to people with disabilities and priority is given to such groups.

Summer activities by the park naturalist include migratory bird day; fish, frog and polliwog programs; bug day; creatures of the night; fine feathered friends; nutty nature; trees, bees and butterfly knees; eco-logic and many others.

Outdoor science buffs should also consider the St. Louis Science Center summer program and day camps at 5050 Oakland Ave. in St. Louis.

On the hills that rise from the Missouri River is a moist, lush mixture of forests, plants and animals. This diverse forest wildlife community is influenced by the rolling topography, fertile soil and climate. Here four of nature's five biomes and major natural communities come together in a transition zone known as an ecotone. Plants and animals common in the Eastern deciduous, Northern forest, Southern Gulf coastal forest and the Western plains all live together in the park.

Flora common to the park includes spice bush, gray coneflower, little blue stem, Indian grass, paw paw, bitternut hickory, basswood, northern red oak, white trillium and others. The hickory forest found in Babler is actually many varieties of trees, shrubs, ferns, moss and fungi. These plants provide food, shelter, atmosphere and moisture for the plant-eating animals. Carnivorous predators also depend on forest plants and animals for survival.

Mammals commonly seen in the park include raccoon, turkey, whitetail deer, about 40 bird species, Eastern chipmunk and striped skunk.

Junior Naturalists are busy at Babler. Visitors can often see their drawings and reports proudly displayed much like my kids' handiwork on the refrigerator door. The Junior

Naturalists know we have 79 species of trees in the state.

The kids' outdoor education worksheets are often posted near a display of mounts that include perch, bluegill, long-eared sunfish, five-line skink, cave salamander, green tree frog and flying squirrel. Plants include puccoon, red maple, Indian pipe, coreopsis, box elder, Queen Anne's lace, Jack-in-the-pulpit, dwarf sumac, slippery elm, coral berry, Eastern wahoo, thimbleweed, flowering dogwood, reindeer moss and white ash.

The dozen binocular microscopes in the center of the visitor's center offer nature students of all ages a chance to examine a number of nature objects including fur, bone, antler, teeth, rock and minerals, feathers, shells and plant material.

Fossils are evidence, preserved in stone, of animals or plants that lived in past geologic times. The inland seas that covered Missouri and the mid-continent throughout much of the Paleozoic time were mostly warm, shallow seas teeming with animal life. Many of these marine organisms are preserved as fossils in the sedimentary rocks in the park. Some of the most common are displayed in the visitor's center and they include bryozoans, sponges, corals, brachiopods, pelecypods, castropods, cephalopods, blastoids and various plan fossils.

Fossils and the geological formations in the park are the result of eons of movement and pressures on the Earth's thin outer crust. Constant volcanic action caused huge slabs of land to collide and stack themselves, making mountains and valleys. Forced molten lava, the continents have been crusted together and split, changing their locations on an expanding sea floor at a rate of only a few feet each century. They have been jolted along a course that has affected plants and animals not only in Missouri but also around the globe. Take time to read the interpretive display to learn about the eras and their impact on the Ozarks and plains to the west.

If you like nature, you can attract lots of it to your backyard. A display in the center shows you how to build and maintain bird feeders and suet feeders, and how to build a bat house, nesting boxes and lots more.

Dr. Edmund A. Babler monument.

The big aquarium tanks hold native fish, and specimens change often. A regular in the 200-gallon tanks is a largemouth bass. Don't forget to look it up when wandering about the visitor's center. Along the ceiling are a number of mounts that include an American kestrel, purple martin, goldfinch and a river otter in a small diorama depicting its life under ice.

Birding: The park publishes a list of common birds found in the park. Ask for a copy of the checklist that includes sharp-shinned hawk, red-tailed hawk, wild turkey, great horned owl, red-head and red-bellied woodpeckers, brown creeper, Carolina wren, golden-crowned kinglet, Eastern bluebird, Northern mockingbird, oven bird, yellow-rumped warbler, Eastern towhee, five species of sparrows, purple finch, horned lark and many others.

Most of these species can be seen from the roadside during the appropriate seasons. Spring warbler watching is considered good and pine warblers can be seen in the conifers beginning in April. The old-growth regions offer a chance to see five species of woodpeckers, including the crow-sized pileated woodpecker that carves triangular holes for nesting in the spring and early summer. If time is limited, hike the two-mile nature trail that starts near the visitor's center. The trail descends a valley and meanders along a ridge where forested layers vary and many tree species are maturing in the secondary recovering forest.

Day-use areas: The Alta Picnic Area has a Civilian Conservation Corps (CCC) made shelter with shake shingles, stout rocks and picnic tables inside. The shelter has a stone fireplace and accents. Look for the blue water tower and you'll find this shade picnic area that has parking for about 50 cars and mowed lawns for field games. The Guy Park Picnic Area also has a CCC shelter and day-use areas. The Walnut Grove Picnic Area has a baseball backstop and mowed areas.

Other day-use areas have a terrific blend of manicured areas, cozy picnic sites and rugged woodlands. In some places grasses and wildflowers are allowed to grow to maturity along the roadways.

Swimming: The six-lane pool opens Memorial Day to Labor Day from noon to 6 p.m. on weekdays and until 7 p.m. on Friday, Saturday, Sunday and holidays. A daily pass is required and discount passes are available. Near the pool are four basketball goals and two backstops for softball or baseball. A number of picnic tables and grills are also near the pool. There is a shallow kiddies pool at the facility, where swimming lessons are offered during the summer.

Near each corner of the L-shaped pool are teal-colored canopy tents and deck chairs on the cement deck. The concession stand offers Nachos, hot dogs, chili dogs, sodas and snow cones.

A swimming test may be required before you enter the diving area. Coolers are not permitted in the pool.

Fun facts: In 1942, part of the park was used as a prison-of-war camp. A CCC-era building at the park is on the National Historic Register.

Kids' view: You can hike through a paw paw grove and discover the aromatic spicebush. Spicebush was used during the Civil War as allspice. Paw paws are the only food source for the zebra swallowtail butterfly.

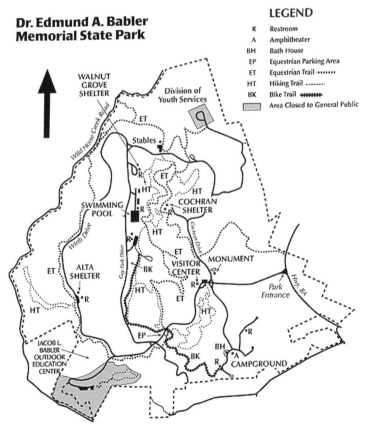

Dr. Edmund A. Babler Memorial State Park

LEGEND

R	Restroom
A	Amphitheater
BH	Bath House
EP	Equestrian Parking Area
ET	Equestrian Trail ········
HT	Hiking Trail ········
BK	Bike Trail +++++++
	Area Closed to General Public

Bring your bike and canoe to Castlewood State Park.

CHAPTER 20
Castlewood State Park
Land: 1,802 acres Water: Meramec River

One of Missouri's premier recreation and historic resort areas during the early 1900s has been reinvented as Castlewood State Park. From 1915 until 1940, St. Louisans by the thousands visited the scenic area for canoeing, jitterbug dancing and sunning on Lincoln Beach along the south bank of the Meramec River. Some even gambled in card rooms shaded by the mixed woodlands and greased with high-dollar stakes. During the area's heyday, it was not uncommon for urban trains to drop off 10,000 weekend resort-goers at three small depots along the foot of the Meramec bluff.

A grand staircase that the fun-seekers used still exists and leads to the ruins of the three resort hotels and many summer cabins once located in the area. Historic black and white photographs in the park office bring to life this era depicting ladies in long swimsuits and picnickers with hats and clothing of the era between the First and Second World Wars.

One of the first piped and pressurized water systems outside of St. Louis was to these upscale hotels and cabins. An old water pump once used to force water from a shallow well along the river to cisterns atop the bluff still stands in the park.

In this bygone era, daytime activities were centered on canoeing, swimming and "indoor ball," now called softball. The evening was filled with dancing on a huge open floor and who knows what back at the hotel. Many people who visited the park nearly 80 years ago were bachelors with club or group names like Happy Hollow, Wigwam, Galions, Gin Creek and Nuthatch. Young ladies stayed in dorms called the Wagner Electric Girl's Club and the Catholic Corona Club.

Huge barns along the river housed canoes, and local farmers sold fresh foods to these hard partying groups. Enjoy the history and think about the partiers from a simple time.

The park strides both sides of the river and offers hiking, day use, nature study, floating and fishing. It provides an enclave of peace from the bustle of the nearby metro areas.

Information and activities

Castlewood State Park
1401 Kiefer Creek Road
Ballwin, MO 63021
(636) 227-4433

Directions: Along eight miles of the Meramec River.

From the south on I-44 or I-55

Take the Hwy. 141 exit and travel north to Big Bend Road. Turn left and travel west to Ries Road. Turn left and continue until reaching the park entrance at the intersection of Kiefer Creek and Ries roads.

From I-270

Take the Dougherty Ferry Road exit and travel west on Dougherty Ferry to Big Bend Road. Turn right on Big Bend Road and travel west to Ries Road. Turn left and continue to the park entrance at the intersection of Kiefer

Creek and Ries roads.

From the north on U.S. Hwy. 40/61

Take the Clarkson exit (near Chesterfield Mall) and travel south. Clarkson crosses Manchester Road and becomes Kiefer Creek Road, which leads to the state park.

From Hwy. 100/Manchester Road (three options)

Take Kiefer Creek Road off of Manchester/Hwy. 100. Kiefer Creek Road will lead into the state park. Or take Ries Road off of Manchester/Hwy. 100. Follow Ries Road to the intersection with Kiefer Creek Road at the park entrance. Or take New Ballwin Road off of Manchester/Hwy. 100. When New Ballwin Road intersects with Kiefer Creek Road, turn left and continue to the park.

The A-frame park office has a shady porch and pay phone. Inside the tiny park office are some terrific old black and white photographs of historic park use, including a picture of the "Happy Hollow Club." Other photos include the old hotel, crowded beaches, church, riverboat, store, Lone Wolf Club, lifeguards from the 1920s and the Red Dog Saloon. There is also a large photo of the limestone Castlewood above the drinking fountain. A trailhead is next to the office.

Emergency number: 911 system.

Hiking: There's something for everybody on Castlewood 28 miles of trails. The Wolf Trail, for example, is a tight twister for bikers, while the Stinging Nettles is flat and easy. Elevation changes can total 300 feet on Castlewood trails.

The River Scene Trail is steep with loose gravel. Atop the palisade bluff are rocky overlooks with a bench and no railings, so watch your toddlers. To your left is the vaulting Castlewood, which is depicted in a photo at the park office. Views include wooded alcoves, gravel shoal and the gentle river about 230 feet downward. If you look closely, you might also see some cyclists plying along the shoreline trail. Go slow down the loose gravel path to the trailhead. There are nearly 200 wooden steps and the trail is open to hikers only in the boardwalk area. The rest of the trail is open to bikes.

Grotpeter Trail (Blue, 3-mile loop) tracts along Keifer Creek thought moist bottomlands. Horses and bikes share this loop. This is the most challenging hiking and riding trail in the park. Hikers can get on the trail from several locations. More than a mile of the trail is along bottomlands.

Lone Wolf Trail (Black, 1.5 miles) also traverses a bluff with views of the river and descends to the creek valley for hikers and bikers. The trail's namesake is the Lone Wolf Club, a tavern used during the resort days at the beginning of the last century.

Stinging Nettle Loop (Yellow, 3-mile loop) runs through the bottomlands and old dredging site at the river. Don't touch stinging nettle, which produces a prickly irritating fluid. The Cedar Bluff Trail (Yellow, 2 miles) is reached from the Stinging Nettles Trail and covers two hilltops and around blackberry brambles.

The park roads are great for dog walking, but keep Rover on a leash.

Nature: Park visitors can enjoy upland forests of the eastern Ozark border that feature white oak and hickory near the park entrance. With permission, you can also ramble around the floodplain forest where silver maple, hackberry, elm and sycamore prosper. During the spring, dogwood and redbud offer splashes of color along park roads and along the trails.

Many think the best way to see the park and appreciate its natural beauty is by floating the river. In fact, a well-known day float is from Times Beach to the eastern park take-out. Approach the gravel bars quietly, and you might see kingfishers and herons hunting for dinner. Hawks also fly the river corridor, sailing on the invisible currents between meals.

Staff says evening hikers might hear owls and witness bats doing their acrobatic flights eating thousands of insects each night. Crow-sized pileated woodpeckers frequently are heard rapping on standing dead timber, while deer and many other common animals avoid much human contact. Mammals commonly seen at the park include coyotes, striped skunk, woodchuck, squirrels, rabbits and songbirds.

Biking: With lots of elevation changes and hard-surface

**Hikers will discover rocky overlooks and palisade bluffs.
The river is 230 feet below on the River Scene Trail.**

park roads and packed earth trails, bikers flock to the park
for challenging riding. Traffic can be heavy on the Cedar
Bluff and Stinging Nettles trail, especially on weekends.

Equestrian trails: Trail riders have a hard-surface parking
area near the bridge. Across from the parking area for horse
trailers are a playground and additional day-use parking.

Fishing: Angers must limit their catch of spotted bass to
12 daily. Large- and smallmouth bass must be at least 12
inches, and you may take six daily. There are 125 species of
fish in the Meramec River including walleye, rock bass,
white crappie, spotted bass, paddlefish, drum and catfish.

Learn more about the improving Meramac River at
www.conservation.state.mo.us.

Boating: There is river access where you can carry in a
canoe or small boat. Nearby is a sand and gravel shoal
where canoeists can easily launch and land. A restroom is
near the landing area. There are 14 public boat ramps from
the city of Arnold (Mississippi River mouth) to M-185 along
the river. The river is about 100 miles long.

Day-use areas: Bring your pitching wedge because you
can carefully hit practice shots in the park's open spaces,
but special rules do apply, so always check with staff or the
bulletin boards to see which areas are open. The day-use
area near the Bluff Overlook Trail features a volleyball

court, open spaces, picnic tables and shelters, swings and play apparatus with benches for parents.

Castlewood has a grand mix of day-use spaces. Some are open and sunny, great for field games, while other are shady and cozy, perfect for family picnics. Grills and drinking fountains abound. Many of these day-use areas are at trailheads. Private picnicking is not a problem at Castlewood.

Kids' view: The 230-foot limestone bluff is really high.

Bring the canoe because the river is gentle and there are lots of shoreline takeout points and places to explore. It's quiet at the river early in the morning.

Fun facts: A firefighter's training center is at Castlewood and Keifer roads. It's a building that can be lit on fire for practice.

Bring your bike and canoe. The park is the site for adventure races (teams compete in three categories: biking, run and upstream float). The park also offers park prowls, night hikes and other programs. Call the park office for detailed information on special programs for groups. If you like Castlewood, plan a trip to the area it inspired, the Meramac River Recreation Area.

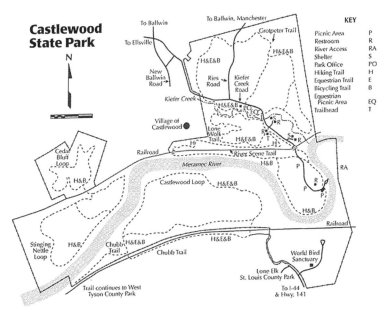

The best way to see Hawn State Park is on foot.
Whispering Pine Trail is ten-miles long.

CHAPTER 21

Hawn State Park

Land: 4,953 acres   Water: Pickle Creek

S tately pines, steep cliffs and sandy-bottomed streams
that run clear give Hawn State Park a superb
character not often found in public parks. The best
way to experience this park is on foot along bluffs, pine
needle-strewn forest floors and along scenic Lamotte
sandstone box canyons. The park has 15 miles of trails,
from the moderately difficult Whispering Pine Trail to the
easy-walking White Oak and Pickle Creek trails.

If you enjoy windswept overlooks, waterfalls and
cascades, you'll love Hawn's back country that is filled with
majestic pines and their cool shade during the summer.
This park is the finest hikers' park in the state.

Sandstone at the park is coarse and grainy. Aside from
the raw beauty of sandstone, the material holds
groundwater and helps produce acidic soil that offers

habitat for some exceptional plants.

Scattered blocks of sandstone and the forested hills of the Ozark Border can be seen from the car as you drive around the park. There are spectacular views in all directions that will convince you that this is one of the most scenic parks in the state. The cool forests and sheltered haunts of the park will often make you feel like you are in a forest hundreds of miles to the north. The headwater canyons and sandstone shelves along Pickle Creek have some of the cooler climate habitats for hikers to enjoy. Bring your most comfortable boots for a memorable, diverse hike.

Aside from the distinctive natural history of the park is the historic importance of nearby Ste. Genevieve, the oldest incorporated town in Missouri, founded in the 1720s. Ste. Genevieve was an important port along the Mississippi River. In 1852, the Old Plank Road was constructed to connect Ste. Genevieve and the iron and lead mines of Iron Mountain. Lumber for building and upkeep of the 42-mile-long road, which was 2 inches thick, came from area oak and pine forests. The plank road paralleled the northern boundary of the park and present Route 32.

Helen Coffer Haw, a former schoolteacher, donated the initial acreage for the park in 1952.

Information and activities:

Hawn State Park
12096 Park Drive
Ste. Genevieve, MO 63670
(573) 883-3603
(877) I Camp Mo; Camping Reservations
www.mostateparks.com

Park office: The office offers brochures, maps and firewood sales. In front of the park office are some interesting horse-drawn farm implements on display.

Directions:

From St. Louis

Hawn State Park is 60 miles south of St. Louis and 20 miles west of Ste. Genevieve. From south St. Louis, take I-55 south to Exit 150. Exit onto Hwy. 32 and travel west 11 miles to Hwy. 144. Turn left onto Hwy. 144 and travel 4 miles to reach the state park.

From Farmington

Hawn State Park is 13 miles east of Farmington. Take Hwy. 32 east 9 miles to Hwy. 144. Turn right onto Hwy. 144 and travel 4 miles to reach the park.

Emergency numbers: 911 system; hospital, (573) 756-6451.

Campground: Hawn State Park offers 50 basic and electric campsites. Services available include reservable sites, a dump station, showers, water and laundry. For reservations, there is a required two-night minimum stay on weekends from April through October and major holidays from May 15 through Sept. 15.

Loop 1-9 has electric sites. They are intimate and along Pickle Creek. They have a vault toilet and are just south of the loop that contains sites 11-45.

Most of the campsites are cushioned by a layer of red pine needles and a canopy that filters the sun. Sites on the outside of the loop are backed up against the woods and a rocky bluff at the creek. Site 19 has wonderful pencil-straight pines that seem to scrape the sky. It is also near the playground and small mowed open space. Sites in the 20s have space for tents off the camping pad. If you like sunny camping, try sites in the low 30s. These sites also have some mowed spaces between them.

Walk-in sites are 46-50 at the end of the loop. The special-use area is also near the walk-in sites, with a short path near site 36. A vault toilet for the walk-in and group sites is also near site 36. The special-use area has water, but no electricity.

Sites in the high 30s are near the showerhouse and sunny. Site 37 is particularly sunny. The showerhouse has five courses of brick and rough sawn siding. There are five unisex showers and coin-operated washers and dryers. The laundry has a utility sink and a countertop for folding your clean clothes. Site 42 is covered with red pine needles and site 45 might be one of the nicest sites in the unit. It has some privacy and a sense you are camping in a grove. Sites

10 and 12 are much the same way.

The amphitheater is behind site 41 where naturalists offer outdoor education programs. The campground is usually full on holidays and summer weekends.

Hiking: Whispering Pine Trail (10 miles) was constructed in 1976 and 1977 with the help of the Ozark Chapter of the Sierra Club. The trail consists of two loops: the north loop is about six miles long and the south loop is about four miles. The trail provides the opportunity for day hikes of varying lengths or a longer backpacking trip. It meanders through a beautiful mixed hardwood and pine forest, which is home to a variety of animals such as bobcat and wild turkey. Extensive exposures of sandstone and granite can be explored along the banks of Pickle Creek and the River Aux Vases. Mosses and ferns create a luxurious effect on the moist overhangs that occur along the two streams. The Whispering Pine Trail can be reached by turning left at the park entrance and proceeding to the picnic area, where a parking area is provided. Water is not available at the trailhead, but can be obtained at the park office or the campground.

Pickle Creek Trail (one mile) begins at the picnic area between the park office and the campground. Once near it, you'll hear the rushing water. The entire trail follows Pickle Creek, which is a beautiful stream. The trail provides a point-to-point hike, although a loop hike is possible by returning on a portion of Whispering Pine Trail that traverses the bluffs on the opposite side of the creek. The campground is about 100 yards from the trailhead of Pickle Creek.

Nature: The Pine Savanna Demonstration Area is maintained by fire. Once naturally occurring fires enhanced the open tree canopy and prairie-like vegetation of the savannas. Today, fire carefully controlled in time and frequency is used to maintain several landscapes. A sample of this careful burning is near the park office. Notice how the mature trees are merely singed.

Also interesting at the park is the fauna. For example, a variety of frogs inhabit the area including the Illinois chorus frog, gray tree frog, Eastern narrow mouth toad,

Many of the campsites are cushioned by a bed of pine needles and shady.

green frog, pickerel frog and the Northern spring peepers.

The cool, damp and shady hillsides have produced a broad menu of flora that includes orchids (including two rare types, green adder's mouth and rattlesnake plantain), Canadian white violet, partridgeberry, lady fern, spleenwort, hay-scented fern, bulblet fern, marginal shield fern, common woodfern, ebony pinnatifid and others. Ground cedar is an endangered plant that is found in the park and only a few other sites in the county.

Pickle Creek has 20 species of fish, including the uncommon silvermouth minnow. The pine-clad ridges camouflage many types of mosses, ferns, lichen and small mammals. Quiet walking often exposes both the fauna and flora that thrive in the understory. Typical mammals that you might encounter include whitetailed deer, raccoon, broad-headed skunk, pine warblers, chickadees, owls, scarlet tanagers and squirrels.

From May through August, a naturalist provides regularly scheduled interpretive programs on weekends. Programs include nature hikes, slide shows, nature bingo and much more.

Day-use areas: Visitors can choose from 30 picnic sites nestled under pine trees. An open picnic shelter, approximately 100-person occupancy, can be reserved at the park office for $30 per day. If not reserved, the shelter may be used on a first-come, first-served basis at no charge. The shelter includes two outdoor barbecue grills and picnic tables.

Insider's tips: Check out the charred trees and tall pines. Hawn is probably the best hiker's park in the state. Try to visit in the spring when the redbud and dogwoods are in full bloom. Look for pink granite rock when you are hiking the trails. You can backpack in the Whispering Pine Wild Area.

Hawn State Park

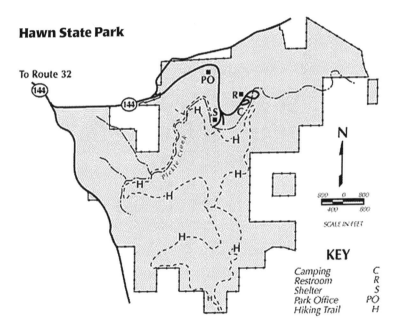

MISSOURI
State Parks

CHAPTER 22
Edward "Ted" and Pat Jones-Confluence Point State Park
Land: 1,118 acres
Water: Missouri and Mississippi rivers

The park was dedicated in the spring of 2004.
In 1804, Meriwether Lewis and William Clark began their journey up the Missouri River at the confluence of the two great rivers of North America, the Missouri and Mississippi. Today, visitors can watch as the Big Muddy and Mighty Mississippi merge into one at Edward "Ted" and Pat Jones-Confluence Point State Park.

The role that both rivers played in the Lewis and Clark expedition and the history of the rivers are interpreted at the park in outdoor exhibits. A short interpretive trail takes visitors to the confluence point.

Restoration of a natural floodplain, which will emphasize native vegetation and natural wetlands suitable for the site's soil, topography and hydrology, is planned for the 1,118-acre park. This will include forests, prairies and marshes with abundant opportunity to preserve native plants.

The confluence point also provides an excellent place for bird watching as millions of birds migrate along the Mississippi River corridor each spring and fall, while others reside in the area. Visitors to the park can relax and enjoy many species of songbirds, shore birds, wading birds, waterfowl and raptors as they watch the rivers flow by.

Information and activities

Edward "Ted" and Pat Jones-Confluence Point State Park
P.O. Box 67
1000 Riverlands Way
West Alton, MO 63386
(636) 899-1135
www.mostateparks.com

Directions: In West Alton off Hwy. 67 east, then right on Riverlands Way just before Clark's bridge.

According to the state's Web site, *www.mostateparks.com* "The mission of Edward 'Ted' and Pat Jones-Confluence Point State Park is to restore, preserve and interpret a quality natural floodplain community that includes diverse flora and fauna while providing numerous recreational opportunities such as hiking, fishing and wildlife viewing. The park will also protect and interpret the unique cultural history of the area and provide excellent opportunities for researching both the natural processes and historical associations of the park's landscape."

Proposed development for Confluence State Park, according to the state's Web site:

• Preserve and interpret the natural and cultural resources associated with the two great rivers.

• Provide recreational and public use facilities that are consistent with the preservation of these resources and the mission of the park, that withstand flooding and that do not exceed the capacity of the land to sustain these activities.

• Provide visitor orientation and interpretive facilities to enhance the public's understanding, appreciation and enjoyment of the resources of the park.

- Provide adequate operational, administrative and maintenance support facilities to protect, secure, restore and maintain the resources of the park.
- Design and develop all structures and facilities to withstand periodic flooding.
- Provide linkage to other trails and greenway systems within the St. Louis urban area.
- Designate tree planting sites and prairie and marsh restoration areas to be used as outdoor classrooms and/or group project sites, as part of the park's urban outreach and environmental education efforts.
- Restore native natural vegetation across the site.
- Check with the state for how the developing is going.

A little history: In 1721, French explorer Father Pierre Francois de Charlevoix wrote of the confluence of the Mississippi and Missouri rivers, "I believe this is the finest confluence in the world. The two rivers are much the same breadth, each about half a league; but the Missouri is by far the most rapid, and seems to enter the Mississippi like a conqueror, through which it carries its white waters to the opposite shore without mixing them. Afterwards, it gives its color to the Mississippi, which it never loses again but carries quite down to the sea...."

Nearly 300 years later, visitors to Edward "Ted" and Pat Jones-Confluence Point State Park can still witness the two great rivers of North America as they join and become one. The Mississippi River, the vital highway down which the products of America's factories and fields travel to the world market, merges with the Missouri River, the wild western river. In 1804, explorers Meriwether Lewis and William Clark hoped the Missouri River was the Northwest Passage leading to the Pacific Ocean. They did not find the Northwest Passage, but at the confluence of the two rivers, they began their epic journey to the ocean.

Just as today's Americans live in a world much changed from that of Lewis and Clark, the two great rivers have changed and continue to change the confluence point. The confluence point is now two miles downstream from the point where the Corps of Discovery entered into the

Missouri River. The expedition's keelboat actually floated atop the present-day confluence point, as it was then the river channel.

Nature: The confluence point is one of the area's best places for bird watching as millions of birds migrate along the Mississippi River corridor each spring and fall. The Mississippi River flyway is used by 60 percent of all North American bird species, including 40 percent of all waterfowl. Common birds seen in the area include great blue herons, bald eagles, geese, gulls, pelicans and many kinds of songbirds.

Insider's tips: Edward "Ted" and Pat Jones-Confluence Point State Park is part of the Confluence Greenway, a 200-square-mile network of conservation, heritage and recreation attractions being developed along the Great Rivers in the heart of the bi-state St. Louis region. For more information, visit ***www.confluencegreenway.org***

Edward "Ted" and Pat Jones - Confluence State Park

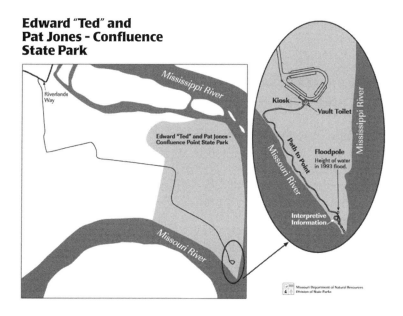

Meramec State Park has a 2,500-square-foot visitor center, motel, cabins, cave tours, conference center and a large campground.

CHAPTER 23
Meramec State Park
Land: 6,896 acres   Water: Meramec River

The grand river and caves define Meramec State Park. It is also defined by a rich history led by American Indians, early white settlers both French and American and mining. Some of this history was brought to life during an emotional dispute over damming the river in the 1970's.

Happily, the park and river have been preserved and celebrated over the years. From Civilian Conservation Corps-era buildings to a modern visitor center, campers, hikers and paddlers will find plenty to keep busy. The rich diversity of the park's environs includes an expanse of nature forests with trees that often get huge on east and north slopes, and steep cliffs. Under these giants and along open spaces are delicate lady slipper orchids in May and brilliant purple coneflower and lavender ray flowers in June.

The glades and forests are some of the finest in Missouri. If this isn't enough, the park features one of the state's first "show caves." Visitors will love the cool moist air at the entrance of the Fisher Cave and witness some unusual plants.

There are many fine foot trails that meander through hollows, thin ridgelines and cherty creeks. Backpackers may camp among the glades and braces of wildflowers in the northern half of the rugged park. The hillside turns golden in the fall and the cooler temperatures make Meramec State Park a great destination for long hikes, biking and camping.

The park borders seven miles of the Meramec River, which has more than 125 species of fish and 40 species of mussel. In the caves are 10 species of bats that take flight nightly amid the mosaic of bluffs, savannas and old fields. More than 650 species of plants have been recorded at the park and park naturalists offer outdoor education during the summer.

Information and activities

Meramec State Park
115 Meramec Park Drive
Sullivan, MO 63080
(573) 468-6072
(877) I Camp Mo; Camping Reservations
www.mostateparks.com

Directions:

From St. Louis

Meramec State Park is about 1 hour, 15 minutes from the St. Louis area. Travel west on I-44 to Exit 226/Sullivan/Hwy. 185 South. After exiting, turn left over I-44 and continue for three miles south on Hwy. 185. The state park entrance is on the right side.

From Cuba/St. James/Rolla

Travel east on I-44 to Exit 226/Sullivan/Hwy. 185 South. After exiting, turn right onto Hwy. 185 and continue for three miles. The state park entrance is on the right side.

From Jefferson City

Meramec State Park is about 1 hour, 45 minutes from Jefferson City. Travel south on U.S. Hwy. 63 to the Vichy Airport. Turn west onto Hwy. 68 and continue to St. James; take I-44 east to Exit 226/Sullivan/Hwy. 186 South. After exiting, turn right onto Hwy. 185 and continue for three miles. The state park entrance is on the right side.

Emergency numbers: 911 system; ambulance, (573) 468-4186.

Visitor center: The light gray, 2,500-square-foot visitor center is open 9 a.m. to 4:30 p.m. daily, April through October. During the off season open from 8 a.m. to 3:30 p.m. A telephone is near the hard-surface parking lot. The visitor center was dedicated in 1989.

The objective of the visitor center is to interpret the upper Meramec River.

Inside are dioramas, board displays, a 3,500-gallon aquarium with 19 species of fish and a 20-minute slide show about the park shown upon request. There is also a video about mussels of the Meramec River. The accompanying display features unusual mussels that include the fat mucket, scale shell, fragile paper shells, snuff box, lilliput, fingernail clams, pond horn, mucket creeper, round pig toe, sheep's nose and many other oddly named mussels.

Mounts found in the center include smallmouth bass, American eel, belted kingfisher, bank swallow, blue star plants, speckled crayfish, stoneflies, rock bass, darters and hellbenders.

The hellbender is a giant salamander that makes its home in streams and rivers in the Ozarks. It typically hides by day under large flat rocks with good circulation and oxygen-rich water. Near this display are big pictures of the horny-headed chub, bullfrog, lamprey, Blanchard's cricket frog, red spotted purple butterfly, woodcock, bobcat, warblers, Ozark minnow, Southern red-bellied dace, water snake, soft shell turtle and many backlit pictures of native fauna.

In the large aquarium are a number of species of fish including black crappie, green sunfish, gar, drum, white

The park has 22 air-conditioned motel rooms.

bass and long-ear sunfish. Next to the aquarium is a wall-mounted display that details "Life Along the Bank." It has a touch quiz that asks, for example, Which riverbank animal is the main predator of frogs? You'll have to visit to discover the answer!

One of my favorite displays is common butterflies. By the way, butterfly watching is becoming increasingly popular, almost like birding. Examples include the goatweed butterfly, giant swallowtail, spicebush swallowtail, Baltimore checker spot, red-spotted purple, tiger swallowtail and zebra swallowtail.

The Ozarks' river and streams have eroded deeply into the bedrock, revealing a vast network of ancient subsurface drainage known as caves and springs. More than 400 caves and 300 springs have been discovered in the upper Meramec Basin; together, the springs and cave streams represent about 20 percent of the water flowing out of the upper basin.

Geological formations include sandstone that makes up about 35 percent of the basin's bedrock. It is composed mainly of grains of quartz held together with silica, lime and iron oxide. These grains once were part of an ancient beach that slowly weathered from the river bluffs and accumulated in the riverbed as sandbars. Chert is also a common rock in the park and is associated with basin dolomite because it is as hard as glass and breaks with equally sharp edges. It was used by early man to make projectile points (arrowheads, etc.). Although brittle, chert is practically insoluble and makes up more than 95 percent of the basins river gravel. It is the also the best rock in the basin for finding fossils. Dolomite makes up about 60 percent of the river basin's bedrock. Rainwater charged with carbon dioxide slowly dissolves dolomite, leaving holes. For this reason caves and springs are often in dolomite deposits.

A mounted otter is near the touch table, which gives visitors a chance to feel a number of nature items. Also in this area of the visitor center is a display about the America Indian which exhibits primitive tools, hammer stones, chert river cobble, flakes, arrowheads, shell-tempered jars, shell scrapers, shell hoe blades and fishhooks made of bone. Indians relied heavily on the river as a place to find both fish and game. They ate many animals that are rarely eaten today such as mink, muskrat, beaver, heron and mussel.

The sheltered valleys, bluffs and caves provided protection from storms and heat. More than 350 archeological sites have been discovered in the basin and more than 80 percent are within one-quarter mile of the river or a tributary.

These Indians relied on many foods and natural medicines, including hickory nuts that were easily collected and stored. Pawpaws also ripened along the Meramec River in mid-September and have a sweet banana-like flavor. The leaves of the young willow contain a compound like aspirin and were used to relieve pain, swelling and fever. The spicebush made a flavored tea, while horsetail rush has so much silica that it was used like sandpaper for polishing or cleaning utensils. Elderberry was used to treat burns and help with labor inducement. Burr oak acorns are the largest in North America. Ragweed seeds were also collected and used for food.

When white settlers came to the valleys, they settled a number of locations during the 1830s and later. Early accounts of the Meramec River reports that it was frequently blocked by uprooted trees, which made it difficult to use for transportation. Although much less dependent on trade than white men, the Indian has established a well-worn trail along the northern rim of the basin that became known to the white men as the "Osage Trail." Parts of the trail became a wagon road and then in the 1850s a railroad was added. In the 1930s, this wagon road became U.S. Route 66. Today much of I-44 follows the original trail.

As the region developed, people from St. Louis would ride the train along the northern rim of the basin and catch a ride to the river. This early appreciation of river quality led to the establishment in 1926 of Meramec State Park, the first of four state parks along the river.

Birds are no longer fed outside the wildlife observation because black bears began to feed at the station. Feeding timid black bear can change them into bold troublemakers.

Campground: The park has 210 campsites and three group sites, including 147 reservable sites, 62 first-come and three group camping sites. Many prime sites are reservable, including waterside sites. Near the fee booth are mowed open spaces where there are some informal volleyball courts and some tent campers. About 100 yards from the fee booth is a shower house. Every site has a ground-mounted fire ring and picnic table. There are also soft drink vending machines and coin-operated washers and dryers in the campground.

Sites 1-19 are premier and across a narrow park road from the peaceful Meramec River. Each of these shady sites can accommodate large RV units. These sites are dry and hard-packed.

Site 60 is lightly shaded, breezy and a perfect place for a pop-up camper or tents. The sites in the 60s are about 50 percent shade mixed with open grassy areas. Sites in the 70s have 12- to 14-inch caliper trees offering shade and some additional space for horseshoes or other small-scale field games. A drinking fountain is near site 73. Site 76 is T-

Many of the cozy cabins are near the dining lodge.

shaped, hard-surfaced and accessible for campers with disabilities. Sites in the 80s are half-shady. Sites 83-84 are excellent for pop-up campers or tents. Sites 85-86 are near a quiet road.

Sites in the low 90s are sunny. Sites in the low 100s are mostly sunny with scattered trees about every 30 to 50 feet. There is some open space near site 111 for small-scale field games.

Sites 22-59 are electric sites. This loop has sycamore and oaks that offer light shade and a vault toilet near site 29. Sites in the 30s have slightly larger trees towering overhead, offering a canopy of shade on those hot summer afternoons. Site 45 is at the end of the loop and somewhat private. However, you can see from one end of the campground to the other without much vegetation obstructing the view.

Some of the sites in the 40s are along a slightly narrowing hard-surface park road. Sites in the 50s can accommodate big RV rigs and are near the drinking fountain and modern play apparatus.

A 300-year-old burr oak tree is near the campground fee station. It's a fantastic tree with at least a six-foot diameter and broad canopy that casts a mushroom-shaped shadow across the camping area.

Sites in the 120s are either along a natural area or the river. All of the sites in the 130s and sites 141, 143, 145, 147 and 149 are against the woods. Along this straight stretch of campsites is 138, which is private and near a drinking fountain that is shaded by skyscraping hardwoods. Behind the sites in the 130s are some 150- to 200-year-old trees complete with twisted branches and burls. Each tree is this section seems to whisper a story of pioneers, dense forests and now squealing kids and campers.

Sites in the even numbered 140s are in a small mowed open field. Park staff says Meramec is popular with young families for a number of reasons, the campground being one of them.

Sites 1-20 have hard-surface pads and are across the park road from the river. Large RV units traditionally occupy many of the sites in the teens.

Pencil-straight trees heavily shade sites in the 150s. This area has huge beech and ash trees that offer at least 75 percent shade. Sites in the 160s are across the park road from the river and have gravel pads.

Sites 178-180 are set back off the road and gently into the woods. Just steps from the river, these sites allow tent campers to get off the pad and into a lightly wooded area. Loop 181-188 are often filled with tent campers, who enjoy mostly shady sites. Shower Building No. 2 is next to sites 187 and 188. Site 186 is gloriously sunny.

Remember, skunks and raccoons can ruin your camping experience. There isn't much problem here at Meramec, but you should not feed any animals and keep you trash and food in the appropriate receptacles. It's also a good idea to keep food in your car or camper.

In loop 189-210, canoers use basic sites near the small boat-launching ramp. This is a terrific place to begin a paddling trip. The high stone bluffs and quiet waters are a popular place for paddling. This loop is shady with gravel pads and is best for small units and tents. Site 196 has room to park a boat next to your site and is next to wooded area. Site 198 is also a terrific site on this small loop. All of the sites on the outside of the loop are backed up against the woods. Site 207 is near some big trees and site 210 can hold a big RV unit. All of these sites have a view of the rocky green and brown bluff that ascends skyward from the river.

Organized groups have three locations with minimum amenities. Group camping area C has a shower building and hard surfaces. The River Trail is also nearby.

The amphitheater has eight bulky benches and naturalist programs are offered to campers and visitors. Video and multi-media presentations are offered. The black bear program I attended was marvelous. The amphitheater is near Fisher Cave.

Cabins: Cabins have a small microwave oven, built-in stovetop, pots, pans, coffee pot, refrigerator, toaster, linen, heat and towels. There are no televisions, clocks or telephones. For more information, call 1-888-MERAMEC.

Cabins 1-8 have one bedroom; cabin 9 offers two bedrooms and cabin 20 has four bedrooms that can accommodate up to eight. Duplex cabins are 10-19 with eight of the cabins featuring two bedrooms and one other with 3-5 bedrooms that can accommodate up to 12 people.

Cabins typically have modern kitchen appliances, carpeting, mini-blinds, table, chairs and linens.

Cabins 1-8 (one bedroom) are along a ridge and private with small a porch and picnic table. The brown cabins are air conditioned and have stone chimneys. Each porch has two chairs that look over the quiet part of the parkland. Each cabin is unique and has a timber play apparatus and basketball goal nearby. According to staff, cabins 5 and 6 are the most requested in this loop. Cabins 7 and 8 have plenty of space between them and have slightly larger porches than the others. All have hard-surface parking and mowed areas for field sports.

Cabins 9-20 are behind the dining lodge. Most of these cabins are clapboard-sided duplexes, but are nevertheless private and popular. Each has a small outdoor deck that views a forested valley. Many of these cabins enjoy about 40 percent sunlight during the day.

Cabin 9 is at the end of the loop and one of the more isolated in this group. Cabins 18/19 are the closest to the dining lodge and outdoor dining patio. They also share abundant open space.

The Fireside Restaurant dining lodge has hardwood floors and benches at the flagstone entrance. The air-conditioned dining lodge has a warm and superb stone fireplace, pay phone and a low retaining wall outlining the building. The patio has metal tables and a brilliant view of the rental cabins and mowed areas along the park road. The dining lodge usually offers a Friday night seafood buffet, Saturday night prime rib special and Sunday buffet from 11:30 a.m. to 3 p.m. The restaurant reduces its hours after Labor Day each year. The Deer Hollow trailhead (1.8 miles) is near the dining lodge.

Motel: The park has 22 quiet rooms. Check-in is at the park store. Each room has a wide bay window and air conditioning. The rooms are modern with brown carpet, full baths, wall-mount televisions and floral fabric patterns. A pay phone is in front of the two-level motel that is outlined by a deck and great wooded views. Next to the motel is a playground that is connected to the lodging via a sidewalk. A conference center is next door.

Hiking: The park has six trails that equal sixteen miles of hiking along rocky or packed gravel on hillside, hollows and riverside paths. All the trails are easy with hiking times of an hour or less.

The Natural Wonder's Trail (1.33 miles) begins at the visitor center and is rugged along some remote areas of the park including the Meramec Upland Forest Natural Area, the largest undisturbed Ozark chert forest in the state. The counter-clockwise trail passes a grove of pines along a spring-fed creek, beaver ponds and open spaces. This trail has great diversity.

The Wilderness Trail (10 miles) to the natural area has backpacking opportunities (registration is required). Other trails are the Bluff View (1.5 miles), Deer Hollow (1.8 miles and connects the lodge with a cave), River Trail (.8-mile) and Walking Fern Trail (.5-mile). Pick up a trail map that offers topographical features, safety information and ethics of good trail use.

Boating: The Meramec River is an excellent paddling destination for the eastern side of the state. A number of float trips are available, including five and 10 miles. Canoe rentals are available across the street from the park store. It's a busy launch area behind the park store. Restrooms are located under the two-story park store that sits along the 150-car parking area.

Fishing: Smallmouth bass take four to six years to reach 12 inches in the waters. It can take 10 years to reach four pounds. The daily limit on spotted bass is 12; large- and smallmouth have a 12-inch minimum and you may take six daily. Shoreline fishing and from canoes is available throughout the park.

Fisher Cave: The entrance to the cave is near the campground entrance. Tours are offered to explore the subterranean passages that feature outstanding calcite deposits. Experienced naturalists guide visitors on the 90-minute (two-thirds-mile) interpretive walk. The cave is a cool 57 degrees year-round, so a light jacket and long pants are a good idea. Visitors should be able to fit through 15 narrows and stoop 50 inches for 100 feet. Most of the cave is spacious, but not accessible to wheelchairs or strollers.

Tours are offered from June-August daily at 9:30 a.m., 11:30 a.m., 1 p.m. and 3 p.m. In September they are offered Thursday - Monday at 1 p.m. and 3 p.m. The cave is closed on Tuesday and Wednesday. The cave is closed from the middle of October to April 15. There is an admission fee.

Meramec State Park is on the Ozark Plateau, an area known for its many caves. Inside the park are 40 caves; many are gated. When Fisher Cave drained, many calcite deposits (speleothems) were created over many years by mineral-rich drops of water. From small structures to huge columns, the deposits are colorful and sculpture-like.

The cave hosts six species of bats, four types of salamanders, two species of frogs and many invertebrates including amphipods.

Caves are natural conditions of state property and you enter caves at your own risk. Adequate training and equipment are essential for any cave exploration. Some caves require a permit.

Nature: The park offers a broad menu of outdoor education programs including black bears are back, the element: fire, snakes alive, man's floral needs, rock hikes, cave tours and many others.

Flora and fauna among the bluff include Eastern red cedar, sumac, Virginia creeper, lip fern, sedge, little blue stem, white oak, aster and goldenrod.

Birding in the park is excellent along the road borders, mature bottomlands and remote areas. Birds that you might see include yellow-billed cuckoo, vireo, Northern parula, America redstart, hooded warblers and others. Crow-sized pileated woodpeckers and owls are common all year. My favorite areas are along the savanna looking for various sparrows and in the toeslope forest for scratching birds.

Conference center: The Hickory Ridge Center has a big round window next to a small playground and the motel. It can be used for meetings and other gatherings. A small bar and movable tables and chairs rest upon the shiny tile floor. The conference center seats about 50.

Day-use areas: Shelter No. 1 is a CCC-era building that can protect about 15 picnic tables from the sun and elements. Shelter No. 2 is a more modern shelter, and like Shelter No. 1, had plenty of open spaces for big family reunions or group outings. Both have vault toilets, nearby water and play equipment.

Insider's tips: The park has some of the finest trees in the system. The park store sells Italian ice frozen treats. Bring your canoe. There are also many private canoe rentals in the area. The park is only minutes from fast food and other services. Late September is a great time to watch the hummingbird migration. There's a great mountain bike trail across the river at the Meramec Conservation Area. Be careful of flooding at certain times of the year. Osprey are common in the spring and fall.

Meramec State Park

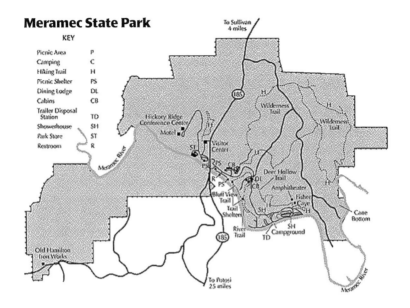

Robertsville State Park is a rustic, get-a-way-style park.

CHAPTER 24
Robertsville State Park
Land: 1,225 acres Water: Meramec River

Rich soils and a gently rolling landscape attracted settlers to this abundant river valley in Franklin County during the mid-1800s. Edward J. Roberts, who is buried in the small cemetery in the park, was the original owner of the park property and other tracts in the area. He was also a tax collector, mason, election judge and merchant.

His store not only served the 100 or so residents of "Robertsville" but also a stream of train passengers who stopped at his all-purpose store. Like the history of many small train stops, the area and its businesses disappeared when the train routes evolved toward stops at larger cities. In 1979, the state purchased the property, with the help of the Land and Water Conservation Fund, from a group of investors who abandoned plans for a fancy resort and golf course.

In many ways, Robertsville is a young park that has a future that might include additional amenities. Given its location along two miles of the Meramec River, Missourians are increasingly discovering its unique wetlands, float trips, fishing and wildlife.

Information and activities

Robertsville State Park
P.O. Box 186
Robertsville, MO 63072
(636) 257-3788
(877) I Camp Mo; Camping Reservations
www.mostateparks.com

The park office is attached to a three-bay maintenance barn and across from a day-use area. The office is open when the staff isn't working in the field.

Directions:

From St. Louis

Robertsville State Park is 50 miles from the Gateway Arch; the trip will take about one hour. Travel west on I-44 to Exit 247 (Union/U.S. Hwy. 50 East). After exiting, take the first right turn, within one-quarter mile. Continue past the Harley-Davidson dealership to the next right turn, which is Route O. Travel five miles on Route O before turning at the first left after crossing the Meramec River.

From Jefferson City

Robertsville State Park is 89 miles from Jefferson City; the trip will take close to three hours. Travel east on U.S. Hwy. 50 for 90 miles to I-44. Take I-44 east toward St. Louis; remain in the right lane and exit almost immediately at Exit 247. Turn right at the bottom of the ramp onto Route O; continue for five miles. Turn at the first left after crossing the Meramec River.

From Springfield/Rolla

Robertsville State Park is 170 miles from Springfield and 70 miles from Rolla. Travel east on I-44 to Exit 247 (Union/U.S. Hwy. 50 East). Turn right at the bottom of the ramp onto Route O; continue for five miles. Turn at the first left after crossing the Meramec River.

Emergency numbers: 911 system; local public safety, (636) 257-3788.

Campground: The camping area has 12 basic and 14 electric sites. The getaway campground is quiet, gently rolling and open March to December; check-out time is 2 p.m. On your way to the campground, you will pass a quarter-mile-long prairie-like field.

Sites are gravel. Site 1 is ideal for a tent while site 13 is big enough for a large RV rig. Site 3 is tucked into the wood and private. Site 14 is on a slightly higher elevation and like the rest of the sites is backed up against the woods. Most of the sites are best for medium-sized rigs. Across from site 17 and 22 is some overflow parking spaces for visitors.

Site 5 and 27 are for campers with disabilities and are hard-surfaced. Site 6 is under cedars and ideal for a pop-up camper or tent. It is also close to a water bib. The bathhouse has brown horizontal siding and a hose bib across the driveway from Sites 7 and 8. Many of the sites have some vegetation between them. Site 24 is slightly wider than some of the other sites and can accommodate parking for a boat trailer or vehicle. Sites 11 and 27 are open and sunny near a flush toilet. Site 12 is at the end of the loop adjacent to a small grassy area that children could use for field games.

All sites have a hard-surface pad where metal leg picnic tables are set. Each site also has a ground-mounted fire ring and lantern post.

Site 26 is on a low rise and is best for small RV units.

There are four showers for each sex and stainless steel sinks inside the tidy facility. Coin-operated washers and driers and firewood are also available.

Hiking: The Spice Bush Trail (one mile) is accessed from a trailhead parking lot off the main park road. It is a moderately easy hiking loop.

Boating and floating: About 20 vehicles with boat trailers could park in the hard-surface lot that is surrounded by a scattering of picnic tables and grills. Also beneath the low bluff of the Meramec River is a vault toilet for boaters and anglers. The hard-surface one-lane ramp's launching condition can change often and is best for car tops and canoes. Low water is typically the problem.

The Meramec Valley has some heavily populated

communities, but the clear stream-fed river retains a wilderness feeling and some excellent floating and fishing. The 100-mile river is floatable along its entire length - and on many of its tributaries. Along the way are caves, steep bluffs, springs and wonderful scenery. Much of the river is quiet and away from the paddling crowds.

The primary tributary of the Meramec is the Bourbeuse River that is wide, slow and less clear. Big River is also a good float trip and passes some rugged country and picturesque valleys. Canoeists should also consider the nearby Courtois and Huzzah creeks that are clear and about a two-hour drive from St. Louis. Canoeists will find the paddling sporty during the right seasons and conditions. Interestingly, the pronunciation of Huzzah is "Hoo-za."

Cemetery: The Roberts Family cemetery is three-tenths of a mile from the main park road under the large utility lines. Although you have to park in a nearby day-use area, the short hike along a mowed two-track path to the cemetery is airy and quiet. A four-foot wrought-iron fence outlines the small cemetery with ornate columns at each corner.

The headstones are simple and worn, but the large ball marker identifies James E. Roberts (1852-1886) and Mary F. Roberts (1848-1920). Roberts was a farmer. Records

Roberts Family Cemetery is a short distance from the main park entrance.

indicate that he grew 10,000 pounds of tobacco in 1850. He also owned 25 slaves who allowed the farm to prosper and also grow oats, potatoes, sweet potatoes and livestock.

Day-use areas: Newer metal-roofed picnic shelters are a hallmark. Also, once inside the park about a half-mile, the park become increasingly wooded, offering shady areas and private spaces for picnics and family outings. A number of young trees dot the play area where a newer play apparatus has a red roof, twin slides and climbers.

Insider's tips: Although rustic and small, the campground often has open sites, even on summer weekends. It's a quiet getaway. Bring your canoe and spin-casting rod. Local anglers report that small spinners and light-colored twister-tail jigs work well in the Meramec River.

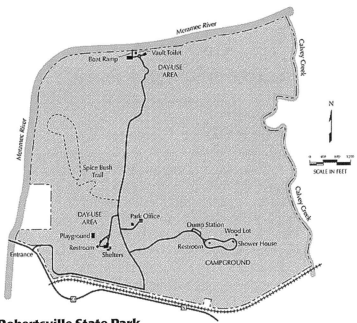

Robertsville State Park

Wall-to-wall historic displays and a great gift counter welcomes travelers to the visitor's center that is dedicated to America's most famous highway.

CHAPTER 25
Route 66 State Park
Land: 419 acres

T he recently remodeled visitor's center has wall-to-wall historical displays and colorful Route 66 memorabilia. The park showcases the history and mystique of a highway that has been called "The Main Street of America." Visitors will see the period architecture of the buildings and towns that graced the roadways of Missouri from the 1930s to the 1960s, and sometimes zany souvenirs travelers bought on their journey across Missouri on Route 66.

The first thing you see upon entering the visitor's center is the historic Route 66 highway sign. Also in the hall are colorful neon lights, samples of restaurant menus, old key chains, napkin holders, photographs of roadside attractions, pictures of old gasoline stations, humorous signs, newspaper clippings and scenes of life during the heyday of the once-important highway.

The Diamond Restaurant, for example, had 25 "modern" tourist cottages and was the world's biggest eatery for a long time. Photographs and details of many other motels are also featured in the exhibit, including a towel from the art deco Coral Court motel that fell out of favor because it didn't have enough privacy, according to the report.

Route 66 was opened as a federal highway in 1926 and has a special place in American popular culture. Spanning some of the most remote country in the United States, from Los Angeles to Chicago, Route 66's fame is primarily due to its role in social changes taking place during the first half of the 20th century. The highway has come to represent American mobility, independence and spirit of adventure. It became one of the greatest migration routes in our country's history and has been labeled by author John Steinbeck as the "Mother Road."

To drive Route 66 during its heyday was to experience both large cities and small towns in rural America. Gasoline stations were not that plentiful and speed limits were slow. Many people have fond memories of childhood vacations along Route 66. A portion of the original Route 66, including a historic bridge across the Meramec River, runs through Route 66 State Park.

The visitor's center and gift shop are open daily from 9 a.m. to 4:30 p.m. year-round.

Information and activities

**Route 66 State Park
97 N. Outer Road, Suite 1
Eureka, MO 63025
(636) 938-7198**
www.mostateparks.com

Directions:

From downtown St. Louis

Route 66 State Park is about 26 miles from downtown St. Louis. Take I-55 south to I-44 west. From I-44 west, take Exit 266/Lewis Road; follow the road to the right and then curve to the left. Continue past the West Tyson County Park entrance to the stop sign at Lewis Road. After crossing Lewis Road, you will see the visitor's center on the left. By continuing across the bridge, you will enter the park grounds.

From I-70 and I-270

Route 66 State Park is about 25 miles from I-70/I-270. Travel south on I-270 to I-44 west. From I-44 west, take Exit 266/Lewis Road; follow the road to the right and then curve to the left. Continue past the West Tyson County Park entrance to the stop sign at Lewis Road. After crossing Lewis Road, you will see the visitor's center on the left. By continuing across the bridge, you will enter the park grounds.

From I-55 and I-270/I-255

Route 66 State Park is about 16 miles from I-55. Travel north on I-270 to I-44 west. From I-44 west, take Exit 266/Lewis Road; follow the road to the right and then curve to the left. Continue past the West Tyson County Park entrance to the stop sign at Lewis Road. After crossing Lewis Road, you will see the visitor's center on the left. By continuing across the bridge, you will enter the park grounds.

From Jefferson City

Route 66 State Park is about 120 miles from Jefferson City. Travel east on U.S. Hwy. 50 past Union to I-44. Take I-44 east to Exit 266/Lewis Road; take a left after exiting and cross the highway overpass. Stay on the outer road, which will curve to the left. Continue past the West Tyson County Park entrance to the stop sign at Lewis Road. After crossing Lewis Road, you will see the visitor's center on the left. By continuing across the bridge, you will enter the park grounds.

From Kansas City

Route 66 State Park is about 265 miles from Kansas City. Travel east on I-70, crossing the Missouri River at St. Charles. Take I-270 south and continue to I-44. Travel west on I-44 to Exit 266/Lewis Road; follow the road to the right and then curve to the left. Continue past the West Tyson County Park entrance to the stop sign at Lewis Road. After crossing Lewis Road, you will see the visitor's center on the left. By continuing across the bridge, you will enter the park grounds.

From Springfield, Mo.

Route 66 State Park is about 190 miles from Springfield, Mo. Travel east on I-44 to Exit 266/Lewis Road. After exiting, turn left and cross the highway overpass. Stay on the outer road, which will curve to the left. Continue past the West Tyson County Park entrance to the stop sign at Lewis Road. After crossing Lewis Road, you will see the visitor's center on the left. By continuing across the bridge, you will enter the park grounds.

More on the visitor's center: I loved the Burma Shave signs and the colorful old motels that many of us remember from our family vacations in the 1950s and 1960s. Displays almost seem endless and include old gasoline pumps, cups and mugs from roadside restaurants, ash trays, graphic brochures, old maps, a drive-in theater display (including an old speaker we once hung on our window), Route 66 signs and the history of Times Beach.

Lyrics to
"Get your kicks on Route 66" song,
by Bobby Troup (1946):

If you plan to motor west travel my way,

Take the highway that's the best,

Get your kicks on Route 66.

It winds from Chicago to L.A.,

More than 2,000 miles all the way.

Get your kicks on Route 66.

Now you go though St. Looey, and Joplin, Missouri and

Oklahoma City is mighty pretty.

You'll see Amarillo, Gallup, New Mexico, Flagstaff, Arizona,

Don't forget Wenonah, Kingsman, Barstow and San Bernardino,

Won't you get hip to the timely trip, when you make that California trip,

Get your kicks on Route 66.

Route 66 became a destination itself featuring curio shops, snake farms, mom and pop motor courts and memorable scenery. But as traffic increased after World War II, heavily used Route 66 became a victim of its own success. By 1985, high-speed interstate highways that bypassed towns and limited access to roadside attractions had replaced America's main street.

Route 66 isn't dead yet, however. Much of the old road is still here, as are many of the attractions that made it memorable. People are still here to offer blue-plate specials and "service with a smile." Organizations like the Route 66 Association urge travelers to leave the interstate and experience the rustic road that has forever meant going somewhere. It's time for another generation to "get their kicks on Route 66."

Gifts and souvenirs: The wonderful center features dozens of retro Route 66-themed gifts including caps, shot glasses, books, banners, postcards, flags, salt and pepper shakers, lapel pins, jackets, videotapes, refrigerator magnets and much more.

Fishing: The Meramec River is one of the most diversified rivers in North America. More than half of the fish species in Missouri are found in it. Anglers can enjoy fishing on the Meramec River from sunrise to sunset. Fishing is prohibited on any nearby ponds.

Boating: Route 66 State Park provides a boat ramp for easy access to the Meramec River. There are no fees for use of the ramp.

Day-use areas: In addition to bicycling and walking, the picnic grounds - nestled among shade trees - offer visitors a relaxing place to sit and have a snack, or just time to enjoy the serene splendor of nature.

The Forest and Dogwood shelters can accommodate up to 75 people each and are reservable for a fee. To reserve a shelter, please call (636) 938-7198.

Insider's tips: The park has 40 species of birds and several biking trails. The park also has an equestrian trail. Information about Times Beach and the dioxin devastation and cleanup is also detailed at the visitor's center. You will also learn there are 5,700 caves beneath the surface of

Missouri. Many of the show caves once were part of the commercial attractions along the old highway. Air conditioning (and TV) were not invented in the early days of Route 66, which caused weary travelers to sit outside their rooms and visit with other guests. That was certainly part of the good old days.

Many visitors will relive their childhood vacations when they view the dozens of displays in the Route 66 visitor's center.

One of the best displays captures the highlights of each decade, including when Jack Keroac wrote "On the Road," and extolled a road trip to the youth and discontented.

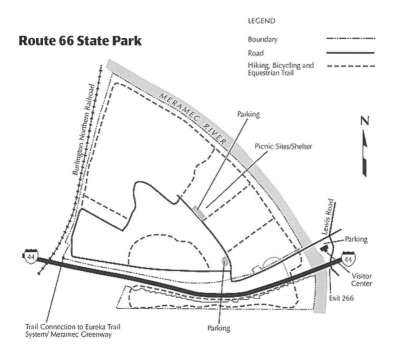

Route 66 State Park

St. Francois State Park.

CHAPTER 26

St. Francois State Park
Land: 2,735 acres
Water: Big River and Coonville Creek

The soul of St. Francois State Park is its clear streams, wooded ridges, thick hollows, blufftop views and mossy rock outcrops. The stunning beauty of the park, the floatable river and Pike Run Hills can make a believer out of anyone.

The park is inviting and quiet even though it is off a main highway. The hills are cloaked in dense mixed hardwood forests and sunny dry glades along the southern slopes.

The first white settlers came to the area to work in the lead mines. Several decades later, moonshiners came to the area for the cool, crystal-clear water. Moonshine was named because "it seemed to work out better if concocted in the night under the light of an Ozark moon." Moonshine, by the way, is probably not good for the soul.

When the Civil War began, it divided many families and

imprinted the area with a colorful history. Sam Hildebrand, for example, was a guerrilla fighter who joined the Confederacy to avenge the cold-blooded killing of his three noncombatant brothers by the Union's Missouri Militia. Hildebrand was known to hide in the park's blufftop caves and became a resentful bushwhacker who pinned down many Northern troops. Fortunately, all is safe today.

Information and activities

St. Francois State Park
8920 U.S. Highway 67 North
Bonne Terre, MO 63628
(573) 358-2173
(877) I Camp Mo; Camping Reservations
www.mostateparks.com

The small brown park office is perched on a ridge and attached to the three-bay maintenance barn.

Directions:

From St. Louis

Take I-55 south to the Festus/Crystal City exit. Exit onto U.S. Hwy. 67 south and travel about 22 miles. The entrance to the park is on U.S. Hwy. 67 on the left side. It is marked by a set of large brown highway signs.

From Cape Girardeau/Poplar Bluff

Take U.S. Hwy. 67 north to Bonne Terre. The entrance to the park is on U.S. Hwy. 67, about 4.5 miles north of Bonne Terre, on the right side. It is marked by a set of large brown highway signs.

Emergency numbers: Hospital, (573) 358-1400; 911 system.

Campground: The park road to the campground is through a canopy of mixed hardwoods. Along the route are some shoreline access and day-use areas. The 110-site campground has modern facilities including hot showers and many electric sites. A bulletin board also offers information on nearby churches, firewood sales hours and other handy details. The stone and wood-sided showerhouse has soft drink vending machines, a pay phone and coin-operated laundry machines. Firewood is sold during the evenings on weekends, weekdays by request. The campground also has a playground with benches for weary adults to watch the kids on the equipment.

St. Francois campground is known for many pull-through sites, big RV rigs and family camping.

Site 2 is against a natural area. Sites 2-22 are along the river and they have small paths to the water. Many of the sites have roofed picnic tables. Many sites are shaded by 12- to 14-inch caliper trees. Many of the sites also have filtered sunlight. For shady sites try 12, 13 and 15. Sites 16 and 18 are large enough for an additional vehicle or maybe a boat trailer. Sites in the 20s are backed up against the woods. Site 30 is shady and a terrific site near a trailhead. Site 31, however, is sunny.

A vault toilet is near site 36. Site 39 is great for a big rig, while sites 41 and 42 offer some mowed space for small field games or an extra tent. Sites in the high 40s and low 60s are idea for families because they are near both the showerhouse and play equipment. Most of these sites are pull-throughs. The amphitheater is behind the showerhouse and used for evening programs and a staging area for naturalist activities.

Sites 64-69 may be best for pop-up campers and tents. Site 70 is shaded by red cedar and a bit of open space surrounding it. Other sites near it (107-109, for example) are small. Sites in the 70s are on a higher elevation and backed up against the woods. A water bib is near sites 78 and 88. Sites 78 and 80 are best for a smaller RV rig. At the end of the loop is a slightly larger site 80. Sites in the high 80s are on a higher elevation. Site 89 is a terrific tent site under a small grove of cedars. This loop is popular among families.

Site 96 is sunny. Sites in the low 100s are near the vault toilet and water bib. These sites are also open. The campground host is often seen patrolling on his golf cart. He keeps a brochure rack at his site near the newer showerhouse. A new play area was built near the showerhouse in 2003.

Hiking: The park has four trails that cover 17 miles. The

The park has many day-use areas including horseshoe pits and two shelters.

short Missouri Trail is point-to-point.

One of my few criticisms of Missouri parks is the lack of interpretive self-guided nature trails. But it's not a problem at St. Francois. The Mooner's Hollow Trail (2.7 miles) is in the Coonville Creek Wild Area, a remnant of Ozark terrain with a rich natural history.

The 10-station trail has a terrific illustrated pamphlet that can be obtained from the office. You simply match the write-ups in the booklet to numbered stations along the easy trail.

Along the trail, you will learn to listen to Ozark streams and view deposits that have been carved by its water power. Station No. 2 oversees a clearing and level ground that's near the babbling stream and was used by pioneer settlers. Prairie dock, Queen Ann's lace and brown-eyed Susans now grow where red cedar and dry-loving plants once thrived. The bent cedars you see along the trail got that way from a heavy snow in the winter of 1981-82. Station No. 3 gives hikers a chance to touch some chert and dolomite stones that have been rounded by the tumbling action of the water. Along the trail are many seeps and small springs. The Coonville Creek has 18 species of fish and cherts. Also in the clear water are many aquatic insects like stonefly and caddisfly that make their homes among the smooth rocks and gravel.

Glades are like deserts, you will learn. The openings in the forest often have thin soil where grasses flourish. Grasses and wildflowers like dock, rose gentian and purple coneflower can be seen along the hike.

Nearly 40 percent of the water in Coonville Creek is from seep springs. This constant water supply provides a good habitat for certain northern plant species, many of which are rare in Missouri such as marsh fern, sedges, swamp loosestrife and swamp ragweed. Common trees in this section of the park include post oak, flowering dogwood, hickory, white oak, sugar maple, sassafras, Eastern redbud and red oak. I also noticed some musclewood trees whose trunks look like muscular arms.

Also around some of the cool seeps and boggy soils are plant communities called fens. These sheltered, moist areas host some rare plants such as swamp wood betony, swamp thistle and grass pink orchids. These narrow shady valleys (fens) are often isolated areas where some plants from the last ice age have survived near the cool and wet streambeds.

Pike Run Trail (11 miles, yellow arrows) is shared by backpackers and equestrians. Swimming Deer Trail (2.7 miles, green arrows) follows the Big River from the campground.

Fishing: Fishing is good on the three miles of Big River that meanders through the park. Anglers should call the park office at (573) 358-2173 in advance for river conditions. Smallmouth bass and catfish are most commonly taken on live bait. Many stretches of both Big River and Coonville Creek are shallow and easily waded, and both streams have easily-accessed banks in the park.

Two river access points in the picnic areas of the park provide convenient canoe launch points along Big River for fishing or floating. Motorized boats are not recommended since the river is too shallow. The sheer rocky bluff walls offer anglers a scenic place to fish. Local anglers report that smallmouth bass fishing is best in the spring using small spinners.

Nature: The park's seasonal naturalist staff offers a

The 110 site campground is shaded by mixed hardwoods.

number of programs including river walks, investigating insects, nature bingo, Missouri Trail, storytelling, junior naturalists program and interpretive hikes.

The mixture of oak/hickory forests and arbitrary pockets of open glades offers a diverse habit for birds. Spring is the best time for birding the park. It's a time when all of the state's warblers, vireos, thrushes and flycatchers can be seen passing through or nesting. Broad-winged hawks also nest during late spring. Worm-eating warblers can be spotted in the ravines while blue-winged and prairie warblers can be seen in the open glades. Some of the vernal ponds and pools can contain shorebirds and puddle ducks in the spring.

Deer and turkeys are common along the park's trails. So are the lovely dressing of dogwoods and redbuds. The hardwood hollows, rocky ridge tops and abundant creeks offer varied habitats for other mammals including foxes, opossums, wood ducks and raccoons. Always watch the small waterfalls during the wet season for an even broader mix of fauna including aquatic insects, reptiles and amphibians.

Day-use area: Picnic shelter No. 1 is a modern structure with plenty of mowed open spaces for field games. An excellent timber play structure with four swings and slide is nearby. There's also a horseshoe pit in this convenient day-use area. There are plenty of open spaces and picnic tables in all directions.

Shelter No. 2 is a popular picnic location surrounded by about one acre of mowed fields and plenty of amenities for group or family outings.

Insider's tips: A rib restaurant is near the busy entrance to the park. There's lots of river access; bring your rod and reel. Mossy rocks, riffles and small cascades are along Swimming Deer Trail. ST. Francois State Park has 11 miles of equestrian trails.

St. Francois State Park

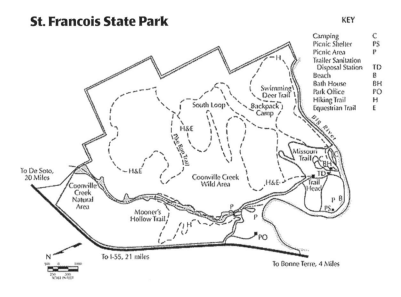

The park's ORV riding area is the center of attention, but there are also many quiet pursuits at St. Joe State Park.

CHAPTER 27
St. Joe State Park
Land: 8,242 acres Water: Four lakes

"Get on your bad motor scooter and ride...and ride...and ride." Okay, how about these motorcycle riding lyrics, "Get your motor runnin'...head it on the highway..." Well, you get the idea. St. Joe is a Mecca for off-road vehicle enthusiasts. You've never seen so many knobby tires and motor-head riders smiling from beneath a coating of mud, bugs and dust. The roar of supercharged machines at this dirt rider's playground is deafening, but no one complains; they love it, and they are far from neighbors, cities and towns in Missouri's third largest state park.

About 2,000 acres of the park are set aside for off-road riding.

The ORV riding area and all the lands around St. Joe are known as Missouri's "Old Lead Belt." The rich deposit was mined for more than a century, leaving more than 1,000 miles of abandoned mine shafts and 300 miles of underground rail track. The evidence of mining is scattered about the big park in the form of old footings, pipes and foundations of old buildings. At one time this region produced 80 percent of the nation's lead.

Once away from the screaming ORVs, the park is quiet with up to a thousand acres of savanna-like areas, a matrix of grasslands, distinctive glades, a stand of shortleaf pines, Ozark-like terrain and rolling forested hills. From fishing four clear lakes to rugged hiking and horseback riding, St. Joe has high energy, remote areas and a legacy of reclamation.

Information and activities

St. Joe State Park
2800 Pimville Road
Park Hills, MO 63601
(573) 431-1069
(877) I Camp Mo; Camping Reservations
www.mostateparks.com

Park office: Ice, soda and live bait, as well as safety items such as helmets, are available for sale at the park office. The office staff sells souvenir shirts and hats as well. The park office is open daily from 7 a.m. to 5 p.m. October through March and 7 a.m. to 8 p.m. April through September.

Directions:

From St. Louis

Travel south on I-55. At Festus, take U.S. Hwy. 67 south to the Leadington/Park Hills exit. Turn right onto Hwy. 32 west and travel about 3.5 miles before turning left onto Pimville Road (just before the railroad tracks). After traveling about two miles, Campground 1 will be on the left. The park office, ORV riding area, lakes and day-use areas are an additional .3-mile.

Emergency numbers: 911 system; hospital (573) 756-4581. Public pay phones are at the park office and showerhouse.
Campground: Campground 1 is comprised of three loops.

Sites 1-15 and 101 - 125 are electrical. Sites 16-50 are basic. A centrally located showerhouse (eight shower rooms), playground, pay phone and woodlot serve campers. The campground is usually full on holidays and many summer weekends. The showerhouse also has a coin-operated laundry.

Sites are wooded - in fact, more wooded than most state park campgrounds. Sites 1-15 and 101 - 125 are all pull-through sites with hard-surface pads, tables and fire pits. A vault toilet is near site 8 and 116. A thick wall of vegetation separates many of the sites. Firewood is sold by the bundle.

Site 20 has an elevated and private place to pitch a tent. Sites 6 and 17 are near a field with a scattering of 4- to 6-inch caliper trees.

Sites in the Basic Loop are also wooded, shady and spaced out equally. Near site 37 is an ORV access path. Near site 40 is a vault toilet with burgundy doors. Sites on the outside of the loop are against the woods. On a slightly higher elevation are sites in 46-50.

Equestrian camping: These sites are nicely separated by walls of vegetation and offer hitching posts. Sites 203 and 213 are on a corner and private. Site 211 is T-shaped. Sites 206 and 210 are near the vault toilets. Site 208 is probably

The park has equestrian camping.

the most private and near the Hickory Ridge and Pine Ridge trailhead. Site 214 is pear-shaped and popular. Sites 215 and 216 are wide, shady and private. Frankly, every site in the equestrian campground is excellent.

ORV riding area: The ORV parking lot reminds you of the pit area of a race track where mechanics and drivers coax, repair and rev up engines for the next round of riding in the mine tailings area. Every ORV and rider can be seen whizzing about with an orange flag flapping above their heads.

The area is loud and energetic. Whiffs of gasoline and the "ring-a-ding-ding-ding" of two-cycle engines are everywhere. The parking lot can hold several hundred ORV riders and their rigs.

Trails are subject to topographic changes resulting from erosion, so be alert to changing inclines, sudden drops and changing slopes. Everyone must wear helmets except when driving a vehicle with an enclosed metal cab. Everyone in motorized vehicles, except motorcycles and ATVs, must wear seat belts.

ORV riders under age 16 must be directly supervised at all times.

The riding area is in a former mine site. The state has conducted a number of tests to determine the exposure of lead in the area to see if it poses a health threat to park users. The state's test results indicate that there may be some health risk for children 6 years old and younger. Recreational use of the mine tailings area should not pose health risks to adults. Potential health risks continue to be assessed and the public should use reasonable care.

A small 40-yard-wide swimming beach is near the parking and staging lot. Swimmers must stay inside the yellow markers that outline the sandy beach. The beach is open 7 a.m. to 8 p.m. and there is no lifeguard on duty. Next to the beach is a small single-lane boat-launching ramp.

An outdoor shower is at the restrooms and changing rooms.

Hiking: Yikes, some of St. Joe's trails are really difficult. Other trails are moderate to easy. The Missouri state park system has about 750 miles of hiking trails and 30 of them are here. A trail map is available from the park office.

The park has about 14 miles of hard-surface biking and walking trails. Horses are allowed on about 15 miles of packed earth and gravel trails. The paved trail has five access points and is easy and a superb way to see the park. It's a little hilly on the north, but the elevation changes in the park are from 800 feet to 1,100 feet above sea level. Novice bike riders should stick to the paved path while others may want to take up the challenge of steep rocky descents and the challenge of bike handling. Drinking water is at both campgrounds.

The Hickory Ridge Trail (three miles, green arrows) is at the south end of the park near the equestrian campground. With many connector loops color-coded off the Hickory Ridge Trail, you can easily spend an afternoon amid the forested ridges, shady hollows and many vistas.

The shortest hike is the 1.5-mile Lakeview Trail loop. It connects at the Pim Lake day-use area with a beach at Monsanto Lake.

Swimming: Permitted at Monsanto and Pim lakes only. Both lakes are easily accessible and have swimming beaches. A large shelter with picnic tables is located at Monsanto Lake. There are also benches, a volleyball net, change house and a vault toilet. Pim Lake and beach is smaller than Monsanto, but has benches, picnic tables, barbecue grills, a change house and a vault toilet.

No cans, glass bottles, coolers, fires, alcohol or pets are allowed at the beaches.

The use of metal detectors is allowed on Monsanto and Pim beaches only with written permission from the Division of State Parks. Permits can be obtained free of charge by writing to the Division of State Parks, P.O. Box 176, Jefferson City, Mo. 65102. Permitted use is allowed during daylight hours from Labor Day to Memorial Day, and 7 a.m. to 9 a.m. from Memorial Day through Labor Day. Digging tools must not exceed 12 inches in length and 3 inches in width.

Scuba diving is permitted in Monsanto and Pim lakes. Participants must be certified and must be accompanied by another certified diver. They are required to display a marker indicating their location. Divers must check in and out at the park office.

Fishing: Anglers in search of bass, catfish and crappie can cast their lines into any of the park's four stocked lakes. Monsanto Lake is the largest, about 25 acres and about 30 feet at its deepest point. Apollo Lake and JoLee Lake are the next in size, and the smallest of the four is Pim Lake. Boats with electric motors can be used on all four lakes. State fishing regulations apply. A permit must be obtained for access to Apollo and JoLee lakes.

Boating launch: There is one gravel boat ramp at each of the four lakes in St. Joe State Park that are open year-round. Man-powered boats and boats with electric trolling motors are allowed on the lakes; the use of gasoline-powered motors is not permitted. There are no launch fees. There is no fishing inside the marked swimming areas.

Radio Controlled Flying Field: Model airplane enthusiasts are welcome to frequent St. Joe State Park. A large area with a grass runway maintained by a local organization is set aside for operating radio-controlled airplanes. A vault toilet and picnic tables are available at this area, and users may gain access by checking in at the park office.

Nature: The sprawling park offers a variety of programs and events. They include ORV races, black power club, bicycle scramble and race, equestrian programs, overnight pack dog campout and others.

Visitors to the park during the spring may notice some blackened areas that are the result of prescribed burns to protect the park's habitats. For thousands of years, fires swept across the land. Whether ignited by Native Americans or by lightning, the fires helped shape the prairie, savanna, glade and oak woodland habitats that dominated this region when the first European settlers came to the area.

Fire has such an effect on the plants, animals and their habitats that the lack of it has caused great changes to occur within the natural communities. The controlled use of fire can restore and preserve the natural resources. These burns help control the invasion of brushy plants into prairie and glade habitats and keep the understory of savannas and woodlands open. Oak trees have dominated the forest since the beginning of time. They cannot reproduce in dense shade. These fires help to keep the woodland open so that these magnificent trees can reproduce and thrive.

Insider's tips: Just four miles away on Hwy. 67 are a grocery store, gasoline station and other services. Staff says the record number of ORVs in a single day is 947 vehicles. St. Joe is the third largest state park by land size. This huge size allows the diverse, sometimes noisy park to work well. Kids will love the fording bridge. Don't forget to visit the nearby Missouri Mines State Historic Site. The paved trail is busy on the weekends.

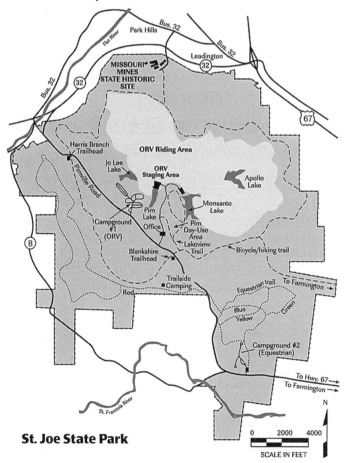

St. Joe State Park

Washington State Park has 15 miles of trails, watercraft rentals, campground, cabins and regional history.

CHAPTER 28
Washington State Park
Land: 2,106 acres Water: Big River

More than a third of a million guests, including 16,000 campers and 5,000 cabin-users, visit the park annually. Located in rocky glades and steep hills with Ozark streams, the park features great views of the Big River, rocky trails, a swimming pool, park store, modern cabins, quiet camping, handsome CCC-era buildings and a blazing spring wildflower bloom. Autumn is also brilliant.

Washington State Park is best known for its Indian rock carvings called petroglyphs. Thousand Hills State Park also has these mysterious rock carvings on horizontal slabs of Cambrian limestone bedrock.

The glyphs hold some mystery. The mystery centers on the fact that similar artworks are found in three distinct and distant locations. Certain cultures along the Big River probably traded with villagers along the distant Mississippi

River. Whatever this trading connection represents, archaeologists believe with certainty that the carving locations - including one here - were the site of major ceremonies. As the authors of "Exploring Missouri's Legacy" say, "There is much we do not - perhaps cannot - know about the petroglyphs here, but we can feel their power and sense that this place was sacred."

In June 1934, Civilian Conservation Corps Company 1743 moved into the park to construct 14 buildings, a picnic pavilion, the 1,000 Step Trail and perform extensive roadside work. The all-African-American company was known for their morale and hard work ethic. In 1985, their work was placed on the National Register of Historic Places as the Washington State Park Historic District. The petroglyphs were placed on the same list in 1970.

Information and activities

Washington State Park
13041 State Hwy. 104
DeSoto, MO 63020
(877) 422-6766 Cabin and Campground Reservations
(636) 586-2995
www.mostateparks.com

Directions:

From St. Louis

Approaching on I-270: Exit onto Tesson Ferry/Hwy. 21 South. Travel south on Hwy. 21 about 45 miles, through Hillsboro and DeSoto. The park is located about nine miles south of DeSoto.

Approaching from I-55: Travel south toward Memphis. Take Exit 174 (U.S. Hwy. 61/67 South to Park Hills/Leadington). Continue about six miles to the exit for Hwy. 110/DeSoto. Turn right at the top of the exit ramp and go about six miles to the intersection with Hwy. 21. Turn left/south onto Hwy. 21 and continue about 12 miles to the park entrance.

From Jefferson City

Approaching from U.S. 50: Travel east on U.S. Hwy. 50 through Union. Turn right/south onto Hwy. 47 and continue through St. Clair. Turn left/east onto Hwy. 30/Hwy. 47 and travel about five miles before turning right/south back onto Hwy. 47. Continue for 21 miles to Hwy. 21. Turn left/north onto Hwy. 21 and travel three miles to the park entrance.

Approaching from I-70: Travel east on U.S. Hwy. 54 to Kingdom City, then take I-70 east to St. Louis. Take Exit 232 onto I-270 Chicago/Memphis. From I-270, exit onto Hwy. 21/Tesson Ferry and travel about 45 miles to the park entrance.

Emergency numbers: Hospital, (573) 438-5451; ambulance, (573) 438-9211; sheriff, (573) 438-5478. There is a telephone near the campground entrance. The hospital is 15 miles south on Hwy. 21.

Park office: The Thunderbird Lodge is a scenic CCC-era stone and timber building that contains the park office where you rent canoes and campsites. It also contains the park store that features camper's supplies, cooking ingredients, coolers, ice, playing cards, batteries, Coleman fuel, sun block, books, field guides, toiletries, candy, walking sticks, stuffed animals, T-shirts, ice cream, board games, towels and coffee. In the small information room just off the store are brochures, restrooms and interpretive wall posters. Live bait includes night crawlers. Thanks to a 2003 tornado, you have a view of the river from the park office and store. Above the Thunderbird Lodge are other CCC-era buildings and a trailhead. Ask about watercraft rentals that are available from Memorial Day to Labor Day.

Campground: The 50-site campground is often full on holiday and summer weekends. Campsites along the main park road are excellent for tent campers. There is less shade in the campground since the tornado of 2003.

Sites 1-25 are less than 50 percent shady. Some of the sites (1-8, for example) are pull-through sites and long and wide enough for larger RV units. Sites 11-14 and many others can accommodate large RVs. Sites 15-17 are best for medium-sized units or tents. Site 19 is at the end of the loop and may be the most private site in this tract. Site 22 is a pull-through and is near a restroom. Site 24 is sunny and

Some of the hiking trails trace rocky ridgelines.

site 25 can hold a big rig.

A split-rail fence outlines the road to basic sites 26-51. This loop is more wooded and flat than the other loop, and it has electricity. A newer play apparatus services the campground and is near the showerhouse.

The wood-sided showerhouse is closed each morning between 7:30 a.m. and 9 a.m. for cleaning. The facility has two coin-operated washers and dryers. There are three showers in each side of the showerhouse.

Cabins: There's a two-day minimum on the weekend for the modern housekeeping cabins that are equipped with full kitchens, placing settings, pots, pans and so on. There are one-, two- and three-bed cabins. The cabins have a modern roofline and nearby pedestal cooking grills and tables.

Cabin 4 is on a rise along the base of the forested hill. Bring bikes and sidewalk chalk for early elementary-age children.

The cabins are wood-sided with screen windows, covered porch and parking notched into the hillside using timbers to restrain the hillside. Cabins 6 and 8 have a small porch that overlooks the woody hollow. All of the air-conditioned cabins have forested views and small mowed areas around them. Cabin 7 is set off the road a little more than some of the others.

Cabin 11 is set off by itself and has a two-car garage. It's more like a spacious ranch house in the suburbs than a state park cabin. Nevertheless, it has a great wooded view, shrouded by trees and is quite private - great for a large family gathering.

Hiking: Washington State Park has nearly 15 miles of trails.

The Opossum Track Trail (three miles, blue arrows going clockwise) is near the Thunderbird Lodge. It tracks along ridgelines and into dense valleys, offering panoramic views of the Big River valley and mining remnants. Miners worked the rocks and soils for a mineral called barite, locally known as tiff, which was used to make paint. The depressions you see along the trail are the remains of the mining operations.

The African-Americans in CCC Company 1743 were expert craftsmen who built the 1,000 Steps Trail (1.5 miles) that begins in the dining lodge parking lot. The trail has stone walking slabs placed by masons.

Rockywood Trail (10 miles, orange arrows) can also be backpacked along the rugged Ozark terrain. The area is mostly oak-hickory with many outcroppings and sprawling cedar glades.

Petroglyphs: There's plenty of hard-surface parking at the petroglyphs, or rock carvings, that remain as evidence of Native American beliefs and ceremonies. The surface carvings give us some understanding and clues as to the lifestyles of these people who inhabited the areas around 1000 A.D. The park is well known for the largest group of petroglyphs yet discovered in Missouri.

These petroglyphs have been assigned to this time period based on the presence of symbols that occurred only during a period when bilobed arrows and ceremonial maces were used. Archaeologists have no way of accurately dating the carvings and their content is the only possible dating technique.

Washington State Park contains three major sets of petroglyphs. There are about 350 symbols at the public viewing spot. This area constitutes about one-third of all petroglyphs found in the state. Little is known about the purpose of these carvings. They are not a form of writing. The figures were probably produced as part of a personal or group thought and may reflect a form of Indian medicine. It's important to consider that Indians relied completely on the natural world and their reverence may be part of the purpose of the compelling artwork.

The presence of animals and animal tracks in the work suggests that they may be part of the ritual of hunters. By depicting the image of their prey, perhaps the artists believed that they could be captured and their spirit controlled, thereby increasing their success.

Some of the carvings might have been a record of symbolism such as the experience of dreams produced by fasting. This was part of the Indians' spiritual life, and some may have had a place in fertility. These might also be memory devices illustrating tales and legends that tell later generation of their lifestyles. The most common pictures are fertile eggs, animal tracks, human figures, thunderbirds, squares and spirals.

For example, the mighty thunderbird sent a bolt of lightning by small birds. The solid lines interspersed with arrowheads possibly denote lightning carried by the small birds. The carvings are both simple and mysterious.

Nature: In 1985, the 79-acre Washington State Park

Upland Hardwoods area was designated as a Missouri Natural Area. There are several types of rare plants on the public lands including evening primrose, Fremont's leather flower and celestial lily. The limestone glades are also home to the rare Eastern collared lizard - a zany lizard that runs on its back legs.

Spring is a wonderful time to hike Washington when Dutchman's breeches, bloodroot and spring beauties blossom. Also in the spring, coachwhip snakes and prairie grasses awaken from winter slumber. Coachwhips are the highest predator at the top of the food chain in the glades.

Other wildflowers include smooth yellow violets, celandine poppies, trillium and blue-eye-Mary's. Tree lovers will find American bladdernut, Kentucky coffee, sugar maple, basswood, pawpaw and many others.

Swimming: The sparkling clean L-shaped pool has a spiral slide, two diving boards and a shallow kiddy's pool in its own fenced area. The pool offers season passes and group/rental rates. There are benches both inside and outside the fence line. A wooded play structure is also nearby. The small pool concession serves cold soft drinks, hamburgers, hot dogs, onion rings, chicken strips, nachos and cheese, pretzels, mushroom fries, dill pickles and ice cream. My favorite was the orange push-up bars. You must eat inside the corded area.

The pool is open noon to 6 p.m. seven days during the summer.

Watercraft rentals: You must be 18 years old to rent the canoes, rafts or tubes. There is a long float of 6.4 miles and a shorter float of three miles. Rentals are offered on weekends in May and September and daily from Memorial Day to Labor Day.

Day-use areas: You can see wooded hills and open glades on foot, from your car and at some of the turnoffs that features CCC-era structures.

Insider' tips: Scenic views are everywhere of limestone glades, uplands, savannas and rolling timbered hills. Stop at the CCC-era octagonal-shaped overlook for a valley view of farmlands and sharp hills (if you look down, you'll see the straight-faced cliff you are standing on!).

Notice the almost Bonsai-like red cedars. Some must be more than 200 years old. The Hilltop Store at the park entrance sells firewood and grocery. For a small park, Washington has many features (pool and store, for example). Look for the famed collared lizard. They are a hoot as they fold up their front legs and race across rocks like cartoon characters.

Washington State Park

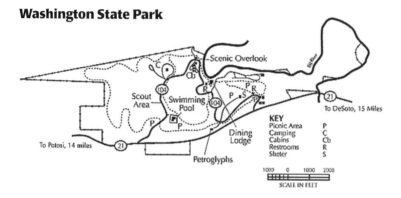

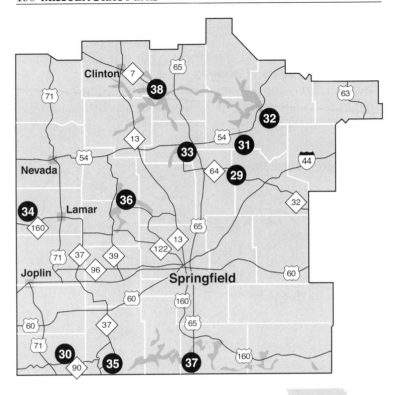

MISSOURI

Lakes Region

29. Bennett Spring State Park
30. Big Sugar Creek State Park
31. Ha Ha Tonka State Park
32. Lake of the Ozarks State Park
33. Pomme de Terre State Park
34. Prairie State Park
35. Roaring River State Park
36. Stockton State Park
37. Table Rock State Park
38. Harry S Truman State Park

Take your buddy fly fishing at Bennett Spring State Park.

CHAPTER 29
Bennett Spring State Park
Land: 3,216 acres
Water: Bennett Spring, Niangua River

The crystal clear waters of Bennett Spring have drawn people since the mid-19th century. During these years, the thriving town of 18 people and was filled with grist and flour mills operated by Peter Bennett and others. The largest, Bennett Mill, burned in 1895.

Today, many visitors come to the steep valley and cold streams for trout and a chance to learn the graceful sport of fly-fishing. The trout population is flourishing thanks to the rainbow trout hatchery on the park's property.

Before the area became a state park, farmers used the land to camp while waiting for their turn at the mill. In 1924, the state acquired Bennett Spring and the surrounding 563 acres of land to make one of Missouri's first state parks. Since then, the park has grown to accommodate every kind of outdoor lover. Canoes are available to rent for tours of the nearby Niangua River, you can stroll 12 miles of beautiful day-hiking trails and lodging includes campgrounds, motel rooms and scenic cabins.

Wooded hills are steep in the valley, and several park roads cross the scenic streams and bridge built from native stone. The heart of the park is village-like and includes views of anglers stroking their fly rods and wading around the chilly trout waters. One of the park's outstanding features is a 100-yard-long natural bridge carved though dolomite by the stream over thousands of years. The bridge is more than 30 feet wide in many places. Other natural features include shallow caves that once housed native Americans, spring-fed ponds, glades and savannas.

Information and activities

Bennett Spring State Park, 26250 Hwy. 64A, Lebanon, MO 65536 (417) 532-4338
(877) I Camp Mo; Camping Reservations
www.mostateparks.com

Directions: 12 miles west of Lebanon on Hwy. 64A in Dallas and Laclede counties.

From St. Louis

Bennett Spring State Park is 161 miles from the I-270 and I-44 interchange; the trip will take about 3 hours, 15 minutes. Go west on I-44 for 148 miles to Exit 129; you are now in Lebanon. At the top of the off ramp, turn right onto Hwy. 5 /Hwy. 32. Stay straight on Hwy. 5 for 1.5 miles, until you reach Hwy 64. Travel on Hwy. 64 for 10.5 miles, then turn left on Hwy. 64A. Travel for one mile until reaching the state park.

From Kansas City

Bennett Spring State Park is 178 miles from Arrowhead Stadium; the trip will take about 4 hours, 45 minutes. Drive east on I-70 for 68 miles to Exit 78A. Go south on U.S. Hwy. 65 for 90 miles to Hwy. 64 at the village of Louisburg. Turn left on Hwy. 64 and drive for 17 miles, then turn right on Hwy. 64A. Travel for one mile until reaching the state park.

From Jefferson City

Bennett Spring State Park is about 95 miles from
Jefferson City and should take about 2 hours, 15 minutes.
Drive west on U.S. Hwy. 54 for 58 miles to Camdenton.
Turn left onto Hwy. 5 and go 25 miles to Lebanon. Turn
right on Hwy. 64 and drive 10.5 miles, then turn left on
Hwy. 64A. Travel for one mile until reaching the state park.

From Springfield

Bennett Spring State Park is about 63 miles from
Springfield and should take 1 hour, 30 minutes. Drive east
on I-44 for 51 miles to Exit 129; stay in the left turn lane on
the exit ramp. You are now in Lebanon. Turn left onto Hwy.
32/Hwy. 5 and stay on Hwy. 5 for 1.5 miles, until you reach
Hwy. 64. Go straight on Hwy. 64 for 10.5 miles, then turn
left onto Hwy. 64A. Travel for one mile until reaching the
state park.

Emergency numbers: 911 system; sheriff, 532-2311.
Campgrounds: Bennett Spring has five campgrounds with
basic electric, and sewer/electric/water campsites. They
offer a dump station, shower houses and laundry facilities.
Water is available April 15 through Oct. 15. Campground
No. 1 is open year round, while campgrounds No. 3, 4 and 5
are closed November through Feb. 24. Staff says
campground 1 is the most popular.

Campground 1 is for big rigs. Campground 5 has 4 basic
sites on a first-come, first-served basis.

A water bib and firewood are across from the
campground check station.

Campground 1 is in a grid pattern and all are pull-
through except the back sites 141-146. The loop is tightly
compacted with plenty of water hook-ups and sunshine.
The best sites are sites 141-146 that are backed up against
the natural area. Sycamore and oaks offer some shade for
campers. I would say it is about 60 percent shady in this
popular campground. There are a few large pines that cast
shade, but midday sun is abundant. The park's contact
station is near this campground.

Sites in Loop 201-224 are reservable and about 75 percent

All of Bennett Spring's 48 cabins are near the fishing and other amenities. Rent one today.

shady. In the middle of the loop are children's swings. A hose bib is near site 221. A split-rail fence courses along the mostly flat loop. Sites on the outside of the loop are backed up against a natural area. There are many oak trees overhead and the sun is dappled by mid-afternoon. There are four duplex sites in this oval loop. Site 215 is best for a smaller RV unit. Site 216 is a tent site. Site 218 is a pull-through and private; this might be the best campsite in the loop. Site 220 is shady and 222 is a bit higher near a hose bib.

Loop 301-319 has a mix of electric and basic sites. The shower house has a phone and laundry. A nice tent site is near the bath house. Some sites have roofed picnic tables and many of the sites have full shade. A hose bib is across from site 304. A walk-in tent site is number 306 complete with a covered picnic table and ground-mounted timbers. Sites on the outside of the loop are basic and back up against a natural area. At the end of the loop is site 310 that has evening sunlight; the rest of the day it's shady. Its picnic table is set off to the side. The water bib is near tent-only site 311 that is on a gravel pad and has a covered picnic table. Sites 314 and 315 are also for tents. Site 319 is near the bath house and sunny all day.

Loop 401- 450, campgrounds 4 and 5, has some

reservable sites and is on a higher elevation. This loop can accommodate larger RV rigs and it's close to many amenities. An occasional boulder rests near campsites. Site 407 is for a smaller unit but has a couple of big rocks around the fire ring. The small haystack-like boulders on site 409 gives you extra places to sit and have a view of the woods down the back of the site. Site 416 is private and you are surrounded by trees and across from a small site, 419, that is best for a pop-up camper. Both are near the modern shower house. Sites 420 and 421 also are near the shower building. Site 423 is small and has great views. Sites 425-427 are duplex sites with cedar trees. Site 426 has cedars that break up the traditional oak trees and is next to an interesting site that gets lots of evening sun. For privacy, consider site 428.

Sites in the inner loop are more private than other loops. Site 434 is ideal for a large unit and site 435 is open and sunny. Site 436 is sunny and best for medium-sized rigs. Site 441 is up a rise and has vegetation that offers some screening and privacy. Neighboring site 443 is sunny. Boulders again dot areas near sites 444 and 445. Site 450 is a clean and neat site that has a view of a wooded valley. This site is also easy to back in to if you have a larger rig.

Loop 501-548 is a first-come, first-served loop. All of the pleasant sites have shade and most back up against natural areas. Eight to 10-inch diameter trees separate many of the sites. Site 517 would allow you to get away from the road with a tent. Near sites in the 540s are the toilet and a separate shower building. Site 554 is one of the shadiest places in the campground. On a slight elevation is site 518. Some of the sites are gravel. Site 519 is near the water bib and you can tent under some medium-sized oaks. Site 540 is for a small rig and gets evening sunlight. Site 520 is great for a medium-sized RV rig. Site 521 is best for a pop-up camper.

Sites in the 530s are smaller. Site 536 is one of the more private sites in the loop. This is a nicely spaced loop with site 531 at the end of the loop offering some privacy and extra space. Site 523 is my favorite in this loop and can handle a medium-sized RV rig, plus parking for a boat if needed. The park road is also wide, making maneuvering your rig easy.

Lodging: Cabins, duplexes and motel rooms are available for daily rental March 1-Oct. 31. Some rooms are even available during winter months. All have refrigerators, cable television, heating, air conditioning and complete linens and utensils. Keep in mind that no pets are allowed in state buildings with the exception of a seeing-eye dog.

Motels: The rooms are pleasant with ceramic tile, mirrors and cedar siding. Most of the lodging opportunities are within walking distance to the fishing and day-use areas and have comfortable bed, table and full bathrooms. There are also patios that oversee a natural and grassy mowed area. Even the colorful bedspreads have the trout-fishing motif.

Cabins: The park has 48 cabins. Take some time to tour the location before you register for a cabin; all are near fishing and amenities. The newer duplex cabins house two bedrooms with double or queen-size beds, parking and air conditioning. Some of the cabins are at the springhead. The four cabins above the springhead are scenic. They are also near walking trails and old fire hydrants that date to the Civilian Conservation Corps era. Each of these cabins has a small porch, grills and picnic table. Huge sycamore trees also provide shade. You'll often see waders and nets drying on the porches of these terrific cabins. The stream is about 75 yards from these cabins.

Cabins 50-55 have small porches, views of a boat launch and mowed areas around them.

The four-plex units often overlook open spaces and are within easy walking distance to the stream. Some are near the pool. Cabins have porch-like decks.

Cabins 16-18 are my favorites and are down a lane and shady. Cabin 21 is also one of the best in the state park featuring shade, on a knoll notched out of the woods and private. It has a small grassy side yard.

Staff at the park store will answer any questions you may have at (417) 532-4307.

Dining: The first building you'll see as you enter the park is the dining lodge, open daily during the trout season. Breakfast and dinner buffets are offered on the weekends. Hummingbird feeders are on both sides of the bulky log-framed entrance. A small gift shop inside the dining lodge sells T-shirts, sweatshirts, hats, postcards, plaques, candles and other items. The salad bar is terrific and lies beneath the vaulted ceiling made from huge beams. The eight-foot-wide fireplace is surrounded by fish mounts and artwork. One of the plaques in the lodge says, "Eat, Sleep and Fish."

At each table are booklets called "Pages of Time" that have clippings from old advertisements from years gone by. For example, the 1954 booklet depicts the prices of stuff during that year. Gasoline cost 22 cents, minimum wage was 75 cents and the life expectancy was 68 years. In 1919, a new car was $466 while a house cost $5,626. Life expectancy then was 54 years. Did you know that Andy Rooney was born in 1919? Yikes, that's not too far away for me. The lodge doesn't serve alcohol due to the proximity to a church.

The chick-fried steak is excellent. The knotty pine dining room inside the lodge was once an open-air porch. Small children can ask for a crayon at their table. Look for the words "Dining Lodged" carved into the lintel above the doors.

Park store: The modern sandstone store sells a variety of fishing gear as well as grocery items, fishing licenses and tags. There are also some benches and a pay phone nearby. The stores sells newspapers, lodging registration, fishing clothes, permits, soft drinks, milk, prepackaged sandwiches, bacon, chips, candy, ice, tissues, diapers, canned goods, flour, T-shirts, toothbrushes, waders, fishing vests, fly-tying supplies, line, fly-tying stations and all kinds of fly-tying materials.

The old main street of Bryce would have passed right in front of the park store. Near the hatchery are remnants of the old village. Rainbow trout helped to transform Bryce from a milling town to a fishing resort. In 1939, the U.S. Postal Service changed the name from Bryce to Bennett Spring. New roads and better cars helped the area grow.

Fishing: The fishing season is March 1 through Oct. 31. Daily permits are required to fish in the spring, and zones are set aside for different lures to be used along the spring and river. The Jim Rodgers Fly-Fishing School operates at

Access points abound at the park. Anglers of every age and skill level are accommodated.

the park, offering basic and advanced casting and fishing classes. Fly-tying and rod making classes are also offered. Learn the various fishing zones before wetting your line. Some areas are artificial baits only.

There is plenty of space for back casting along the stream. That's rare. There also are plenty of fishing access points for anglers with disabilities.

Missouri Department of Conservation Hatchery: The raceways are straight and raise thousands of trout for planting in the nearby streams. Spring is a busy time and the hatchery is across the street from the park store.

Hiking: The Savanna Ridge and Natural Tunnel trails offer hours of scenic views, nature watching and wildlife. Savanna Ridge is a 1.5-2.5-mile hike that takes you through rugged hardwood forest, and gives a scenic view from atop dolomite glades (allow 1.5 hours round trip). The Natural Tunnel trail is a 7.5-mile hike that will take you through several habitats (allow 4 hours round trip), with a tunnel at the end.

Swimming: A fence encloses the outdoor pool that is open during the summer months. Hours vary, but most days it's open from noon to 7 p.m. Swimming in the spring or nearby river is not permissible. There are two lifeguard stands and two diving platforms at the blue pool. There are large mowed areas around the pool.

Day-use areas: Picnicking and newer timber-style playgrounds are scattered throughout the park.

Canoes: Canoes and tubes are rented and launched at the boat ramp near cabins 50-55. Canoes also are rented outside the park at vendors.

Nature and visitor center: The modern center is a wood and stone building overlooking a section of the spring-fed river. Inside are a small spring and several exhibits representing the Bennett Spring and other natural springs around Missouri. A full time naturalist is on duty to offer evening nature programs, guided nature walks and year-round school programs.

There is also information about the Civilian Conservation Corps at the center. Samples of their hand tools include a draw knife, wrench, brush hook, drill, marking gauge, auger, bolt tongs and more. About 250 men worked in the CCC here. The CCC work was completed in 1934-1937. Workers renovated and enlarged the hatchery, established foot trails and built many of the structures including the arch stone bridge that cross the spring branch. The dining lodge, picnic shelter A, dams and park cabins were also the handiwork of the CCC craftsmen. Black and white photographs depict examples of their work.

Also inside the nature center is a cross-section of a white oak that grew near the spring for 180 years when it fell in 1989. The display shows the events in human history while this massive tree was alive. In 1821, for example, Missouri became the 21st state.

Ozark springs drove development and attracted pioneers for more than 200 years. The springs offered water for livestock and power for mills that were often the hub of communities. Today visitors enjoy the unique flora and fauna of springs and, of course, fishing. Missouri is lucky to have public lands and highways that access the state's abundant springs.

The influence of springs doesn't end at the edge of the water. Plants that need lots of moisture thrive on the shorelines and range from the delicate spotted jewelweed to stately sycamore trees. Because the spring branch provides a constant source of food even in the winter, many animals live along the banks. The display in the visitor center depicts many animals that call Bennett Spring home.

Bennett Spring is one of the best known and most developed springs in the state. The spring has a circular pool that is about 50 feet wide. The area's dolomite is overlaid by sandstone guarding deep valleys that are usually dry except after heavy rains. The spring is subject to flooding, which leaves lots of gravel that is sometimes cleared out by state workers. Divers have said the underwater entrance to the spring is about 12 feet high and 30 to 40 feet wide with a ceiling of 22 feet.

Wildlife at the park includes wintering bald eagles, great blue and green herons, mink, beaver, river otter, belted kingfisher, wild turkey, brown creeper, horned owl, indigo bunting, five species of woodpeckers, Eastern phoebe, Carolina chickadee, loggerhead shrike, red-eyed vireo, common yellow throat and a variety of sparrows. The best birding is away from the fishing areas, maybe along the Natural Tunnel trail and other trails behind the nature center.

Interesting flora include redbud oak and flowering dogwood in the spring. And, of course, you can get close-up looks at trout. The park has a comprehensive wildflower list that breaks down wildflowers by their bloom color. White blooms are the most common species. Manna grass is also a native species.

Life in and out of water at Bennett Spring is vital to the life cycles of many insects. Some insects spend their larval or nymph stages in the water before emerging as winged adults. These insects include stonefly, Mayfly, dragonfly, Dobson fly and caddis fly. Other animals use these insects as food sources and fishermen tie flies that imitate the various life stages in an effort to catch trout and other fish. The aquatic insect display at the center gives visitors a chance to see magnified pictures of the insects. There is a wildlife feeding station behind the visitor center. Also here is a display of some flies used for fishing that show how close they appear to the real insects.

Inside the visitor center are a model of a mill, aquariums,

rock samples, restrooms, literature, maps, a donation box for the bluebird project and more.

Nature programs include nature's neighbors, hop to it, tunnel hikes, snakes hike, interpretive spring tours, freshwater animals, tree study, dinosaurs, owl hikes and more.

Insider's tips: Do the spring waters come from Lake Michigan? Visit the park to find out. The state-of-the-art exhibits in the visitor center are some of the best in the park system. Bennett Spring is the fourth largest in the state. It flows more than 100 million gallons daily.

The park has about one million visitors annually. Most of the visitors are anglers and families. Look for, but don't take, polished rocks in the hillside northeast of the spring. The polished gravel and rock suggest that the spring has a strong tumbling effect.

Nearby communities offer full service for park visitors. The rainbow trout is not native to Missouri, but they thrive in the cool spring. Fire destroyed the last spring-side mill in 1944.

Check out all of the unusual items that have been found at the bottom of the spring at the visitor center. The common aquatic insect display is one of the best features at the visitor center. This display is especially meaningful for fly fishermen. A small private church is on the property and right behind the CCC-built lodge.

There's a scale outside the park store so that you can weigh your catch of trout. Bring your bike to Bennett Spring.

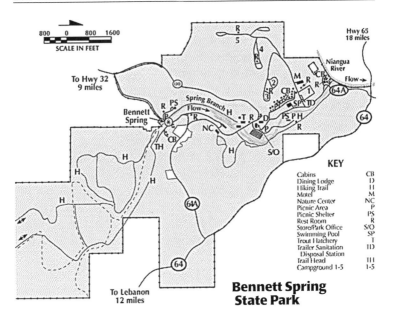

KEY

Cabins	CB
Dining Lodge	D
Hiking Trail	H
Motel	M
Nature Center	NC
Picnic Area	P
Picnic Shelter	PS
Rest Room	R
Store/Park Office	S/O
Swimming Pool	SP
Trout Hatchery	T
Trailer Sanitation Disposal Station	TD
Trail Head	TH
Campground 1-5	1-5

Bennett Spring State Park

CHAPTER 30
Big Sugar Creek State Park
Land: 2,082 acres   Water: Big Sugar Creek

B ig Sugar Creek sits in the Elk River section of the Ozarks Natural Landscape Division. It's nestled in the extreme southwest corner of the state.

The heavily forested Elk River watershed, which includes Big Sugar Creek, is part of the Arkansas River Basin, which extends into Missouri's Ozarks. It has a distinct natural history, with many of its plants and animals being Southern species that are less common or absent further into the state. This basin is also noted for having a distinctive fish population.

Big Sugar Creek State Park was established in 1992 with an initial acquisition of 640 acres. In 2000, the value and significance of the park's natural environment resulted in the designation of 1,613 of the park's 2,082 current acres as the "Elk River Breaks Natural Area." This designation by the Missouri Natural Areas Committee emphasizes the importance of the park's chert woodlands, forests and headwater streams to the natural history of the state. The park offers about three miles of hiking trail.

The clear-flowing stream, bedrock, rocky ledges, solitude and rolling hillside make this relatively undeveloped park a great getaway for nature buffs and hikers. There is no park office, but there are wonderful glades, upland woods (oak savanna that once covered 13 million Missouri acres), and brilliant scenery.

Information and activities
Big Sugar Creek State Park
c/o Roaring River State Park
Route 4, Box 4100
Cassville, MO 65625
(417) 847-2539
www.mostateparks.com
Directions:
From St. Louis
Travel west on I-44 to U.S. Hwy. 71 near Joplin. Take U.S. Hwy. 71 south to Pineville; exit at Route W to 8th Street and continue five miles east along Big Sugar Creek. This will lead you to the trailhead for Big Sugar Creek State Park.
From Kansas City
Travel south on U.S. Hwy. 71 to Pineville; exit at Route W to 8th Street and continue five miles east along Big Sugar Creek. This will lead you to the trailhead.
From Springfield, Mo.
Travel west on I-44 to U.S. Hwy. 71 near Joplin. Take U.S. Hwy. 71 south to Pineville; exit at Route W to 8th Street and continue five miles east along Big Sugar Creek. This will lead you to the trailhead.
From Jefferson City
Travel west on U.S. Hwy. 54 to Camdenton. Take Hwy. 5 south to Lebanon; then travel west on I-44. Near Joplin, take U.S. Hwy. 71 south to Pineville; exit at Route W to 8th Street and continue five miles east along Big Sugar Creek. This will lead you to the trailhead.

Hiking trails: The three-mile trail allows visitors to view distinctive natural features in a 1,613-acre tract in the park that is designated as a natural area. The woodlands found in the Elk River Breaks Natural Area are among the last of a landscape that was once common across the region. They feature open growths of shortleaf pine, oaks and hickory trees over a grassy hillside rich with shrubs and wildflowers. The trail follows a small bedrock stream, surrounded with steep hills on both sides, before climbing up into these woodlands, which offer wonderful views across the rugged Elk River landscape. The trailhead includes a vault toilet and a parking area.

Nature: The woodlands feature open growths of shortleaf pine, Ozark chinquapin oaks and hickory trees over grassy hillsides rich with shrubs and wildflowers. There is a potential for another natural area in the upland portion of the park. There are two Ecological Stewardship Areas in Big Sugar Creek State Park, where two burn units are used to restore and maintain the natural areas.

Big Sugar Creek State Park features an array of plants and animals that are less common or absent further into Missouri. Living in this unusual natural landscape are more than 345 kinds of plants and 134 kinds of birds. Notable and rare plants found in the park include the Ozark Chinquapin tree, Ozark corn salad wildflower, mock orange (a rare shrub) and low prickly pear cactus. Animals found in the park include armadillos, scarlet tanagers and graybelly salamanders.

Insider's tip: Although there is no camping, park office or significant facilities at this time, the park has a master plan that includes these in addition to continued development of the trail system, property acquisition, signage, preservation and an interpretive plan.

Big Sugar Creek State Park

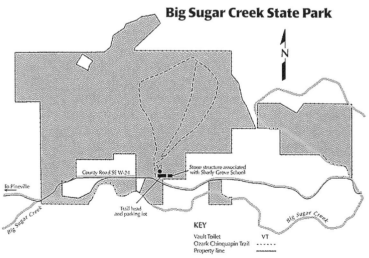

KEY

Vault Toilet   VT
Ozark Chinquapin Trail   · · · · · ·
Property line

Ha Ha Tonka State Park has 250-foot tall bluffs and has the state's 12th largest spring.

CHAPTER 31
Ha Ha Tonka State Park
Land: 3,679 acres
Water: Lake of the Ozarks

Although the park's "karst" terrain (sinkholes, caves, steep bluffs, etc.) is its most notable nature feature, the park's location in a transition zone between prairie grassland and the Ozark forests results in an unusual semi-open forest with a ground cover of prairie grasses and wildflowers called Savanna.

The cultural history of the park is as spectacular as its natural features. The wooded hillside and abundant wildlife first attracted Native Americans. Trappers and pioneers also explored the beauty of the spring and awesome valley. Daniel Boone and his son trekked the steep bluffs and rugged wooded hills, in this part of Missouri.

The original mill burned down in 1836 and later a second mill ground corn and wheat. It was destroyed to make way for the Lake of the Ozarks.

In 1909, Missouri Gov. Herbert S. Hadley proposed the

area as Missouri's first state park, but it didn't happen until 1978. A natural bridge, 70 feet wide, reaches more than 100 feet into the air. The coliseum is a steep-sided sinkhole measuring 500 feet long and 300 feet wide. The Whispering Dell sink basin is 150 feet deep with two bluff shelters - Counterfeiter's Cave and Robber's Cave - both of which were used as hideouts by criminals in the 1830s.

Bluffs of 250 feet tower over the gorge through which Ha Ha Tonka Spring, Missouri's 12th largest, discharges about 48 million gallons of water daily. All of these wonders are the result of the collapse of underground caverns in ancient geological times. Today, the spring issues from the mouth of a portion of the cave that still exists and continues to be sculpted within the earth.

Boardwalks and trails make it simple for park visitors to experience the honeycomb of caverns, spring and sinkholes. Visitors may look into caves, trek through and around sinkholes, or climb from the spring to the castle on wooden steps that circle the spring chasm. A visitor center features a large relief map of the park carved from stone.

High on a bluff overlooking Ha Ha Tonka Spring and Lake of the Ozarks sits the ruin of a stone mansion that represents the most intriguing story associated with the park.

Information and activities

Ha Ha Tonka State Park
1491 State Road D
Camdenton, MO 65020
573-346-2986
www.mostateparks.com

Emergency numbers: 911 system. Ambulance 573-734-1600; Sheriff, 573-346-2243.

Directions:

From south St. Louis

Travel west on I-44 to Exit 129 at Lebanon. At the top of the exit, turn right and travel north on Hwy. 5 for about 30 miles until reaching Camdenton. At the traffic light, turn left onto U.S. Hwy. 54 and travel west 2.5 miles before turning left onto Route D, which will lead into Ha Ha Tonka State Park.

From north St. Louis

Travel west on I-70 to Exit 148 at Kingdom City. At the top of the exit, turn left and travel west on U.S. Hwy. 54 until reaching Camdenton. From the traffic light at the junction of Hwy. 54 and Hwy. 5/7, continue on U.S. Hwy. 54 for 2.5 miles before turning left onto Route D, which will lead into the state park.

From Kansas City

Travel east on I-70 to Exit 78 (Sedalia/U.S. Hwy. 65). Head south on U.S. Hwy. 65 for about 75 miles to the town of Preston. Turn left onto U.S. Hwy. 54 and travel east for about 30 miles. After crossing the U.S. Hwy. 54 bridge over the Niangua arm of the Lake of the Ozarks, turn right onto Route D, which will lead into Ha Ha Tonka State Park.

From Springfield

Travel east on I-44 to Exit 129 at Lebanon. At the top of the exit, turn left and travel north on Hwy. 5 for about 30 miles until reaching Camdenton. At the traffic light, turn left onto U.S. Hwy. 54 and travel west for 2.5 miles before turning left onto Route D, which will lead into the park.

Castle/mansion: The castle is great and so are the views of karst topography and rugged landscapes. The carriage house ruins are first on the short trek to the castle. It was built to house 100 horses, 30 cars and the caretaker's family. The carriage house burnt on the same day as the castle in 1942 when sparks caught its roof on fire.

The hard-surface walk to the castle has six rest stops along the way. From the start of the trailhead to the castle is 521 feet. Along the path are constant lookouts of treetops, rock outcroppings, bluffs, rolling hills and the lake to your left.

Robert McClure Snyder, a Kansas City businessman, bought more than 5,000 acres and began construction of his dream retreat. A magnificent European-style mansion - or a castle - was built, sparing no expense. Material for the 60-room castle included sandstone, walnut and oak lumber all obtained on site. The rooms were grouped on three floors around a central hall rising 3.5 stories. A stone stable, 80-foot water tower and nine greenhouses were built to tend the main house. Today, all that remains are the

Mansion remains at Ha Ha Tonka State Park. The stone castle-like house had 3.5 floors.

sandstone walls.

In 1906, one year after construction began, Snyder was killed in an automobile accident. The dramatic castle and grounds remained unfinished until his sons completed it in

You can walk under the 70-foot natural bridge. The park has 13 trails.

1922.

A number of interpretive signs and overlooks are along the trail leading to the ruins of the castle.

A tank at the top of the 80-foot tower fed water to the mansion. Employees of the estate were housed in quarters beneath the tank.

Visitors center: The first thing that catches your eye is the large hexagonal outdoor exhibit with six reader boards and other information. The sandstone center was dedicated in 1997 and features an outdoor kiosk that interprets the park features. The outdoor exhibit also has photographs of the area's savanna, glades, rock and water features of the park.

A compass is painted on the floor. A butterfly garden is near the entrance of the impressive building. The flowers in the garden provide food or nectar for the butterflies. All are native wildflowers transplanted from other natural areas in the park. Common butterflies you might see include swallowtail, brush-footed sulfurs, hairs takes, Viceroy, mountain cloak, hackberry butterfly and skippers.

People's fascination with this landscape has been evident for thousands of years. The spring, caves, sinkholes, bluffs, plants and animals attracted a variety of people to the area.

The natural beauty that adorns the rugged terrain inspired many dreams.

Some sinkholes in the park are more than 200 feet deep and the sandstone you walk on was once an ancient seashore. Over the eons, sand was cemented into sandstone and tiny sea creatures were cemented together to form dolomite. Much of the chert between the dolomite and sandstone formed an ancient algae reef.

A variety of books are sold in the visitor center, including field guides. Other items offered are postcards, T-shirts, posters and more.

Hiking: The park has many boardwalks, wooden steps and walking trails. Some are challenging and a map is available from the park visitors center and various locations in the park. The coliseum trail (.5-mile) takes you to a natural bridge that reaches more than 100 feet into the air. You can walk under the bridge that is about 70 feet wide. On wet days you can see little seeps that trickle water.

The park has 13 trails; most are short and many merge together.

Geology: Here's what earth scientist Thomas R. Beveridge says about the area:

"The Hahatonka area is a classic example of collapse structures in a karst area and the close kinship of the common karst features is no better demonstrated in any other area of Missouri. Where collapse has not spread ruin, there are cave systems; where the cave system is filled with water and breached by surface erosion, there is a major spring. Where a cave system has collapsed, there are chasms and sinkholes as well as the tumbled ruins of collapsed rock. Where the collapse has been incomplete, a natural bridge is preserved. Steep bluffs mark the remaining walls of the collapsed cave system."

Nature: Common birds in the park include various swallows, Eastern bluebird, red-tailed hawks, belted kingfishers, vireo, warblers, green and great blue herons.

The last common raven in the state was seen at Ha Ha Tonka.

The spring in the park is always 56 degrees. Wintering bald eagles are sometimes seen in the Lake of the Ozarks area. Turkey Vultures soaring overhead are a common sight in the park.

Common wildflowers are black-eyed Susan, New England aster, smooth beardtongue, columbine, Indian paintbrush, spiderwort, Missouri primrose, sunflower, ox-eyed daisy, yellos coneflower, purple prairie clover, common milkweed, blazing star, bluebells, butterfly weed, Queen Anne's lace, purple coneflower, dock and wild sweet William.

The Ha Ha Tonka Savanna preserves an excellent example of pre-settlement lands. Scattered oaks, prairie grasses, open rocky glades and valley woodlands form the savanna much like it was historically.

Fire maintains the natural cycle of the savanna by controlling invading brush that would otherwise crowd out and shade native prairie plants. Fire releases natural nutrients that are recycled into the soil and help determine the kinds of trees and vegetation that grow in the area. Professionally controlled burns increase food supply and openings for feedings, nesting and travel. These fires keep the area looking like they once were.

Day-use areas: The Natural Bridge area has a .5-mile trail, drinking fountain and picnic tables. Picnic tables are also located at River Cave, the old Post Office shelter area and the lake shelter area.

Insider's tips: Read all of the interpretive signs. They include information about the karst region, flora, fauna and cultural history.

Ha Ha Tonka was heralded as one of the "seven beauty spots" in Missouri in 1929. Missouri has the second most number of caves in the United States with more than 5,000. The park has eight caves and seven sinkholes. Learn about the Ha Ha Tonka gorge that is a collapsed cave creating a chasm and island with 250-foot bluff walls.

Prescribed burns are routinely conducted in the late Fall and early Spring each year. The Missouri state park has 750 miles of hiking trails. River Cave is home to 20,000 gray bats, a federally protected species, in the summer months.

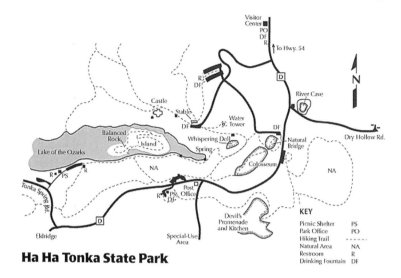

Ha Ha Tonka State Park

Lake of the Ozarks features a huge campground, aquatic trail, stables, caverns, marina and an infinite number of nearby visitor attractions.

CHAPTER 32

Lake of the Ozarks State Park

Land: 17,441 acres
Water: 55,342 acres Lake of the Ozarks

This giant water-based state park is a treasure trove of cultural history, Civilian Conservation Corps architecture, natural history, fishing, camping, caverns and every variant of water sport. There is solitude, but Lake of the Ozarks is well known as a gateway to the area's vast tourist attractions, shopping and high-energy destinations. Lake of the Ozarks is the largest state park in Missouri and offers primitive and modern camping, park store, horse rentals, remote cabins, group camping, boat ramps, marina, day-use areas, mountain biking, shoreline access, butterflies and grand underground adventures.

The park has 20 small glades and two savannas that are rich with their own brand of life. Each terrain supports its own grasses, wildflowers, sedges and other plant and animal life. The park's natural features were augmented in 1978 by the purchase of Ozark Caverns, where half-mile guided tours of the spectacular caves are conducted by lantern light.

The tract is an amazing mix of habitats to explore by boat, car or foot on 12 trails. Steep hills rise from the lakeshore and seepy bogs have boardwalks that take visitors through fens and other Ozark environs. The park has more than 80 miles of shoreline on the eastern end of the Grand Glaize arm of the Lake of the Ozarks.

Oops, I forgot to mention two beaches, an aquatic interpretive trail, suspension foot bridges, boardwalks, endangered species, bald eagles in the winter, nature programs, hundreds of camping sites, a "show" cave and a great staff.

Information and activities

Lake of the Ozarks State Park
P.O. Box 170
Kaiser, MO 65047
(573) 348-2694
(877) I Camp Mo: Camping Reservations
www.mostateparks.com

The park is off Hwy. 42 from U.S. Hwy. 54 in Camden and Miller counties. The park office is in an attractive log cabin. Inside the office is a touch station filled with natural history objects that include chert, turtle shells, bones and other items. There are also a number of animal mounts. Near the park office is another log building that features panel displays, trail information, maps, photographs and other interpretive resources. Access to the Woodland Trail that takes you to the 1,275-acre Patterson Hollow Wildlife Area is behind this log building.

Directions

From St. Louis

Lake of the Ozarks State Park is about three hours from St. Louis. Take I-44 west to St. James. From there, go north on Hwy. 68 to U.S. Hwy. 63. Proceed north on U.S. Hwy. 63

to Vienna. From Vienna, go west on Hwy. 42 until reaching Osage Beach. Take Hwy. 134 into the state park.

From Jefferson City

Lake of the Ozarks State Park is about one hour from Jefferson City. Take U.S. Hwy. 54 west to Hwy. 42. Proceed east on Hwy. 42 to Hwy. 134, which will lead you into the state park.

From Kansas City area

Lake of the Ozarks State Park is about three hours from the Kansas City area. Take I-70 east to Columbia. Exit onto U.S. Hwy. 63 and travel to Jefferson City. In Jefferson City, take U.S. Hwy. 54 west to Hwy. 42. Proceed east on Hwy. 42 to Hwy. 134, which will lead you into the state park.

From Springfield

Lake of the Ozarks State Park is about 2 hours, 30 minutes from Springfield. Take I-44 east to Lebanon. Proceed north on Hwy. 5 to Camdenton where you will take U.S. Hwy. 54 east. From U.S. Hwy. 54, take Hwy. 42 east to Hwy. 134, which will lead you into the state park.

Emergency numbers: 911 system; Lake of the Ozarks Hospital, (573) 348-8000.

Campground: Year-round accommodations for guests include more than 230 campsites that have showerhouses, electrical hookups, modern restrooms and laundry facilities.

A small store and trailheads are across the road from the check-in station. Site 2 is shady and hard surfaced where you can get your tent near a wooded valley. This first loop is sites 1-30 and has a number of tightly packed sites. Sites in the 20s are up a rise and near overflow parking. Site 24 is a pull-through and one of the nicest in this small egg-shaped loop. Sites in the mid-20s are near the vault toilets. Behind the showerhouse are a timber-style play apparatus and grassy areas. Site 30 is a pull-through near the play equipment. Site 31 has a partial lake view and stone wall. Other sites in the 30s have old stone walls running along their edge, and they have plenty of midday sunshine. Site

36 is best for a tent. Sites in the 40s enjoy shade and they are close together and easy to back into. Most of these also have a distant lake view.

Site 46 gets late-afternoon sun at the front of the site. Site 48 is a pull-through in a heavily wooded area. It's also near the bathhouse. Site 50 is also a pull-through with a picnic table that's somewhat isolated from your pad. Site 53 is near a little swale and private. Sites in the 60s are near the amphitheater and

There are eight rustic log cabins and some have distant water views. The cabins do not have running water but there is a showerhouse.

toilet. There are a couple of Y-shaped sites that are great for two families who want to camp together. Sites in the low 70s are shady and tightly packed. Some of the inner loop sites are best for larger RVs. Sites 75-79 are a great mini-loop for big RVs. Sites 81 and 83 have a long-distance view of the water and are shady. In fact, all of the sites in the 80s are shaded. Sites 85 and 87 get some late-afternoon sunlight. Site 88 has room to park your boat, while site 89 is a pull-through with a little stairway down to the picnic table platform. It also has a view of a wooded valley. You are near the water, toilets and drinking fountain. The newer bathhouse has a stone veneer and is near site 96.

Sites 90-182 are in a series of concentric loops. Site 102 is on a rise. Down the hill are many sites with water views. Campers should take a look at the sites before they choose one; some of the sites are a bit uneven. There are also views across this section of the campground due to the small size of the trees. Site 108 is on a dramatic angle; avoid it unless you have a very small rig. Site 109 is cut into the woods and has a water view. Sites in the 120s and 130s are near the bathhouse and small playground. The campground has a number of small open spaces useful for field games. Site 123 is under a big cedar and shady. Some of the sites on the inner part of the loop are close together; others have more space and some privacy. One of the better water views is from site 127 and near a shoreline access point that's ideal for family fishing. Sites in the low to mid-150s are along the water. Other water sites include 158 and 160-169. These are premier sites at Lake of the Ozarks.

Site 160 has extra space around it. It's rare to find quality campsites this close to the shoreline. Above it is site 161, that is equally nice for smaller rigs or a tent. The waterside sites are probably best for medium-sized RV units. Site 165 has extra space on one side of the pad and offers midday sunlight. Sites 174-182 are near the water and strewn with a few boulders. Sites in the 170s have great views near the water; site 177 is the most private in this mini-loop. Site 179 offers a slightly elevated look at the lake's sparkling water. Site 180 has midday sun, and sites 181 and 182 are backed up against a natural area. These sites are near a vault toilet and drinking fountain.

From some of the sites along the water, you could fly cast. There's plenty of room.

Group Camps: Accommodations for groups between 40 to 200. Facilities include cabins, a dining lodge with kitchen, a play court and a designated swimming area. Reservations can be made by calling the park office.

Cabins: The Outpost, located in the heart of the park and surrounded by an oak-hickory forest, has eight rustic log cabins for campers who want to experience the outdoors without pitching a tent. Opened in May 1993, each cabin has tables and chairs, a wood-burning stove and sleeping accommodation for up to six. Outside the cabins are benches, a grill and nearby modern showerhouse and flush toilets. The log cabins do not have running water or electricity. Some have distant water views. Bring your own cooking utensils. The cabins have a ground-mounted fire ring, trash barrels and picnic table. It is a steep scramble to the shoreline, so be careful. The Lake Trail is near the cabins.

Fishing: Lake of the Ozarks is one of the Midwest's most productive fisheries. It's also one of the most developed. Inch by inch, the shoreline is jammed with amusements, marinas, entertainment destinations, private cabins and various developments.

No timber was left in the lake when it was developed, which means most of the structures that hold fish were manmade. Finding deadfalls and brush are the gemstones where fish congregate. Maximum depth in the lake is about 100 feet and it's fed by about 1,000 springs that feed the major tributaries - the Nianqua and Grand Glaize rivers and Gravois Creek.

The lake has 1,300 miles of irregular shoreline. Aquatic vegetation is sparse even in the narrow coves and bays, making fishing difficult at times. Therefore manmade brush piles, especially around boat docks, are the primary fish holding areas. Some anglers call this the "pattern."

Lake of the Ozarks is a fine largemouth bass fishery with tournaments held on many weekends. Crappie and white bass also command attention during the spring and summer. You've got to know how to fish this unique body of water. Oxygen depletion occurs when the water warms, sending fish to varying depths seeking comfortable temperatures. At these times, fish are near the surface up to 10 feet deep.

Bass anglers have thousands of boat docks to fish around, but identifying productive ones is the challenge. Many of the docks have "private" brush piles and can be extremely productive. Here, you can try pig and jigs or plastic trailers in the shadows. During other times, anglers might hunt new brush piles, logjams or deadfalls that will hold bass and crappies. Casting at the base of the bluffs and letting your worm or jig fall to the ledge beneath is also a tested method.

Crappie anglers should key on gravel, creek channels

and coves. Minnows under a slip bobber are the common technique for these slabsides.

Boating/marina: The main lake is your oyster. Visitors can rent pontoon and fishing boats at the Grand Glaize Beach Marina. The marina also rents slips, offers camping necessities and sells fuel, paper plates, batteries, candy, ice cream, live bait, tackle, pre-packaged sandwiches and has a snack bar and coffeehouse. A laundry and firewood are also available. The covered rental slips are filled with pontoons and other boats. There is a lot of boat traffic at the marina.

The marina is five miles from the park entrance.

Mountain biking: All kinds of biking trails and hard-surface park roads are accessible. The park's Trail of the Four Winds is a 15-mile mountain bike route. The elevation changes about 150 feet and the climbs and descents are moderate, so a beginner can ride the trail. Horses also use this trail.

Aquatic trail: Water plays a major role in shaping the character of the Missouri Ozarks. The water trail is nine miles long and takes about two hours to complete. The launch is near beach No.1 and the Grand Glaize beach. Each stop is marked with orange and white buoys that are lettered consecutively. An interpretive booklet is available at the office. The water trails will teach you about rock types, logging chutes of the late 1800s, huge bedrock joints, nature solar heating, the natural history of rock overhangs, green plants, karst topography, caves and glades.

Stables: The state park stables are 3.5 miles from the main entrance. The stables offer half-hour pony rides up to overnight rides with meals and tents. All trail rides are guided and helmets are required for children under 12. Call in advance; they are busy. There are two vending machines and a picnic table at the stable area.

Ozark Caverns: The main natural attraction at the Lake of the Ozarks is one of three "show" caves in the state. Visitors carry lanterns to explore the cave, which features a small stream, seeps and many types of underground geological formations. Discovering what's beneath the surface is fun, low cost and an easy walk. There is an

Geological diversity and a self-guided trails are within the popular state park.

admission fee. During the summer, tours are offered two or three times a day. The traditional tour lasts about a half-hour. There are interpretive signs at the cave entrance. Inside the interpretive visitors center at the cavern's entrance are animal mounts, touch table, displays on cave evolution, bluebird information, artifacts, three aquarium tanks and literature.

About 8,000 people tour the cave annually. Outside the entrance doors is a native wildflower garden that includes Christmas fern, shooting star, smooth yellow violet, sweet William, bluebells, buttercup, hispid buttercup, bloodwort, starry campion, wild ginger and others.

Angel Showers is a focal point of the tour, where a never-ending shower of water seems to come out of solid ceiling rock. Four species of salamander, four types of bats and 16 invertebrates live in the caverns.

Hiking: Huge geological diversity can be seen from the trails. The Ozarks' natural beauty is often best seen by foot.

The Coakley Hollow Self-Guided Trail near the cavern entrance includes suspension bridges, interpretive booklet and learning stations. The trails are chipped and gravel and generally gentle. The trail introduces hikers to a series of Ozark features including sides, lopes, chert, lichens, fungus algae, flowering dogwood, spicebush, seeps, butternut tree, spring-fed stream, aquatic insects, a glade, a fen and geology. Don't get locked out - or in, I should say. Check at the visitor center for the closing time.

The Woodland Trail (6 miles) meanders through the Patterson Hollow Wild Area, which is a patchwork of old fields, pastures, stands of oak-hickory forests and quiet areas where songbirds sing. Trail of Four Winds (16.5 miles) is open to hikers, horses and mountain bikes. It's complete with boardwalks for foot traffic only, rocky outcrops and vistas of the valleys. For a walk along the lake, try the Lake View Bend Trail (1.5 mile), an easy stroll along the base of the cliffs.

Nature: A wildlife checklist brochure is available at the park office. The park has 167 species of birds, 29 reptiles, 15 amphibians and 28 types of mammals. The park has gray bats, red-shouldered hawks and northern scarlet snakes that are endangered species.

Residing in the park are four types of skinks, four types of turtles, Northern fence lizard, white pelicans, central newt, salamanders and mammals that include foxes, bobcats, whitetail deer, groundhogs, mink, raccoons, squirrels, bats, muskrats and others.

Interpretive programs include secrets of the hidden forest, Junior Naturalist hour, talking with trees, bird walks, tree trek and others.

Birding in the park is great. From bottomland forests to glades, savannas and aquatic habits, the park's terrain features diversity amid plenty of mixed outdoor recreation uses. Staff says that some of the best birding are on the Coakley Hollow Trail, Rocky Top Trail and the Bluestem Knoll Savanna. Each of these locations has diverse habitats. The Rocky Top Trail is steep, but leads to a glade with showy spring wildflowers and plenty of songbirds and raptors.

The Bluestem Knoll Savanna is near the park entrance, and like its name suggests, it has plenty of grasslands where lark sparrows and other songbirds are commonly seen and heard. Other species in the park include hummingbirds at the feeders, swallows at the cave entrances, vireo, many types of warblers, several kinds of sparrows and others. Wintering bald eagles are also seen at the lake crossings. The state's captive bald eagle program that started in 1981 has made a huge difference in establishing resident birds. There are about 1,500 bald eagles in Missouri.

A butterfly checklist can be obtained from the park office that includes a list of 10 butterfly families. Individual species include seven types of swallowtails, 11 kinds of skippers, six kinds of hairsteaks, dogface butterfly, fritillaries, comma, painted lady, snout butterfly, Falcate orange tip, six types of dusky wings and many more color species. To attract butterflies at home, plant flora that provides nectar.

Beaches: Beach No. 1 has oaks, playground equipment, benches, volleyball court and changing rooms. A T-shaped floating dock and retaining wall overlook the 125-yard-wide brown gravely beach. The view from the beach is of a wooded shoreline and rocky ledges that peak through the distant towering trees. The nearby mature trees and CCC-built structures are terrific examples of architectural

Lake of the Ozarks State Park has two popular beaches.

quality that is rarely duplicated today. The changing building has massive beams, flagstone steps and rugged siding. The boat ramp is about 200 yards from the beach.

The smaller beach at the Grand Glaize is down a steep grade to a narrow cove. A footbridge and plenty of space for field games connect the day-use area. The beach is about 50 yards long. An outdoor shower at the gray bathhouse allows kids to wash their feet off before they hop into the car. A concrete retaining wall overlooks the beach.

Day-use areas: The picnic and day-use areas are some of the finest in the parks system. Many of them have Civilian Conservation Corps buildings, baseball backstops and other amenities. Group picnics are welcome at the park and facilities are excellent.

Insider's tips: A huge park is diverse and there are infinite numbers of tourist attractions and restaurants nearby. The lake's shoreline is heavily developed. From factory outlets to Pickled Pete's bar, the area is wrought with putty golf, go-kart tracks and fast food stores. The region gets about three million visitors annually.

Private owners opened the caverns in 1951. The state bought it in 1978. Watch for northern rough-winged swallows near the entrance of the Ozark Caverns. Prairie racerunner lizards can be seen on the Rocky Top glade.

Lake of the Ozarks is sometimes called the "Land of the Magic Dragon" because if you look at a lake map, it looks like a dragon. Some of the Civilian Conservation Corps-era log cabins that are used at the beach or for restrooms are some of the nicest in the state park system. Stone bridges in the park are also noteworthy.

The park roads are wide, smooth and winding. Bring your bike. Bring your airplane, also. A small airport is on state parkland.

Lake of the Ozarks State Park

KEY

Shelter	S
Equestrian Trail	E
Hiking Trail	H
Bicycle Trail	B
Primitive Camping	PC

To Eldon

Lake of the Ozarks

Grand Glaize Beach/Pa He Tsi

Picnic Area

Grand Glaize Bridge

Camper Cabins

Kaiser

Park Entrance

Wild Area

Camp Red Bud

Camp Pin Oak

Boat Launches

Marina Beach

Camp Hawthorn

Park Office

To Brumley 5 miles

To Brumley

McCubbin's Point

Trail Center

Grand Glaize Arm

Camp Clover Point

Camp Rising Sun

Fort Leonard Wood Recreation Area

Anderson Hollow Rd.

Riding Stables

Marina/Store

Picnic Area

Beach

Boat Launch

Amphitheater

Swinging Bridges Rd.

Campground

Ozark Caverns

McCubbins Drive

Natural Area

To Camdenton

N

SCALE IN FEET

Pomme de Terre State Park is your gateway to water recreation and views of the oak-hickory forests that blanket the region.

CHAPTER 33

Pomme de Terre State Park
Land: 734 acres Water: 7,790 acres

Like many of the lakes that U.S. Army Corps of Engineers made, Lake Pomme de Terre started as a river. In the 1830s, the Pomme de Terre River was a dividing line between Indians and the settlers of Polk and Hickory counties. Today, the state park is your gateway to water recreation on the nearly 8,000-acre lake.

"Pomme de Terre" means "potato," which translates to "apple of the Earth." Legend says that early French trappers and fur traders named the river for the potato-like vegetation that grew on its banks. Now, oak-hickory forests blanket much of the region. There are also rolling plains underlain with dolomite, limestone, shale and sandstone. In pre-settlement times, the area was a savanna where tall grasses of the prairie intermingled with the Ozark forests of the east.

In 1938, Congress authorized the flooding of the river to create Pomme de Terre Lake. Project planning began in 1947 and construction wouldn't begin until 10 years later. The dam and lake were completed in 1961, at a cost of $14 million. The lake can expand from 7,800 acres to 16,100 acres as excess run-off is impounded to prevent downstream flooding. There are about 113 miles of shoreline.

The state park has campgrounds (255 sites) on two sides of the lake, the Pittsburg and Hermitage sides.

Information and activities

Pomme de Terre State Park
HC 77, Box 890
Pittsburg, MO 65724
(417) 852-4291 (Pittsburg)
(417) 745-6909 (Hermitage)
(417) 852-4567 - marina
(877) I Camp Mo; Camping Reservations
www.mostateparks.com

Directions: The park has two areas, one each near Pittsburg and Hermitage, south of U.S. Hwy. 54 in Hickory County.

Pittsburg Area

From Springfield

Travel north on U.S. Hwy. 65 to Louisburg and turn left onto Hwy. 64. Proceed about nine miles and continue right on Hwy. 64 toward Pittsburg. Turn left at Hwy. 64B, which leads to the state park.

From Kansas City

Travel south on U.S. Hwy. 71 to Harrisonville. Take U.S. Hwy. 7 south to Clinton, where you will take U.S. Hwy. 13 to Collins. From there, take U.S. Hwy. 54 east to Hermitage. In Hermitage, turn right onto Hwy. 254 and travel to Carsons Corner; continue straight on Hwy. 64 toward Nemo. At the four-way stop in Nemo, turn right, staying on Hwy. 64, and travel over the lake. Turn right onto Hwy.

64B, which leads to the state park.

From Jefferson City

Travel west on U.S. Hwy. 54 through Preston. Turn left onto Route D and travel to the four-way stop in Nemo. Continue straight, now on Hwy. 64, and travel over the lake. Turn right onto Hwy. 64B, which leads to the state park.

From St. Louis

Travel west on I-44 to Lebanon. Take Hwy. 64 west through Louisburg, passing the turnoff for Bennett Spring State Park. Continue right on Hwy. 64 toward Pittsburg. Turn left at Hwy. 64B, which leads to the state park.

Hermitage Area

From Springfield

Travel north on U.S. Hwy. 65 through Urbana. Turn left onto Route NN and continue for about nine miles to the four-way stop at Nemo. Continue straight on Hwy. 64 for two miles, then turn left at CR 246. Travel about one mile and turn left onto the state park road.

From Kansas City

Travel south on U.S. Hwy. 71 to Harrisonville. Take U.S. Hwy. 7 south to Clinton, where you will take U.S. Hwy. 13 to Collins. From there, take U.S. Hwy. 54 east to Hermitage. In Hermitage, turn right onto Hwy. 254 and travel to Carsons Corner. Continue straight, now on Hwy. 64, then turn right at CR 246. Travel about one mile and turn left onto the state park road.

From Jefferson City

Travel west on U.S. Hwy. 54 through Preston. Turn left onto Route D and travel to the four-way stop at Nemo. Turn right onto Hwy. 64 and continue two miles to CR 246. Turn left and travel about one mile before turning onto the state park road.

From St. Louis

Travel west on I-44 to Lebanon. Take Hwy. 64 west to Louisburg. At Louisburg, turn right onto U.S. Hwy. 65 and continue through Urbana. Turn left onto Route NN and travel to the four-way stop at Nemo. Continue straight on Hwy. 64

for about two miles. Turn left at CR 246 and continue for one mile before turning left onto the state park road.

Emergency numbers: Ambulance (417) 745-6415, Citizens Memorial Hospital (417) 326-6000, Hickory County sheriff (417) 745-6415.

Campgrounds: The Pittsburg side offers 127 campsites, while the Hermitage side has 128 campsites.

On the Pittsburg side, sites in the 400 loop are first-come, first-served. A truck with ice and wood goes through the campground in the morning and early evenings on weekends only from Memorial Day through Labor Day.

Loop 101-121 offer water and electrical hookups. The hard-surface park road circles though the wooded campground that has small shelters that your picnic tables can fit under. Sites are shaded by oaks and the loop is about 70 percent shady. The vault toilet is across from site 104. Site 111 is at the end of the loop, and is one of the more private in this section. It is also near a small natural area. Sites are tight and close to your neighbor. Site 112 is shady and on a low knoll about two feet above the roadbed. Open are sites 114 and 115 and they get lots of morning sunlight.

Loop 201-240 offers electric sites and is about 70 percent shade. Site 201 is a fully shaded site. A sunny morning site is 204. Look for a burl the size of a basketball on the tree at this campsite. This loop's sites have a little more space between them.

Occasionally there is a little vegetation and trees offering some screening. Site 209 gets a spot of morning sun near its front part. Sites in this loop are on varying elevations and gently rolling. From site 214 to site 234, you can see glimpses of the lake. Other sites at the end of the loop have views of the woody slopes that drop to the lake. The vault toilet is near site 216. Sites 218 and 219 are great with access to the water.

Site 221 is slightly elevated and looks down on a narrow lake cove that is maybe 40 yards across. Site 222 is also an excellent site that has an expansive lake view and is large enough for big RV rigs. Sites 224-227 also have a water view and can accommodate big rigs. Campers can scramble

The park has small boat launches and a larger marina with park store.

down the slope to the lake for some fishing. Fishing can be good from a protected cove there. Sites 228-229 also enjoy water views. Site 233 has a small cedar tree and lots of shade. This loop is left a bit natural instead of closely mowed. I like that. Up the rise are sites in the high 230s. They are shady all day long, but do not have lake views. Sites 238 and 239 have plenty of space around them.

Loop 301-338 offers many fine sites with expansive views of the coves and lake. There is community water and electricity in this loop. The loop is on a peninsula and is the western-most camping area. Most of the pads are paved, with various elevations and oak trees that tower overhead. Sites 301-303 are best for pop-up campers. Site 304 is hard-surfaced and can accommodate a larger RV unit. Site 308 is also hard-surfaced and has a partial water view. Many of the sites on the inside loop have additional room for a tent or screen room. Site 310 is a pull-though and has a great view of the narrow cove and tree-lined lakeshore.

Site 311 has a terrific view and is on a rise above the cove. In the distance, you also can see a single-lane boat ramp and fishing pier. Site 316 is a new site with a gravel

pad and a great view. Site 317 is a pull-through at the north
tip of the loop. It is the best site in the loop. Site 319 is also
a pull-through with a view through the cedars to the quiet
watery cove. Some vegetation separates the rest of the sites
in the 320s, and they are more private than many nearby
campsites. They also get lots of midday sunlight. Many of
these sites have footpath access to the shoreline. Site 330
has a big cedar and is next to a very sunny site 333
complete with a small mowed side yard. Site 337 is on a
sunny knoll with oaks and cedars providing shade.

Loop 401-429 has a small shower building with flush toilets
and nearby playground. Sites 401-402 are wide open and
sunny. Many sites in the lower 400s have water views. All of
the sites on the inside loop have electrical hook-ups. Sites in
the low 400s are great for two families who wish to camp
next to each other. Most are hard-surfaced pads. Site 410 is
near the vault toilet and water bib. Site 413 has a limited
water view, on a knoll and can contain a large RV unit. It also
has privacy and space around it. Some of the sites in the
teens have vegetation that offers some privacy and have
views of the bays and lake. Site 417 has one of the best views
of the lake. It's also near a small natural area. Site 418 is very
private with water views. Site 421 is best for a big RV unit
because it's wide and flat. Down the hill we go to site 423 that
has lots of room. Sites in the high 420s are within easy
walking distance of the playground and rest room.

The Hermitage Area campground is sunny. Here's the
details about this camping area.

A near bonsai-like Eastern red cedar tree is next to site
101. This loop has many small to medium sites with lots of
sun. Notice the many other mature red cedars along this
loop. From site 115, you have a water view down into a tree-
lined cove that often has great blue herons working along
the brushy shoreline.

The loop with sites 201-259 has electrical hook-ups and
some trees. You can see from one end of the tract to the
other. Sites have gravel pads, tables and fire rings. Both
sides of the park's campground have views of the narrow
coves and rocky shorelines. Site 205 has a distant water
view and shade for the hot summer afternoons. Sites 210-

215 have a place where you can pull your boat ashore and camp nearby. Site 215 has direct walking access to the water. Sites in the teens are small and offer ready access to the shoreline and a view of the 7,240-foot dam about a half-mile away.

Sites in the 220s are mostly sunny. All of the sites are smooth and flat. Sites 228 and 229 are partly shady sites that have views of the long dam. Sites in the 230s also have water views. Most of these sites have one 8- to 10-inch caliper tree per site. Sites in the 240s and 250s can accommodate large rigs.

Sites in the low 300s have a good view of the lake and coves. Sites 312-314 are attractive and shady. These and others in the teens have water views of craggy shorelines and small bays. Some say the views are the best in the park from this part of the campground. The outside of the loop is large and shady; the inside of the loop offers smaller sites. Sites 319 and 321 are notched into the woods.

Hiking: There are two hiking trails, one on the Pittsburg side (Indian Point Trail) and one on the Hermitage side (Cedar Bluff Trail). Indian Point Trail is three miles but can be reduced to 1.5 or 2.5 miles by using the connector trails. The trail takes you along a peninsula shoreline to Indian Point Overlook. Cedar Bluff Trail begins at either the beach or the campground and is a 1.5- or 2-mile hike depending on whether you use the connector trails. This hike is along a peninsula shoreline.

The main trails have blue arrows and the connector loops have red arrows. Most of the hiking in the park is easy.

Fishing: The lake has hundreds of narrow coves for fishing. The lake is known for its muskellunge fishing experience, but you can also try to catch bass, walleye, catfish and crappie. There are two boat launches on both the Pittsburg and Hermitage sides of the park, as well as two public beaches. The State Park marina is on the Pittsburg side. There is a small daily charge to fish off the marina. The marina store sells bait and artificial lures including plastic jig bodies and spinners. Crappies like yellow jigs. A fish bragger board is in the store also. There is a Fishing Hot Spots map for the lake. Live bait is sold at

The marina store sells bait, ice cream and serves breakfast and lunch. You can fish from the docks.

the marina store from a large aerated tank. Fishing licenses are also sold at the store.

Muskies have been stocked in the lake since 1966. Many 36-inch muskies are taken from the lake; 48-inch muskies are rare. It takes about 28 hours of skilled angling to catch an average-sized muskie of 36 inches, according to park information. In the spring anglers work the coves, especially Copper Cove and other back coves. Yellow bucktails is a popular bait. Try large spinners of yellow and chartreuse also. Try working the lures parallel to the shore so you can stay in the strike zone longer. Some experienced anglers use jerk baits in these areas. Once the surface temperature of the water reaches 80 degrees, the muskie fishing falls off. Muskies like low light conditions.

The lake has had some periodic walleye planting in recent years. Other improvements to the fishery include placing hundreds of cedar trees to attract fish. Hundreds of the 3- to12-inch cedars have been placed in 1 to 20 feet of water. There are four lake maps available that detail the location of fish attractors.

The average Missouri angler spends about $1,200 annually on fishing, which means about a $832 million boost to the state's economy. All of this also funds about

15,000 jobs.

Some anglers fish for crappie under the floating marina. Lots of fish are visible from the marina docks. The weedy shorelines, brush overhangs and standing timber offer lots of fishing opportunities. There also are expansive stretches of gentle shoreline from which the entire family can fish.

Limits are crappies nine inches, 15 daily; black bass 13 inches, six daily; walleye 15 inches, four per day; and muskies, 36 inches, one per day.

Make sure you help stop the spread of zebra mussels. Routinely inspect and wash your boat between put-ins. Even your bait bucket can spread zebra mussels; replace bait between put-ins as well.

Marina: Inside the tidy tan store you'll find sunscreen, T-shirts, aspirin, bait, pop and juices.Yahoo, hand-dipped ice cream is served. It's a very clean store and eating area. There are picnic tables on the floating dock.

In the marina, you will find a breakfast /lunch menu. The park marina sells ice, gasoline and food. The food is topnotch in the sparkling clear little concession. A flush toilet with parking is near the small boat launch ramp. Under the metal roof are all types of boats moored for storage. Views from the marina features wooded shorelines and gentle water. There are two boat ramps on the Hermitage side of the park.

Swimming: Above the beach are a rest room and benches. The swimming area is outlined by solid yellow markers. A timber-style play structure, cedar trees and a parking lot for about 45 vehicles are next to the small 100-yard-long sandy beach. From the four benches you can see the dam at the end of the cove, campgrounds and rocky shorelines. I love the aged red cedars with their sinew-like bark. Standing dead timber and brushy coves are also apparent around the beach.

Both sides of the beach are brushy and there are some picnic tables and pedestal grills.

The beach at the Hermitage Area is available only to campers and has a shower building, bike rack, hard-surface parking and small naturalist's office. There are vending machines and it's a much nicer beach than in the Pittsburg area. The views are of the rocky ledge-like shoreline and rolling tree-covered hills. Sixty to 70 cars can park in the parking lots. The day-use area features grills. The beach is about 125 yards long and tall hickory trees shade the access road. There is also lots of room for field games behind the gravely brown sand.

Day-use areas: There are about 45 picnic sites in the park.

Nature: Some of the natural wonders you'll want to see are the Post and Chinquapin Oak trees that are in the park. Some of these trees are more than 200 years old, but they do not display the characteristics of a 200-year-old tree. Instead of being tall and slender they are short and round; this indicates that they had adequate space to grow, proving that the area was once a meadow.

Junior Naturalist programs include butterflies are beautiful, bug study, insect survivors, bug hunt on the trail, bug bingo, bug mania, Indian point day, history in the trees, bird box building and interpretive hikes.

Insider's tips: Firewood is sold only at the marina store. The mission of the Missouri park system is threefold: To preserve and interpret the finest examples of Missouri natural landscapes, to preserve and interpret the finest examples of Missouri's cultural landmarks, and to provide healthy and enjoyable outdoor recreation opportunities for all Missourians and visitors to the state. There are 2,000 campsites in the Missouri state park system. Hunting is allowed in nearby Corps of Engineers lands.

The Pomme de Terre Outfitters is between the park units and offers lots of outdoor supplies. Corps of Engineers facilities include beaches, hiking trails, developed campgrounds, primitive camping, group picnic areas and more. For example, Nemo Park has a nice beach. Both state park beaches are within driving distance from the campgrounds.

The annual Ozark Market Days is always held on Saturday of the July 4th weekend.

Pomme de Terre State Park

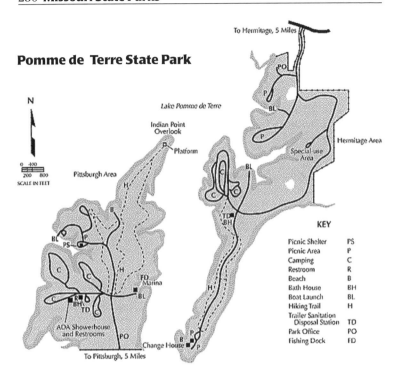

N

Lake Pomme de Terre

Indian Point
Overlook

Platform

Pittsburgh Area

Hermitage Area

Special-use
Area

0   400
200   800
SCALE IN FEET

Marina

FD

ADA Showerhouse
and Restrooms

Change House

To Pittsburgh, 5 Miles

To Hermitage, 5 Miles

KEY

Picnic Shelter	PS
Picnic Area	P
Camping	C
Restroom	R
Beach	B
Bath House	BH
Boat Launch	BL
Hiking Trail	H
Trailer Sanitation Disposal Station	TD
Park Office	PO
Fishing Dock	FD

Prairie State Park is sun-drenched and treeless. A resident elk and bison herd are part of this extraordinary unit that interprets prairie ecology.

CHAPTER 34
Prairie State Park
Land: 3,942 acres

The Missouri Prairie Foundation's brochure says, "It's hard to imagine anything more distinctly American than our legendary prairies."

Although the mammoth expanses of prairies are gone, Prairie State Park is a sun-washed, treeless tract that recaptures our heritage and maintains a waving slice of our precious prairies. The visitors center is particularly well-designed and interprets not only the prairies' extraordinary natural history, but also man's role in this irreplaceable environment. Elk and bison herds are pretty cool to see, too.

"The prairie feeling is a magical mixture of distant horizons, vast blue sky, brilliant floral displays, massive bison, and restless grass," says the state park's literature. We can only imagine the feeling of early travelers as they looked upon the endless sea of grass. Luckily we can have our own experiences of this immeasurable prairie by visiting the state park.

Here you will learn about sod builders, the sponge-like moist prairie, desert prairie conditions and the fires that shaped plant and animal communities. Along the many trails visitors will sometimes see islands in the prairie sea where there are patches of shrubs. These islands, especially in the spring, often embrace raucous nesting birds and offer browsing for deer and small mammals. There is much to see along the trails including a flowing stream, prairie trees and various predators.

One of the best times to visit the park is during the spring and early summer, when splashes of color from the grand expanses of wildflowers are in bloom. The courtship dance of the prairie chicken also takes place in the springtime. Some experts say Prairie State Park is the best destination of all the parks during this time of the year.

For information and activities

Prairie State Park
128 NW 150th Lane, P.O. Box 97
Liberal, MO 64762
(417) 843-6711
www.mostateparks.com

Directions:

From Joplin

Prairie State Park is 35 miles north of Joplin; travel time is about 45 minutes. Travel north on Hwy. 43 about 25 miles to Hwy. 160. Turn left/west onto Hwy. 160 and continue for about two miles before turning right/north onto Route NN. Proceed one mile to Central Road (gravel surface); turn left/west and continue for three miles. Turn right/north onto 150th Lane and proceed 1.3 miles to the park's visitors center.

From Kansas City

Prairie State Park is 110 miles south of Kansas City; travel time is between two and 2.5 hours. Travel south on U.S. Hwy. 71 to the Hwy. 160 (Lamar exit) and turn right/west onto Hwy. 160. Continue about 16 miles to Route NN and turn right/north to proceed one mile to Central Road (gravel surface). Turn left/west onto Central Road and continue for three miles before turning right/north onto 150th Lane. Proceed 1.3 miles to the park's visitors center.

Emergency number: Sheriff, (417) 682-5541.

Visitors center: The low-slung visitors center offers a paved handicap parking space with an adjacent pathway leading to its entrance. The ramp to the entrance is an average 6.2 percent grade with a railing and is level before the doors. Inside are a spacious lobby with information and helpful staff to answer your questions. A water fountain and public restrooms with front-transfer toilets are available. Three landings lead to the lower level. This level has interpretation activities, a panoramic view of the prairie, a wonderful diorama of prairie life and a museum. Views of the prairie and the diorama may also be observed from the upper level.

The parking lot at the visitors center is gravel and two flags fly overhead.

Immediately inside the center is a wall-size diorama call the "Hidden World of the Prairie," where an assortment of native animal and plant mounts is detailed. Animals include killdeer, mole cricket, slender grass lizard, scissortail flycatcher, rough-legged hawk and others. In the middle of the exhibit hall is a full-size mounted America bison that is surrounded by a number of native flora and fauna including brier, box turtle, least shrew, Eastern meadowlark, bull snake, black-eye Susan, pale purple cornflower, prairie beard tongue, brown-headed cowbird, gay feather, crested hair grass, rattlesnake master, Indian grass, short-eared owl, blue sage, bluestem grass, purple aster and much more. This display is a giant glass cube that offers 360-degree views of the bison and native wildlife and vegetation.

Southwestern Missouri was one of the last regions of the state to be settled. Many settlers preferred the eastern part of the state that had easy access by the river, timber for homes and plenty of water. The southwest's first residents landed primarily along timbered creeks or abutting the prairie forest margins. They ventured little into the prairie expanse, since it was difficult to till. Most early settlers relied on subsistence farming and raising livestock. The visitors center displays settlers' tools and equipment including harnesses, nails, pumps, cultivator blades, plows, shoes from draft horses and horse collars.

Early farmers planted alfalfa, winter wheat, millet, corn and hay. They also constructed rock fences and barbed wire fences. Today, electric fences contain the park's bison herd.

Fire ruled the prairies. Some prairie fires you can step over and they creep slowly; other fires accelerate through seven-foot grasses at a perilous rate. No matter who lived on the prairie, Indians, settlers or farmers, nature's fires indeed ruled, replenished and ultimately restored the rambling grasslands. However, farming changed all that. Fires set by lightning once swept vast regions of unbroken tallgrass prairie and shaped the character of the grasslands. Today, these lifegiving fires must be set on purpose. By burning an area every two or three years, old vegetation is cleared, promoting new lush growth and spectacular floral display. In addition, some animals need the growth. These fires also prevent brush and trees from invading the grassland.

The Missouri sea of grass once covered 13 million acres. Today, a new sea of crops and pastures has all but swallowed up the once endless prairie horizons that are now just islands. But the beauty of the prairie is still found at Prairie State Park.

Some plants and animals live only on the prairie and need specific conditions to flourish. For example, prairie chickens need lawn-like areas grazed by bison. Prairie mole crickets have not been found when heavy grazing occurs. Marsh hawks nest in brushy sumac clumps, while certain butterflies lay their eggs on specific plants.

In the drawers beneath the observation windows that look out on the prairie are color photographs of the area's mammals, birds and reptiles. There are also drawers filled with samples of turtle shells, a butterfly collection, insect collection, pelts from beaver and deer, galls, Golden Guides, magazines and fossils. In the small lecture room at

Views of the prairie are everywhere and the areas natural history is part of America's heritage.

the rear of the center are more interpretive displays that include information about bison. More on that later.

The "scoop on poop" can be learned at the visitors center. Many times when you are hiking, you can learn more about animals by learning about their remains. Scat is one of the indicators. The center has examples of scat from bear, otter, bats, rabbits, elk, raccoon, whitetail deer, opossum and bobcat.

At the observation window are binoculars, bird identification cards and a bird song identifier.

Bison: These beasts are the largest land mammal in North America. Bison move across the prairie rapidly while eating mostly grasses, leaving other plants alone. This resulted in areas with shorter grass and abundant wildflowers that attract many nesting birds and insects.

Bison are rich brown, but their calves are pumpkin color. Calves are born without horns or humps, and cows are pregnant 9.5 months. The 50-pound calves are typically born between May and July. Bulls can weigh 1,600 to 2,000 pounds and sometimes exceed 12 feet long. Remember, buffalo are native to Asia and Africa. In the lecture room there are samples of bison horn, fir, bone tools, fiber and hides. Bison are not buffalo.

There is a herd of elk that can sometimes be seen with binoculars from the visitors center. Ask the naturalist about the herd's location and tips on spotting them.

From January through March, the visitors center is open Wednesday through Saturday from 8:30 a.m. to 5 p.m. and Sunday from 1 p.m. to 5 p.m. From April through December, the visitors center is open Tuesday through Saturday from 8:30 a.m. to 5 p.m. and Sunday from 1 p.m. to 5 p.m.

Hiking: The Gayfeather Trail is recommended by the naturalist for its

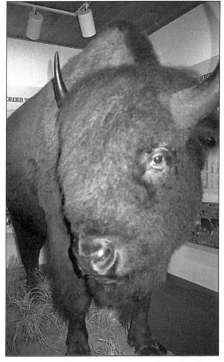

The park has a resident herd of bison. Bulls can weight more than 1,600 pounds.

wildflowers and a chance to see the elk. Guided groups often use a half-mile trail near the visitors center.

Pick up a copy of the 27-page Trail and Nature Area Guide that details natural history features in the tract. Trailheads have small gravel parking lots that are outlined by rail fences. The park has four main hiking trails; some pass through electric fences that are designed to manage the bison herd. Hikers should step through the insulated wires at these points.

The park also publishes an animal checklist and listing of wildflowers that detail blooming dates and color. There are at least 10 wildflowers that have pink blooms and 33 white bloomers that mostly blossom from April to July. The park has 23 species of reptiles, 12 types of amphibians and 22 species of mammals. Butterfly lovers can spot nearly 100 species along the easy-walking trails.

Drovers Trail (2.5 miles, red markers) travels the center of the. The Gayfeather Trail (1.5 miles, green markers) passes the Regal Prairie Natural Area that features nearly undisturbed communities of plant and animal life.

Camping: Prairie State Park offers limited basic campsites and a backpack camp. A gravel road takes you into wooded camping. The campsites are grassy and rustic. Each site is private. The restrooms are down a dirt footpath from site 2. There is a back pack camp located on the Coyote Trail.

Day-use area: The picnic area is near a stream under shady trees. The parking lot is compacted gravel. One site has an accessible pad with an extended end table. All sites have pedestal grills. The vault toilet has compacted gravel parking adjacent to a concrete path. Some users may need assistance, as the clearance in front of the doors is only four feet wide.

Insider's tips: Begin looking for the bison herd as soon as the prairie flats begin. Bring a picnic lunch; there is a single table outside the visitors center that has a great view of the prairie. An endangered variety of milkweed blooms in select areas during June. Look for prairie chicken and listen for their drumming. Wildflower buffs will love this state park.

Prairie State Park

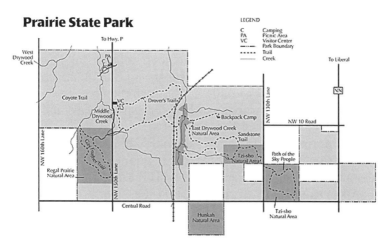

Outdoor recreation and trout fishing comprise one of the state's finest parks. The unit has a scenic hilltop lodge, fish hatchery, camping and cabins.

CHAPTER 35
Roaring River State Park
Land: 3,973 acres   Water: Roaring River

Midwest Living Magazine called Roaring River "a place of rainbows and sunrises." It's impossible to disagree.

In fact, the spring-carved valley and wood-cloaked hills have cradled human activities for centuries. Today, visitors continue to take energy from the deep hollows, tall ridges and productive trout streams. The spring that gushes more than 20 million gallons daily first attracted native Americans, then Europeans who built mills and a small community.

Outdoor recreation and great trout fishing now dot this part of the Ozarks. Visitors love the mountain-like terrain, deep blue spring and cedar glades. Did I mention fishing? For thousands of fly fishermen, Roaring River is a world-class destination. Good fishing, a productive hatchery, great dining and tall tales are just some of the features that attract increasing numbers of sport fishermen.

Early settlers began to arrive in the 1800s, when native Americans had already moved to reservations in Oklahoma and Kansas. Many newcomers to this beautiful region were farmers from Kentucky and Tennessee. The early settlers often chose sites along spring-fed streams that offered clean drinking water and natural refrigeration. The rushing water also provided the energy to power mills for grain, timber, wool and cotton.

Today, this water supplies a hatchery, which grows fish and attracts thousands of anglers to the park, cabins and scenic inn annually. The park also has 187 campsites, 26 guest rooms, 26 secluded cabins, conference facilities and a terrific restaurant. All in all, Roaring River is one of the finest state parks in the system.

Information and activities

Roaring River State Park
Route 4, Box 4100
(417) 847-2539: Park Office
(417) 847-2330: Lodging Reservations
(877) I Camp Mo: Camping Reservations
www.mostateparks.com

Directions

From Springfield

Roaring River State Park is 65 miles from Springfield. Travel west on U.S. Hwy. 60 for 39 miles to Monett. Turn left/south onto Hwy. 37 and continue for 19 miles to Cassville. Take Hwy. 76/86 west through Cassville to Hwy. 112. Travel south on Hwy. 112 for seven miles to the park entrance.

From Joplin

Roaring River State Park is 66 miles from Joplin. Travel east on I-44 to Exit 26/Sarcoxie. Take Hwy. 37 south for 42 miles to Cassville. Take Hwy. 76/86 east through Cassville to Hwy. 112. Travel south on Hwy. 112 for seven miles to the park entrance.

From Rogers, Ark.

Roaring River State Park is 28 miles from Rogers, Ark. Travel north on U.S. Hwy. 62 for 15 miles to Garfield, Ark.;

turn north onto Hwy. 37. Continue on Hwy. 37 for four miles to Seligman; turn right onto Hwy. 112. Travel nine miles east on Hwy. 112 to the park entrance.

From Eureka Springs, Ark.

Roaring River State Park is 20 miles from Eureka Springs, Ark. Travel north on Hwy. 23 for 10 miles to Eagle Rock; turn west onto Hwy. 86. Continue on Hwy. 86 for six miles to Route F. Turn left onto Route F and continue west for four miles to the park entrance.

From Branson

Roaring River State Park is 50 miles from Branson. Travel south on U.S. Hwy. 65 for seven miles. Turn right/west onto Hwy. 86 and continue on through Eagle Rock. Turn left onto Route R and continue west for four miles to the park entrance.

Emergency numbers: Law enforcement, (417) 847-4774; hospital, (417) 847-6000; ambulance, (417) 847-4774.

Lodge: The modern hilltop Emery Melton Inn and Conference Center includes motel rooms, a coffee shop, a full-service dining room, conference and meeting rooms, a gift shop and a swimming pool. The parking lot at the inn is carved from the hillside. A ground-mounted bike rack is along the red pavers at the double-door entrance to the inn. The inn opened in 1998 and rooms feature nine-foot ceilings and solid wood doors. It's a quality place.

The vaulted ceiling inside the lodge has a full-size canoe hanging down and a gaping fireplace, cozy leather chairs, stained glass, wide-screen television and gift shop that sells warm socks. Also in the lobby are an elk head mount and others. Tin buckets also are hung from the ceiling and fabrics depict outdoor scenes and adventures. Astute visitors will notice the trout-fishing theme in etched glass, framed artwork, fish mounts and country-style signs.

Behind the customer service counter are newspaper machines and two brochure racks filled with colorful information about nearby Branson.

The Tree Top Grille is inside the new inn and offers the finest in casual dining and a stunning view of the park. The

Roaring River fish hatchery.

Tree Top Grille offers a wide variety of luscious entrees in a rustic atmosphere. In addition to restaurant service, the Grille provides catering for weddings, parties, banquets and theme picnics in the park. The restaurant has round tables and treetop views. The brass fixtures complement the modern eatery's décor.

The Fishing Hole Sweet Shoppe features hand-made pizzas, cakes, pies and breakfast specialties. This could be a dangerous place for your waistline.

Meeting is big business at the conference facility that has six meeting rooms inside the inn. It is ideal for any type of banquet with all conference services from technical support to catering and activity planning. The Riverview Room is one of the larger conference rooms that features antiques displayed on the walls and a canvas canoe.

The gift shop off the lobby features mugs, hats, upscale gifts, T-shirts, jewelry, candles, field guides, candy, framed artwork, walking sticks, CDs, books, signs, warm socks and much more.

Cabins: Cabins 4-9 are behind the CCC Lodge along the shady ridge. There are about 15 flagstone steps up to the brown cabins. Notice the stone gutter and carefully hand-laid walls and flat stone walkway. Each cabin has a porch, hanging swing and shade. Cabin 4 is at the entrance to a stone step walkway that takes you to a wonderful observation platform. From this wooden platform, you can view the trout-filled raceways, Civilian Conservation Corps-built hatchery buildings and anglers tossing fly lines fore and aft.

Each of these cabins has a small porch light and they define the word "cozy." They are air-conditioned and popular with anglers who merely walk down to the stream and begin waving their rods. Fishing hours, by the way, are 6:30 a.m. until 8:15 p.m. These cabins are also near the CCC Lodge store (Orvis Shop) and the hatchery where many anglers go to salivate while watching the huge brood stock fish circle their in-ground tank.

Cedars border the cabins in loop 12-20. Most of the cabins on this rise are duplexes with cedar siding. They have a view of the campground and, unlike cabins 4-9, all have a small side yard that is good for children's outdoor playing.

Cabins 21-24 also are two-story units. They are along a wooded hill and over look campground No. 3. Cabin 27 has a large yard for children. The Fire Tower Trail (3.5 miles) is near this group of tall cabins.

Park store: The CCC Lodge offers tackle, camping supplies, fishing rods, fishing licenses and tags, and the Lunker Snack Bar, featuring hand-dipped ice cream. A large fireplace greets visitors browsing for snacks, T-shirts, mugs, bug dope, soap, Orvis fishing products, fly-tying supplies, fly line, artificials of all manner, flies and lunker board. The stone store is next to many fishing access points near hard-surface parking. Upstream from the lodge is the hatchery.

The Dry Fly Deli is under the spectacular CCC Lodge. The biscuits and gravy breakfast is terrific! I guarantee it. They also serve barbeque sandwiches and soft drinks. A restroom and phone are nearby. The huge slab of fieldstone at the entrance is fantastic. While admiring the carefully laid fieldstone, check out the round wood pegs that secure the timber framing. You can still see the hand-crafted marks on the timbers.

Campground: Roaring River State Park offers basic and

electric campsites and group camping areas. Services available include reservable sites, a dump station, showers, water and laundry.

Campground No. 1 (loop 1-57): There is a coin-operated laundry behind the historic schoolhouse near the entrance to this loop. This loop is mostly shady; however, sites 1 and 2 are sunny. The entire loop is electrified. Many of the sites have covered picnic tables that are great for eating or storing equipment if the weather turns soggy. There are some huge sycamore trees; in fact, some are 2.5 feet in diameter, casting a broad canopy of shade. Many of the sites are backed up against a rocky ledge along the cool valley floor. There are a half-dozen pull-through sites in this section. Site 15 is a spacious pull-through site. Site 18, ideal for a large RV, is near a water bib. Site 19 offers midday sun. Most of the sites in this loop can accommodate larger rigs. A vault toilet is at the end of the linear campground road where there is access to the Pibern Trail (1.5 miles). My favorite site is 24 near the end of the loop.A small gravely creek can run after rainstorms. Site 26 is near some big trees and backed against a natural area. Site 28 gets midday sun and site 29 is popular with big rig campers.

Site 31 has some grassy spaces surrounding it, while other sites in the 30s are tight and have covered picnic tables. Site 41 is shaded by a jumbo sycamore. It also has some grassy side yards for small-scale field games. Site 42 is sunny; site 44 is great for a big rig, but be careful backing into the site due to the narrow entrance. Sites in the 50s are near the Paradise Valley Resort entrance, where there are a small store and privately-owned recreation offerings. Sites in the 60s and 70s can be a bit small but they are near the showerhouse and pool. The stream runs through the campground where fly fishermen can access the water with an easy walk from any point in the campground. There is plenty of room along the river for back casting.

Campground No. 2 has a modest showerhouse with board and batten siding. Sites 78-118 comprise this loop. The loops are nicely wooded as you enter, but many of the sites receive midday sun. Sites 80 and 81 are backed up against the cliff face and shady. Site 87 is open and sunny

The lodge has a coffee shop, lobby, dining room, swimming pool and gift shop.

and across from a huge sycamore tree. Site 90 has some mowed space around it. Sites in the 90s and low 100s are along the creek. The creek is easily waded, scenic and productive. Sites in the 90s are some of the finest in the state park system. The gentle ripple of the stream offers campers an extra feature in this scenic campground. Site 99 is a pull-through, near the water and sunny. Sites 104-107 are sunny sites along the stream.

Campground No.3 has reservation sites 156-171. All others are first-come, first served. The historic Roaring River School is near the entrance to the campground. The campground has a wonderful showerhouse designed for campers with disabilities.

Nearly half of the sites in Campground No. 3 are along the stream. The nature center is at the northwest end of the campground near sites in the 120s. The showerhouse has vending machines. Generally speaking, this camping area is sunnier than the other two tracts. Most of the classic river in this area is fly-fishing only. There are four duplex camping sites and about a dozen electrical sites at the western end. At many of the sites, you can pitch an extra tent or tent camp off the pad. There are four pull-through sites in this loop. Site 121 is near the showerhouse. Sites 134-148 are electric and, according to staff, they are very popular. They are at the bend in the stream and an easy walk to the showerhouse and nature center. Large RVs might want to inspect this popular area before pulling in. The river along the low 150s has some hard-surface access points for anglers with disabilities.

The valley's bountiful resources, particularly its water, attracted settlers beginning in 1820. The constant rapid flowing of the spring-fed Roaring River appealed to millwrights who saw the chance to use the reliable source of power. In a brief span of time, the water resources and the resulting milling industry attracted lots of people to create the need for a school. Local tradition suggests a log school once operated in the area. As in most rural areas, one-room schools were common. It's believed the school library once had 100 books in its collection. Multiple ages and grades were in a single room, which required a teacher to divide her attention and for older kids to help the little ones (which is now again popular in modern schools).

As one class recited, the other classes reviewed their lesson or read silently. Pranks during class time usually resulted in standing in the corner or take a dose from a hickory stick. According to a local resident, teachers sometimes participated in recess games. Interestingly, it was a privilege to be assigned to retrieve water. Two students went to a nearby string and filled a tin bucket with fresh water. Everyone drank from the same dipper. In 1927, a high school was added to the building. Locals built a partition that divided the elementary students from the high schoolers. About the time of World War II, one-room schools were phased out as districts consolidated. The school was closed in 1952.

Group camping: Camp Smokey, the park's organized group camp, is available to nonprofit organizations, Missouri youth groups and for special occasions such as family reunions and wedding receptions. The camp includes a dining lodge and kitchen, sleeping quarters for 100 and a recreation hall. Camps must be reserved well in advance for use from April 15 to Oct. 15. Please contact the park office at (417) 847-2539 for application procedures.

Hiking trails: The River Trail (.7-mile) parallels the Roaring River between the lodge and campground No. 3. This trail remains an example of the outstanding trail work done in the 1930s by the Civilian Conservation Corps.

The name of the Devil's Kitchen (1.5 miles) Trail is derived from an odd rock outcrop that forms a room-like enclosure. Civil War guerrillas and outlaws used this room, according to legend, as a hideout. Entry and exit points for the trail are near the junction of Hwy. 112 and the hatchery road, and in the small picnic area across from the lodge. The trail is marked with blue and yellow arrows. A self-guided interpretive brochure for this trail is available at the nature center.

The Pibern Trail (1.5 miles) includes a variety of distinct habitats, including both dry and moist limestone forests, tall bluffs, north- and south-facing slopes and a small Ozark stream. Access points to the trail are found at the north end of campground No. 1 and behind campsite 55. The trail is marked with orange arrows.

The Eagle's Nest Trail (2.3 miles) is on the south side of the Roaring River near campground No. 2. It begins behind campsite 81 and follows the river for some distance before ascending to one of the highest points in the park. Located on a cool, shaded hillside beneath lofty limestone bluffs, this trail provides a pleasant jaunt on a hot summer day. The trail is marked with yellow and green arrows.

The short Deer Leap Trail (.2-mile) leads to an overlook and boardwalk above the fish hatchery and the beautiful spring that feeds Roaring River. If you look closely, you may see the axle from a water wheel that is believed to have been associated with a grist mill operation in the mid-19th century. Access points to the trail are next to the waterfall and near the hatchery pools.

There are three access points to the Fire Tower Trail (3.5 miles): one from Camp Smokey, one at the wild area parking lot on Highway F, and one off Deer Leap Trail. The old lookout tower, about 1.5 miles from Camp Smokey, once stood sentinel over the surrounding countryside and is the namesake for the trail. Most of the trail is in the

Roaring River Hills Wild Area. This area offers rugged Ozark terrain, dense hardwood forests, scenic views from atop open dolomite glades, the dynamic stream environment of Ketchum Hollow, and an excellent opportunity for wildlife photography. The trail is identified with yellow and brown arrows.

Fishing: The Roaring River, stocked daily during the trout season by the park's hatchery, which is managed by the Missouri Department of Conservation, is known for its premier trout fishing. Fishing licenses and tags are available in the CCC Lodge, which also sells fishing equipment, tackle, camping supplies and groceries. Take your catch-of-the-day to the park's cleaning and fillet station and enjoy fresh fish for your next meal. The filleting station is a fun place to hear anglers' stories and tips. It's a short downhill walk from the lodge. Remember to purchase your fishing permit from the lodge.

Much of the river's edge is of high banks and gravel bottoms. Check with the park office about fishing rules, but artificial lure areas are identified where no putty, dough balls, natural bait or food bait may be used.

One of the most popular flies, according to the Orvis shop staff, is the crackleback on a No. 16 hook. Others that are recommended include Dave's hoppers, olives, white Millers, sulfur dun, pale morning dun, pale evening dun, long-tail evening dun, cream midge, double trouble, renegade, blue dun, Adam's, mosquitoes, copper John's, hare's ear, pheasant tails and many bugs. The eagle hair caddis on a No. 18 hook is a popular choice during the early summer; so are wooly buggers.

Spinner fishermen will find rooster tails effective, especially in light colors. Trout worms for spinner anglers work well in the spring. The clerk at the Orvis shop claims the lucky lady is one of the best for hardware tossers. Powerbait is also popular and all of these baits can be bought at the CCC Lodge Store near the statue. The store also sells waders, reels and fly-tying supplies.

There are many access points along the river. Several access points have nearby picnic tables, paths, parking and play equipment. The access points are kid safe.

Swimming: The square swimming pool, across from the gable-roofed park office, is open from Memorial Day weekend to Labor Day. There are two lifeguard stations. The pool is open to all park visitors for a nominal fee. The pool is usually open noon to 6 p.m. and slightly longer hours on the weekends. A small poolside concession sells goggles, swim toys and light snacks. You can rent the eight-foot-deep pool for parties. The small kiddies pool is elevated and shallow.

Nature center: The Ozark Chinquapin Nature Center features interpretive displays of the park's natural history, including animal and nature exhibits. The nature center sells a variety of books, guides and Roaring River souvenirs, and also has a few live animals on display. Some plant beds that feature native plants surround the old CCC building. Species in the planting pockets include sumac, coneflower, prairie coreopsis, river oats, black haw, Ozark chinquapin, bellwort, columbine, rose verbena, butterfly milkweed, red bud, Ox-eye daisy, Ozark corn salad, poppy mallow, bloodroot, Carolina anemone, Indian plantain, spiderwort, Jack-in-the-pulpit, Jacob's ladder and many others.

The nature center also identifies many mature trees in its front yard.

One of the most successful programs assisting Americans during the Great Depression was President Franklin D. Roosevelt's Civilian Conservation Corps, known simply as the CCC. The program provided training and employment to more than 3 million young men during the nine years from 1933 to 1942. Enrollees were sent to camps in every state of the Union to work on conservation projects, fight fires, assist during emergencies and to build parks, roads, bridges and buildings. Each man was paid $30 a month plus housing, food and clothing. Of that amount, $22 was sent home to his family. For most, camp life didn't end with the completion of the CCC service. They either enlisted or were drafted into the military for World War II.

The 1713 CCC Company was stationed at Roaring River State Park from June 1933 until November 1939. During their stay, they made numerous general forestry improvements and completed many construction projects including cabins, foot trails, bridle paths, bridges, dams, picnic shelters, fish raceways, the fish hatchery, a bathhouse (now the nature center) and the swimming pool.

The CCC planted more than 3 billion trees, developed more than 800 state parks, built 46,854 bridges and 4,622 fish rearing ponds, restored 3,930 historic structures, built 3,116 lookout towers, 8,065 wells, 1,865 drinking fountains, 27,191 miles of fence, and 204 lodges and museums. Incredible. Some of their finest work is here at Roaring River and other Missouri state parks.

Park programs can include bluegrass music, Missouri fossils, hatchery tours, guided hikes, diving in the Roaring River, black bears, snakes of Missouri, kids fishing day (free hot dogs!), caving and much more.

Nature center winter hours: From November through February, the nature center does not have regular hours. Check in at the park office before heading to the nature center.

Summer hours: From March through October, the nature center is open daily from 9 a.m. to 5 p.m.

Hatchery: The many raceways are filled with darting trout in different levels of development. Some of the raceways contain young fry while others house the fish that are nearly ready to be released into the Roaring River. Hatchery tours are every Saturday at 2 p.m. Coin-operated trout feeders are located along the raceway.

Proceeds from the fish feed are used to maintain the trout program. It takes 1.5 pounds of feed to produce one pound of trout. Feeding the fish is fun, especially the older ones. Try tossing a single pellet of fish food away from them and learn how well they can see the food. This given you some idea about how well they can see flies and bait.

The hatchery building is where the young fish are hatched until they are three to four inches long, usually at four months old. Then the fish are moved outside to the smaller raceways to continue growing. Parent fish can be seen in a round tank. They are kept to supply eggs and milt (sperm) and they are called "brood stock." One strain of brood stock is maintained at Roaring River. The strain is the Missouri Arlee of rainbow trout, which spawns in

February. Females produce about 900 eggs per pound of body weight.

Fish are moved from raceway to raceway as they grow, and are stocked in the river with an aerated tank mounted on a truck. The tank holds up to 800 11-inch fish. Sometimes a fish pump is used move large numbers of fish. Fish can actually be safely pumped from one end of the hatchery to the other through a six-inch pipe.

The Roaring River produces more than 170,000 pounds of trout annually. It takes about 15 months for fish to grow to release size. They are stocked at the end of the day at a ratio of about 2.5 fish per tags sold the same day the previous year.

Behind the hatchery is the spring-head (a cave-like area), where there's a pond and some big trout that typically swim lazily near the surface. Evening visitors will see lots of bats exiting the cave, ready for their night sorties. This spring is the 20th largest in the state and is the beginning of the Roaring River and is the only water for the hatchery. The coolness of the spring and mossy opening is an easy walk from the hatchery.

The Roaring River carves it way through three miles of the park on its way to Table Rock Lake four miles downstream from the park boundary. In 1979, divers explored the spring and made it all the way to the bottom, nearly 224 feet deep. There is a huge dome room, which is an air-filled chamber that can only be reached from under water.

Day-use areas: More than 50 picnic sites are scattered throughout the park. A children's playground facility is in the main picnic area and along the river in front of the CCC lodge. Two picnic shelters can also be reserved for large family gatherings or special outings. Both shelters are covered and can accommodate up to 75 guests. The shelters include outdoor grills, picnic tables, electrical outlets and restroom facilities. Contact the park office at (417) 847-2539 to reserve the shelters. There is a fee. If not reserved, the shelters are available at no charge on a first-come, first-served basis.

Shelters can be reserved at the park office.

Insider's tips: The Roaring River is near Table Rock Lake and all its water recreation prospects. Plan a visit to Whisker's Bar and Grill about 10 minutes from the park on Route 86.

The climbing drive to the park is scenic, sporting rolling mountain views, ledge-like outcroppings and winding roads. There is an outdoor worship service at the amphitheater on Sundays at 9:30 a.m. The Roaring River also offers fly-fishing classes at the CCC Lodge. Rooms with balconies have a wonderful view of the rolling mountains. Kids should bring their bikes. The campground and other rolling roads are fun places to cycle. Eagles winter in and around the park. Kids will find the park a great place to learn to fish. Access points are many and safe. Take an evening stroll; the inn is attractively lit after dusk. A small zoo, private trout farm, RV parks and motels are nearby.

Roaring River State Park

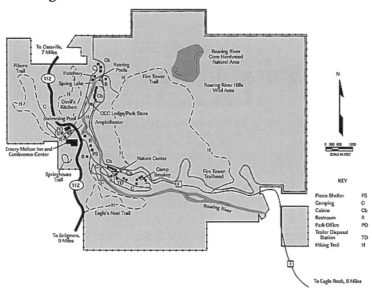

The Stockton Lake-area is a major recreation destination complete with marinas, shopping, camping, festivals and events.

CHAPTER 36

Stockton State Park
Land: 2,175 acres
Water: 25,000-acre Stockton Lake

Stockton Lake has 298 miles of shoreline, 12 parks (include the state park), 25,000 acres of water surface, swimming, 14 boat ramps, 10 campgrounds (including 74 sites at the state park), day-use areas, marinas and more. In many ways the state park is a starting point to explore the vast lake and its environs. Speaking of the lake, there also are scuba diving, water skiing, sailing, power boating, fishing, canoeing and excellent wildlife viewing.

The rolling woodlands of Stockton State Park are on a peninsula that juts northward and divides Stockton Lake to its two main tributaries, the Sac and Little Sac rivers. The area in and around the Stockton State Park peninsula has a sweeping history; extensive archaeological work in the Stockton area indicates that man has occupied the river valleys for more than 10,000 years.

French explorers discovered that the Osage Indians occupied the area until the 18th century, when the Osage chief signed a treaty with representatives of the U.S. government. The first permanent settlers wouldn't come until the 1830s. Back then, the area was known as Lancaster, later changed to Freemont and then to Stockton in 1859.

The lake was created when the U.S. Army Corps of Engineers constructed a dam across the Sac River in 1970. Since then, it has become a favorite for water sports, especially sailing because of the dependable southwest breeze. The park also offers nature hikes, evening programs and Junior Naturalist programs during the on season.

Information and activities

Stockton State Park
19100 S. Hwy. 215
Dadeville, MO 65635-9771
(417) 276-4259
(417) 276-5329 - marina and inn
(877) I Camp Mo; Camping Reservations
www.mostateparks.com

Directions:

From Springfield

Stockton State Park is about one hour from Springfield. Travel north on Hwy. 13 to Bolivar, where you will turn west onto Hwy. 32. At the square in Stockton, turn south onto Hwy. 39 and travel about 4.5 miles to Hwy. 215. Turn left at this intersection onto Hwy. 215 and travel east/southeast, crossing Stockton Lake on the "mile-long" bridge. Hwy. 215 runs through the state park.

From Joplin

Stockton State Park is about 1.5 hours from Joplin. Travel north on U.S. Hwy. 71 to Lamar; then take Hwy. 160 east to Greenfield. Turn left/north onto Hwy. 39 and continue for about 20 miles to Hwy. 215. Turn right at this intersection onto Hwy. 215 and travel east/southeast, crossing Stockton Lake on the "mile-long" bridge. Hwy. 215 runs through the state park.

From Kansas City

Stockton State Park is 2 to 2.5 hours from Kansas City. Travel south on U.S. Hwy. 71 to Nevada; then take U.S. Hwy. 54 to El Dorado Springs turn south on Hwy. 32 follow this to Stockton. At the four-way stop in Stockton, turn south onto Hwy. 39 and travel about four miles to Hwy. 215. Turn left at this intersection onto Hwy. 215 and travel east/southeast, crossing Stockton Lake on the "mile-long" bridge. Hwy. 215 runs through the state park.

Emergency numbers: 911 system; Cedar County sheriff and fire, (417) 276-5133; ambulance, (417) 276-3400; Cedar County Memorial Hospital, (417) 876-2511.

Campground: Sites 27 - 34 and 41-74 are electrical and reservable. Campsites 23 - 38 offer 50 amp service. Campsites 15 - 22 & 39 - 74 have 30 amp service. The other two small loops have a handful of electrical sites. Check in at the park office as you exit southbound Hwy. 215 to enter the park. Most of the hard-surface sites can accommodate large RV rigs. Firewood is sold at the marina site. Overall, the campground is tidy and clean.

Sites 17 and 18 are two of the shadiest sites in the campground. Site 23 is open but has some grassy space nearby and a little privacy. Site 24 is against a natural area, as all along this stretch are. Sites 25 and 26 have their picnic table notched into the woods. Other shady sites include 30 and 39 near the playground, A-frame-like showerhouse and open space.

The entrance to sites 41 - 74 is near the dining lodge. Also at the entrance are a playground and newer showerhouse with a small laundry with coin-operated washer and dryer. On the three-sided reader board near the showerhouse are a list of nearby churches, maps, emergency numbers and other information.

Sites in the 40s have water views and plenty of sun. Sites in the 50s are against natural areas. Sites in the high 50s have additional privacy. Here are also duplex sites for families who want to camp next to each other. Sites 64 and 65 get plenty of afternoon sunshine. Sites 69 and 71 are near the restroom and backed up against the woods. There is not a lot of privacy on the sites on the interior of the loop. Eight- to 12-inch diameter trees offer some shade and visual separation along the interior loop.

The showerhouse has three showers and two sinks. The coin-operated laundry has one dryer and washer with a three-foot folding table and white utility sink.

Sites in this loop are about 75 percent open and sunny. Firewood is sold pre-bundled.

A small footpath leads you to the park's amphitheatre near the campground.

Lodging: The Stockton State Park Inn features both condominiums, motel units and camper cabins open March through October. The 800-square-foot condos offer full housekeeping, two bedroom units with kitchenettes and walkout patios with a grill. The condos are equipped with queen-size beds, color TV and large bathrooms with tub/shower and vanity. The spacious kitchens come with a full-size refrigerator, electric range and microwave oven. Utensils and linens are provided.

Motel units feature cozy rooms with single and double beds and color TV. Also, Stockton State Park Inn is conveniently located near the dining lodge. Each motel unit is air conditioned and has brown Berber carpeting, floral bed sheets, draped windows and wood siding. Some of the duplex units have patios and ground-mounted fire rings. There isn't much shade around the motel units.

Duplex and motel units have hard-surface parking.

Camper cabins are now available. These rustic log cabins provide the experience of camping without a tent or recreational vehicle. The cabins provide accommodations for up to four adults and two children, with a queen-size bed, a full-size futon and a carpeted loft for sleeping bags. Camper cabins have electricity, heating and air conditioning, but do not include water or restrooms. Each cabin has a dining table, ceiling fan and microwave/toaster oven. Cabins also include refrigeration, picnic table, pedestal grill and campfire grill.

The cabins are located in the campgrounds so campers can use the campgrounds restrooms and showerhouses from April 1 through October 31. During the winter months, vault toilets and water are available in the park. Parking is designed for each unit and can accommodate two vehicles and a boat trailer. People preparing to use the camper cabins should bring everything they would for a regular camping trip, including bed linens or sleeping bags and cooking supplies.

From March 29 through October, all lodging is open. For rates, availability and reservations, call the park marina at (417) 276-5329.

Dining: "Welcome Aboard," says the sign that greets you inside the restaurant. The dining lodge in Stockton State Park is a smoke-free environment that boasts a beautiful view of Stockton Lake and offers fine dining featuring a full breakfast, lunch and dinner menu. Inside the lodge you'll find a sailing theme with boat wheel fans, brass light fixtures, and wall-mounted trophy fish. The catfish is excellent!

The staff at Stockton State Park Dining Lodge will also cater banquets or parties. Contact the lodge at (417) 276-5329 for more information.

From November through March, the dining lodge is closed. From April through September, the dining lodge is open from 7 a.m. to 7 p.m. Sunday through Thursday and 7 a.m. to 8 p.m. Friday and Saturday. From May through August, it is open from 7 a.m. to 8 p.m. Sunday through Thursday and 7 a.m. to 9 p.m. Friday and Saturday. During October, it is open from 8 a.m. to 7 p.m. Sunday through Thursday and 7 a.m. to 8 p.m. Friday and Saturday.

Fishing: A quiet cove or secluded shoreline is not hard to find at Stockton Lake. Anglers can expect to catch a variety of fish including bass, white bass, crappie, walleye, catfish or bluegill. Fishing is not allowed near the boat ramps or the marina area; there are no motor restrictions on the lake. Check with the park office for a map of the manmade structures in the lake. More than 100 cedar trees were sunk in the lake to provide fishing habitat.

There are fishing tournaments on the lake. There is 29-foot clearance under the various bridges. Live bait is at the marina store and a small vendor is about five miles either way from the campground (Hwy. 215 and Y or Hwy. 215 and 39). There

Stockton Lake has 298 miles of shoreline to explore.

is a fish cleaning station at the floating marina store.

Although Stockton Lake isn't famous in the Ozarks as a fishery, the lake is under-fished for most species. Walleye action can be outstanding as the state continues to stock about 30 fingerlings per acre on alternative years. Summer walleye are found along rock ledges using a small jig and minnow rig.

Largemouth anglers will love Stockton Lake. Of the three bass species, largemouth comprise 90 percent. Seven- to nine-pound specimens are sometimes taken in the standing timber and timber-lined channels. Walleye also are found in standing timber at depths of 10 to 25 feet. The Price Branch area is considered the best crappie hot spot, according to the staff at the marina. Here are deadfalls, rocks and drops that can hold crappies during any part of the year. Try tube jigs during the spring high waters.

Boating: The park has concrete boat ramps at both the marina and at Hartley Cove. There are no launch fees or motor restrictions at Stockton State Park.

A sailing regatta called the Governor's Cup is held on the lake each summer. About 30 mono-hull sailboats compete during the two-day event. Sailors will find information on the reader board near the marina store.

Marina: Stockton State Park Marina offers the finest facilities in the entire area and is the only marina on the Little Sac arm of Stockton Lake. The wood-sided marina is equipped with a full-service dock and has fishing equipment, sunglasses, snacks, live bait, limited tackle, fishing maps, batteries, fuel, boat maintenance supplies, hunting and fishing licenses as well as lake and guide service information. The marina sells ski and tubing equipment and rents boats and covered slips with electric hook-ups. You will also find a variety of snacks and drinks, including ice cream and all the necessary supplies for a day of fun at the beach.

Stop by the marina for Stockton Lake souvenirs, such as T-shirts, beach towels and hats, to name a few. Beer and ice are also sold. Fish feed is sold which may be fed to the dockside sunfish that rise to the surface as soon as a kibble is tossed into the water.

Boat rentals include fishing boats, 16-foot aluminum with 15-horsepower motor, pontoon, 24-foot with 90-horsepower motor, bass boats and sailboats.

There are no fishing or swimming from inside the marina cove.

If you need propane for your camping comforts, the Country Depot can service you at the intersection of highways 215 and Y or Stockton Mini-Mart at Hwy. 215 and 39.

Swimming: A beach, with a restroom and change house, is at the north end of the park. The beach is not supervised by a lifeguard and is open from 8 a.m. to 8 p.m. Memorial Day weekend to Labor Day. Also nearby is a picnic area with tables and outdoor grills.

Day-use areas: Stockton State Park is a terrific place for holding family and corporate outings. Two large open picnic shelters that accommodate up to 100 guests can be reserved for a small fee. The north shelter, which overlooks the lake, is a reproduction of the Civilian Conservation Corps and Works Progress Administration work done in the 1930s. The north shelter includes electrical outlets, picnic tables, an outdoor grill and access

Stockton Lake State Park Marina.

to a restroom. The south shelter is near the marina boat launch and features great water views, picnic tables, an outdoor grill and access to a restroom. If not reserved, the shelters are available at no charge on a first-come, first-served basis.

There are also three main picnic areas off of Hwy. 215 as you enter the park that are open to all visitors during park hours. These areas are equipped with outdoor grills, picnic tables and a children's playground.

There are also playground facilities at the north shelter and both loops of the campground.

Nature: The major focal point of this park is the endless hours of fishing serenity.

Insider's tips: The Great America Raft Race is held on the lake at the end of July each year. The Stockton Black Walnut Festival is held in late September and features more than 100 arts and crafts booths, pioneer demonstrations, a parade, old cars and lots more.

The dam is 5,100 feet long and 750 feet wide at the base. Walleye fishing is improving on the lake due to an aggressive planting program. Hunters should plan a trip to Carl's Gun Museum in El Dorado Springs. There are more than 1,200 collector guns on display.

President Harry Truman's birthplace is between Stockton and Prairie state parks, in Lamar. There also is a Sonic drive-in restaurant in Lamar. A small cemetery is within the park, with worn markers that are mossy and unreadable. The south picnic shelter is terrific.

Stockton State Park

Table Rock State Park is in the middle of the craggy
Ozarks and minutes from Branson.

CHAPTER 37

Table Rock State Park
Land: 356 acres
Water: 43,100-acre Table Rock Lake

Table Rock State Park is in the middle of the craggy
Ozarks and minutes from one of the country's most
popular recreation areas and entertainment venues.
Southwest of the sprawling park is Branson. The sparkling
lake has nearly 800 miles of shoreline and is nationally
known as a largemouth bass fishery.

Table Rock Lake Dam is on the main stem of the White
River, about six miles from Branson. The dam produces
millions of dollars worth of electricity and provides flood
control for a huge drainage basin. But for park visitors, the
lake is all about fun. The huge lake also offers all kinds of
water sports, about 20 public campgrounds, nearly 20
public beaches, a dozen boat launches, three visitor centers
and many other recreational and entertainment facilities.

The state park marina features docked boats with colorful covers, boat rentals, a diving shop and fishing information. Table Rock State Park is actually embedded in vast Corps of Engineers land holdings and features some of the best access to the lake. The clarity of the lake makes the park and surrounding public contact points popular with swimmers, divers, boaters and anglers.

Information and activities

Table Rock State Park
5272 State Hwy. 165
Branson, MO 65616-8901
(417) 334-4704
(417) 334-2628 - marina
(877) I Camp Mo; Camping Reservations
www.mostateparks.com

The park office has a wall-mounted brochure rack with plenty of information about neighboring Branson. A picnic shelter is behind the park office.

Directions:

From Springfield

Table Rock State Park is 47 miles south of Springfield. Take U.S. Hwy. 65 south about 42 miles to Hwy. 165. Turn right at the traffic light onto Hwy. 165. The main park entrance is five miles up on the left; watch for the park signs.

From Harrison, Ark.

Travel north on U.S. Hwy. 65 for 32 miles, then take a left onto Hwy. 265. When Hwy. 265 intersects with Hwy. 165, turn left and travel for about three miles. The main park entrance is on the left; watch for the park signs.

Emergency numbers: 911; Coast Guard, (417) 739-5496; Water Patrol, (573) 751-3333.

Park store: Boat rentals include pontoons and kayaks, plus fishing and ski boats. Also available are personal watercraft and a 49-passenger catamaran. Enjoy parasailing and scuba diving. Lessons are available from experienced instructors.

Campgrounds: Table Rock State Park has two

campgrounds offering 161 basic, electric and
sewer/electric/water campsites. Both camping areas are
nestled among oak and hickory trees. Services include
reservable campsites, a dump station, showers and water.
In-season camping for Table Rock State Park runs from
March through November. One boat per campsite may be
parked on the grass.

Campground 1: During November, the water hookups
remain operational unless temperatures drop below
freezing. From December through February, one heated
showerhouse remains open. Cedar trees welcome you in
this mostly electric campground. Sites in the 30s - 50s are
large enough for big RV rigs and enjoy a mix of sun and
shade. Sites in the 40s - 60s are generally sunny. Sites 167 -
172 are duplex sites. These sites have a view of the covered
marina and sparkling waters where boats and anglers play
from sunup until dusk. Sites in the low 70s are shady and
near the toilets. Site 183 gets midday sunshine and is
surrounded by cedars.

Sites 100 - 103 are best for pop-up campers and have a
distant view of the lively marina. Site 104 is for campers
with a disability. Sites 107 and 109 have a clearer view of the
marina. Sites in this stretch have covered picnic tables. No.
110 has enough room to park a small fishing boat. Site 111
has a towering oak and site 112 can handle a large RV. In
fact, most of the sites in this loop can accommodate large
RV rigs. The small showerhouse has a telephone and
laundry. Site 123 is across from the modern showerhouse.

Sites 119 - 138 are open and sunny and popular with big
rigs. They are sewer/electric/water sites near the dump
station and showerhouse. The amphitheater is at the gentle
and flat Chinquapin Trail (.5 mile) that is accessible for
visitors with disabilities. The nearby playground has had
recent upgrades.

Campground 2: During November, the water hookups
will remain operational until temperatures dip below
freezing. Site 200 is under an oak and shady. Next to it, site
201 has midday sunshine. The sites on the outside of the
loop are against a natural area. Sites 202 - 214 are hard-
surfaced and mostly shady with filtered afternoon sunlight.

The showerhouse was renovated in 2003. Site 212 is next to it. Site 214 is shaded by cedar and oaks and is quite private.

A thin wall of vegetation separates some of the sites. Sites 270 - 282 are near the water with limited steep-bank access. The views are marvelous and shady along this loop. Site 276 has excellent water access, as the lake laps the shoreline only a few yards from the camping pad. Sites 280 and 281 are among the most private sites in the campground. These sites offer shoreline anglers great access. These sites are also sunny in the afternoon and along the shoreline. This section features great views of the marina and boats that ply the gleaming waters. Site 219 is sunny all day. Site 222 has shade provided by an oak, while sites 224 - 227 are mostly open. Site 228 is the shadiest site in the area.

Sites 231 and 233 are near the restroom. Site 239 has a small side yard with a picnic table ready for your spread. This campground has some interesting rock outcroppings and wildflowers.

For reservations, there is a required two-night minimum stay for weekends from April through October and major holidays from May 15 through Sept. 15.

Fishing: Table Rock Lake is one of Missouri's premier fishing destinations. Anglers can expect to catch a variety of fish including bass, crappie and other warm-water species. Fishing is allowed 24 hours a day except in the day-use area, which is open from 6 a.m. to 10 p.m.

The Table Rock Lake fishery is composed of large- and smallmouth bass, spotted bass, white crappie, paddlefish, catfish, white bass, walleye, bluegill, sunfish and carp. There are also other species, but the large lake is managed for three primary types: large- and smallmouth, and spotted bass. About 85 percent of the bass are largemouth. Growth rates in the lake are excellent where 190,000 pounds of catfish are taken annually. Walleye reproduce naturally. Some of the best spawning areas are in the James and King river arms.

The 43,100-acre lake has an average depth of 73 feet. In front of the dam it can reach a depth of more than 220 feet. The nearly 800 miles of irregular shoreline varies from

Table Rock Lake has 43,100 acres of fun. There is nearly 800 miles of irregular shoreline.

gravel to solid bedrock, offering anglers seasonal opportunities. Underwater structures vary from stump fields to silt. Since there is almost no aquatic vegetation, finding the stumps and other cover is essential to angling success.

During the summer, most bass are taken in 20 to 30 feet of water along thermoclines in the main lake. Many daytime anglers also work the shallows in the King, White and James arms of the lake. Anglers in the main lake often use worm rigs and jigging spoons. Plastic worms in the grape color range are said to be a winner.

Boating: There are no fees to launch your boat into the lake, and all of the surfaces are concrete or asphalt. There is a boat ramp near the picnic shelter and park office. A rigging lane and vault toilet are nearby. The marina is a marquee feature of the park.

The concession consist of a marina and provisions store with snack bar. Boat rentals include pontoons and kayaks, plus fishing and ski boats. Also available are personal watercraft and a 49-passenger catamaran. Enjoy parasailing and scuba diving. Lessons are available from experienced instructors. The marina is closed from November through

February and is open daily from March through October. **Hours are as follows:**

- March and October: 8 a.m. to 5 p.m.
- April: 8 a.m. to 6 p.m.
- May and September: 8 a.m. to 7 p.m. daily.
- June, July and August: 7 a.m. to 8 p.m. daily.

The Spirit of America, a 48-foot sailing catamaran, can take up to 49 passengers on excursions twice a day. Snacks are available onboard. Or you can be your own skipper by renting a pontoon, personal watercraft, fishing boat or 20-foot ski boat that can accommodate eight people. Skis, fishing rods, knee boards and waterboggans are also rented. Rentals range from two hours to all day. But if renting a boat and cruising the beautiful lake aren't enough excitement, you can take an eight- to10-minute parasailing flight. You won't get wet, unless you do it yourself.

The marina store has a bulletin board that details boats for sale, fishing guide services and other useful information. The full-service dive shop features wet suits, tanks, lights, snorkels, goggles, fins, tools, dive markers, how-to videos, belt weight, parts and service. The marina store also sells lots of boat products including lubricants and propellers, some fishing tackle, batteries, live bait, coolers, ice cream, film, hats, candy, submarine sandwiches, soft drinks, coffee and water-related toys. Look for the fat green sunfish when walking around the floating marina store and public docks. You can also purchase carp food from a vending machine and feed the large bug-eyed rough fish.

Swimming: Swimmers can enjoy the clear waters of Table Rock Lake at the state park and other nearby beaches. There is no designated swimming beach; however, several shoreline areas offer ample swimming opportunities. Swimming is not allowed near the marina or boat launch areas. Restroom facilities are available near the picnic area.

Scuba Diving: The clearness of the water makes Table Rock Lake a popular place for scuba diving. Diving equipment can be rented or purchased at the marina, and beginning and advanced scuba courses are offered.

Day-use areas: A picnic shelter can be reserved for a fee

Table Rock State Park Marina.

by contacting the park office at (417) 334-4704. It is across from the park office and can occupy up to 100 persons. It's near the boat launch.

Many of the day-use areas are on variable elevations and have small parking lots.

Picnic areas include tables, outdoor grills, and nearby restroom facilities and new playground equipment. There is no charge and individual picnic sites are available on a first-come, first-served basis.

Nature: Most park programs are offered in the afternoon or evening and they include trees as habitat, night beetles, butterfly walk, spider programs and honeybee educational presentations.

Insider's tips: Ya'll are in Branson, complete with every service imaginable including campgrounds, shopping, entertainment, fishing charters, restaurants and boat rentals. The Shepherd of the Hills Fish Hatchery is only minutes from the state park and is the largest trout-rearing hatchery in the state. The hatchery is six miles southwest of Branson and produces about 400,000 pounds of trout each year. The hatchery has exhibits, aquariums, multimedia presentations and guided tours during the summer. Remember to let the kids feed the carp at the marina. The park is 177 miles from Little Rock and 206 miles from Kansas City, Mo.

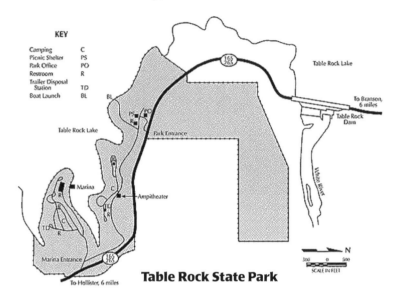

Table Rock State Park

Steep valleys and rocky bluffs surround Harry S Truman State Park.

CHAPTER 38
Harry S Truman State Park
Land: 1,440 acres
Water: 55,600-acre Truman Lake

The sprawling park is on a spine-line peninsula with limestone barrens. The park is nearly surrounded by Truman Lake where fishing, boating and water sports are the main attractions. Steep valleys and U-shaped coves often share the view with rocky bluffs and undulating ridges. Even sheer cliffs and tall bluffs tower above the vast lake.

The making of the lake was hotly contested decades ago because thousands of families were uprooted and more than 4,000 archaeological sites were flooded. The building of the electricity producing dam and lake eventually took place, and the park opened in 1983. The cultures and landscape of the area's dissected hills were diverse and complex, including early Ice Age Indian hunting areas, Osage tribal lands and a place for American pioneers in the early 1800s.

The dam project wasn't the first conflict for the area. In the 1840s, vicious outlaws fought each other and the battles became known as the "Slicker Wars." Apparently, some of the villains used "slick" oak branches to beat captive foes.

The park was deeded to the state in 1983. This is a superb location for a park. The quiet peninsula has a broad menu of wildlife, rocky overlooks and places to access the lake. The lake is large enough for many sailboats, too. From a natural history point of view, the park includes some unusual habitats that are often found farther to the west. Prescribed burns have carefully kept the plains area much like the settlers would have discovered it.

Wildlife viewing is also an important feature of the park. Often visitors will see whitetailed deer and turkeys. Other wildlife include osprey, beaver, red fox, double-crested cormorant (you sometimes see them drying their spread wings), mink, coyote and bobcat. In the winter a group of bald eagles hunt the lake from the treetops. Also watch for shorebirds along the many miles of shoreline and mudflats. The park features elements of Western prairies and the Ozarks. The park office is in the western section of the park. The eastern part of the park is for day-use. Both areas cater to water-based recreation.

Information and activities

Harry S Truman State Park
28761 State Park Road
Warsaw, MO 65355
660-438-7711
(877) I Camp Mo; Camping Reservations
www.mostateparks.com

Directions: West of Warsaw, off Hwy. 7, on Route UU in Benton County.

From St. Louis

Harry S Truman State Park is 256 miles from the St. Louis Gateway Arch. Travel west on I-70 to the Sedalia/Marshall exit. Take U.S. Hwy. 65 south to Warsaw. At Warsaw, take Hwy. 7 west nine miles to Route UU. Turn right and travel three miles to the state park.

From Springfield

Harry S Truman State Park is about two hours from Springfield. Take U.S. Hwy. 65 north to Warsaw. At Warsaw, take Hwy. 7 west nine miles to Route UU. Turn right and travel three miles to the state park.

From Kansas City Metro Area

Harry S. Truman State Park is about two hours from Kansas City. Take Hwy. 7 southeast through Clinton to Route UU. Turn left and travel three miles to the state park.

Emergency number: 911 system.

Campground: A small check-in station offers maps, rules and information about the five camping loops. Scenic and walkable roads meander throughout the rolling campgrounds. Truman's campground is one of the cleanest in the state park system.

Loop 1-21 is called Devil's Backbone. The hard-surface camping sites are surrounded by 10- to 12-inch diameter trees and some are screened by vegetation. A number of large oaks offer filtered sunlight. Sites 6 and 7 are excellent sites for larger RVs. Site 15 has a little slope to the pad. There is a drinking fountain near site 11.

Loop 22-51 is called Raccoon Ridge and has a new water tower and play equipment near the cement block showerhouse, which has a phone and laundry. This loop is on a peninsula. There is seating for adults at the small playground and the road is easy walking. Most of the sites in this linear loop are backed up against natural areas and have ground-mounted fire rings. Sites in the 20s are nicely shaded by oaks and cedars. A beautiful cedar tree is next to site 27. Many of the sites have enough space to pitch a tent in the grassy area alongside the pad. You also could park a small boat trailer at many of the sites.

Sites in the 30s are on a rise and have a scattering of cedars behind them. Sites in the high 30s are more private. Sites 37 and 39 have lake views and are premier sites. Both of these sites can handle RV rigs, and access to the lake is down a steep bank. Site 40 (handicapped accessible site) is also an excellent flat site with a water view in a private location. Sites in the 40s can accommodate medium to large RVs. All of the sites in this loop are electrical. Sites in the high 40s have filtered midday sun and views down the wooded ravine.

Loop 80-119 is a bit rolling. Sites in the 80s are shaded by oaks and separated by thin walls of stringy vegetation. There is a hose bib next to site 82, where medium- and larger RV units can park. The park road is wide and hard-surfaced for easy backing into the sites. Site 85 is on a pleasant rise and offers a view of a wooded valley. Sites in the 90s are along a bend in the road. Sites 90 and 91 are duplex sites. Many of the sites receive midday sun that filters through the oaks. Sites in the 90s are level. Starting at site 97, you are at the end of the loop and have a view of the wood ravine. Sites 98 and 99 are duplex sites for two families. Site 100 receives late afternoon sunshine. All of the sites have lantern hooks. Sites in the low 100s are up a rise and on a little bit higher ground. All size RV units can use these dry sites. Some of the sites in this area have room for a tent off the main hard-surface pad. The rest of the sites in the low 100s have views of the woods and are backed up against a natural area. Sites 114 ands 115 are ideal duplex sites for two families camping together.

Loop 57-149, called Buck Ridge, is on a ridge. Sites in the 50s are private. Sites 49-73 are shady and have plants between sites. Basic site 59 is great for a larger RV unit. Sites in 60s are shady, but get some midday sun. A water bib is near sites 62 and 70. The park road is slightly wider here than in other state park campgrounds. Therefore, children have a little extra space to play or ride bikes and drivers have space to back up their RV units. Sites in the high 60s and low 70s are medium-sized. Site 74 is sunny during the afternoon. The showerhouse is near site 79.

Basic site 121 in Wild Turkey Ridge is a great camping site for a jumbo RV. Site 122, however, is uneven. These sites have a screened view of a lake cove. These sites are on a busier park road, but they are easy to back in to. Site 130 is heavily wooded and has a view through the woods of the sparkling lake. Sites in the 130s are heavily wooded with a canopy of oak branches overhead. Site 133 is at the

The lake has many underwater fish holding features and habitats. There are many access points for anglers.

end of the small loop and quiet. Be careful of several uneven sites in this area. Most of the sites in the 140s are wooded and easy to back in to. Heavy gates sometimes close off the smaller loops during the off-season. A small camper's swimming beach is nearby. Sites in the 150s are the closest to the camper's beach, maybe an eighth of a mile away.

Thorny Ridge has basic sites 152-194 and is gently rolling. At the entrance is a modern showerhouse with laundry facilities. Once you crest the ridge at site 153, you can see the distant shoreline that has rocky outcroppings. A boat ramp is near site 157. Sites in the 160s are flat and also within an easy walk of the single-lane boat launch. Site 163 has a small open space next to it that is great for a family field game. Sites in the 190s are close to the board and batten-style showerhouse. It has a green drinking fountain out front. Sites in the 170s receive plenty of afternoon sunshine and are close to a vault toilet that is along the bend in the park road.

Site 173 has partial view of the water. Sites in the high 180s have a through-the-trees view of the lake. Sites in the low 180s are premier sites at the end of the loop. Sites 183 and

Fish cleaning station.

184 are sunny and offer terrific water views. Site 185 and others in this area allow campers to make their way down to the shoreline where you can fish or wade. Sites in the low 200s are great for larger rigs along the wide park road.

The Bluff Ridge Trail passes the area and offers hikers a chance to compare north slopes with the more open woodlands of the south slopes.

Hiking: The Bluff Ridge Trail (2 miles) contrasts the north slopes of the campground with the more open woodlands of the south slopes. South-facing slopes support woodland communities dominated by post oaks. These tracts have highly variable plant communities with open and dense areas alternating. Common plants in the open area include sunflower, little blue stem, poverty grass and fragrant sumac. The highlight on the trail is the bluffs that overlook the lake. Some large red oaks can also be seen. A prescribed fire program is used to restore the natural community. Historically, the rocky wooded Ozarks hills were more open and covered with glades and savannahs like you would see on the West Wallflower Trail that is near the park office. Today, most woodlands in the western Ozarks are denser and more forested like on the Bluff

Ridge Trail.

The Western Wallflower Trail (.75-mile) is near the campground. Oak trees commonly in the savannahs and glades of the park include chinquapin and post oak species. The oaks are twisted and bent. These oaks are able to withstand the periodic fires because of their thick bark. They thrive in the dry grassy area around the park that is unsuitable for more water-dependent maples, white oaks and northern red oaks. There are lots of whitetail deer and turkeys along this trail. The glades are covered with grasses including Indian grass and big blue stem.

The diversity of wildflowers is intriguing. Wildflowers include the Western wallflower and stickleaf along bluff outcroppings and dry glades. Most of these are common in the southwestern plains. Truman State Park is the only park in the system with a sizable population of Western wildflowers. Prescribed burns and other management tools are being carefully used to preserve these unique habitats.

Boating: The Truman State Park Marina, (660) 438-2423, has lots of boat rentals. Pontoon, Jon and fishing boats are available by the hour or day. There is a two-hour minimum on all boats. They even have big-horsepower bass boats for rent. The marina is only a couple of minutes from the camping areas. The marina also features snacks, fuel, camper and boat storage, covered slips and bait. The store also sells boating supplies, T-shirts, food, candy, toothpaste, charcoal, sun block, beer, milk and coffee.

A small ramp is near site 157 in the Thorny Ridge camping loop. It has parking for about 30 cars and a vault toilet. The view is fulfilling of the rocky shoreline and flooded timber.

Fishing: Serious anglers' mouths water when they see the cover and habitats in the huge lake. The rolling wooded shorelines have downed trees and offer brushy cover along its irregular length. The sheltered bays can be excellent bass fishing locales. Norm's and other guide services operate out of the marina. Norm can be reached at (660) 438-7574. Hiring a guide to help you figure out the big lake is a good idea.

Maximum depth of the lake is about 70 feet, with an

average of about 22 feet. Organic muck is in the shallows and there are large areas of flooded timber and stumps. Some of the flooded timber is in 40 feet of water and provides excellent cover for many species. Submerged vegetation also offers dense cover in shallower water.

Generally speaking, the lake's best quarry are largemouth bass, channel catfish, white bass, hybrid striped bass and white crappie. Other species include walleye, smallmouth bass, carp and bluegill. Largemouth bass represent 90 percent of the bass population, with crappie the second-most popular species anglers chase. White bass are also abundant, but walleye angling is down as the lake matures. Most walleye are taken in the spring, as are white bass. During the spring, bass and crappies will chase black/chartreuse, blue/blue and brown/orange jerk baits and other lures. Jerk baits in the flooded timber work until the warm days of summer when small lures are the rule. Big bass can be taken in the summer among the flooded timber with plastic worms at four to 12 feet deep. Top water lures, crankbaits and spinnerbaits also work well at times in the summer.

Check at the marina store for the latest information on fishing. They have a dry-erase board with lots of up-to-date fishing reports and details. A fish cleaning station is at the marina. You can also have your boat checked at the marina.

Beaches: The 60-yard wide main beach is somewhat near the large marina, covered slips and twin-lane boat ramp and along a narrow cove surrounded by day-use areas. The beach has reddish-brown coarse sand and parking for about 100 cars, flush toilets and lots of picnic tables and pedestal grills. A shelter is rentable and perched near the bathhouse and shoreline. The busy marina is in view.

The camping beach has modern cement-block bathrooms, and views of flooded timber and reddish sand along the water's edge. The beach is about 40 yards wide.

Nature: Naturalist programs include insects, Lewis and Clark history, fur bearers of Missouri, Junior Naturalist activities and others. The lake has about 8,800 acres of standing timber for aquatic habitat. Waterfowl are common on the lake.

Insider's tips: Plan a visit to the Lost Valley Fish Hatchery. The hatchery sits on 78 acres and is the largest warm-water hatchery in the state. Inside the 2,000-square-foot visitor center at the hatchery is a 12,700-gallon aquarium and interpretive displays. Species raised include walleye, bluegill, channel catfish, largemouth bass, hybrid sunfish and others.

A Wal-Mart is about nine miles from the state park. The lake is high-energy and higher horsepower. The park roads are great for walking along the oaks, rolling hills and flatlands. Day-use areas and vistas are plentiful along the winding park roadways. Squirrels are the comics of the park and are seen in rocky glades. The dam is 1.5 miles north of the Osage River and has a concrete spillway and six turbine generators that make 160,000 kilowatts of power. Prickly pear cactus grows in the dry climes of the park. Look for prehistoric-appearing paddlefish cruising along the surface of the lake. There are more than 30 public and private campgrounds in the region.

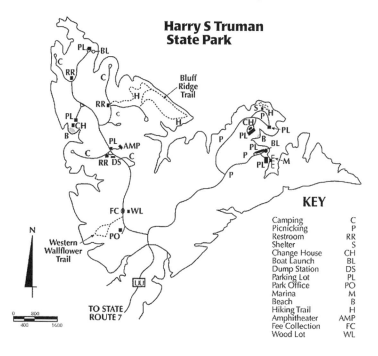

Harry S Truman State Park

KEY

Camping	C
Picnicking	P
Restroom	RR
Shelter	S
Change House	CH
Boat Launch	BL
Dump Station	DS
Parking Lot	PL
Park Office	PO
Marina	M
Beach	B
Hiking Trail	H
Amphitheater	AMP
Fee Collection	FC
Wood Lot	WL

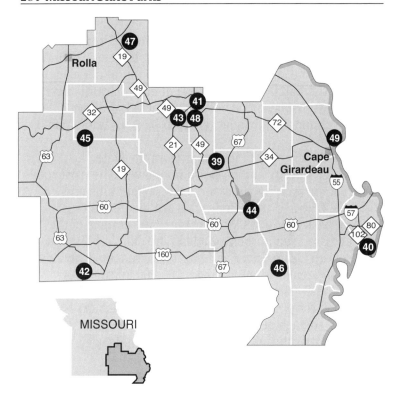

Southeast Region

39. Sam A. Baker State Park
40. Big Oak Tree State Park
41. Elephant Rocks State Park
42. Grand Gulf State Park
43. Johnson's Shut-Ins State Park
44. Lake Wappapello State Park
45. Montauk State Park
46. Morris State Park
47. Onondaga Cave State Park
48. Taum Sauk Mountain State Park
49. Trail of Tears State Park

The park features a wonderful visitor's center, 200-site campground, a rocky Ozark stream, cabins, park store, lodge, boating, fishing, swimming and lots more.

CHAPTER 39
Sam A. Baker State Park
Land: 5,323 acres Water: St. Francois River

Sam Baker grew up and taught school in rural Wayne County. He was elected governor of the state in 1924. The 1,000-foot conical and domed hills that surround the area frame this park as a classic. From the excellent Civilian Conservation Corps-era stone buildings to the rolling campgrounds and river access, Sam Baker is one of the finest parks in the system.

The panoramic views of the St. Francois Mountains are majestic, and if you look vigilantly you can see the tabletop hills and escarpments that thrust to the bottomlands. The views - and the facilities - are exemplary. The morning mist that often hangs along the slopes quickly fades as the sun peaks over the Mudlick Mountains, revealing handsome stone buildings that include Depression-era workmanship. These classic timber and native stone buildings are some of the best examples of CCC-era design and construction in the nation.

The Mudlick Mountains erupted about 1.5 billion years ago and signify the oldest and hardest exposed rocks on the North American continent. Many of the conical domes rise to 1,000 feet, and jumbled blue boulder slopes and moist tracts are habitat to some rare flora and fauna like the rare yellowwood tree and four-toed salamander.

The other classic element of the park is Big Creek, a rocky Ozark stream that rushes at the bottom of the state's deepest canyon-like gorge. Its recreation value is high, its beauty is even greater. All of these natural features began when vigorous volcanoes (and temperate oceans) shaped the countryside of southeastern Missouri. The boulders that have toppled into the canyons over the eons are millions of years old. Touch them, climb on them, and take some time to think about the distinctive history of this part of the "Show Me" state.

Information and activities

Sam A. Baker State Park
Route 1, Box 113
Patterson, MO 63956
(877) I Camp Mo Camping Reservations
(573) 856-4223 Cabin Reservations

Directions:

From St. Louis

Travel south on I-55 to Festus. At Exit 174, take U.S. Hwy. 67 south for about 75 miles. Turn right/west onto Hwy. 34 and travel five miles before turning right onto Hwy. 143, which leads into Sam A. Baker State Park. Campground 1 is near the park entrance; Campground 2, the visitor center, cabins and shelter areas are two additional miles.

From Jefferson City

Travel south on U.S. Hwy. 63 to Rolla. Take Hwy. 72 to Salem. About 13 miles past Salem, take Hwy. 32 east. Travel to Hwy. 21 south. Follow Hwy. 21 south as it turns into Hwy. 49. At Des Arc, turn left onto Hwy. 143, which leads into the park. Campground 1 is near the park entrance;

The campgrounds are often full on holiday weekends.

Campground 2, the visitor center, cabins and shelter areas are two additional miles.

Emergency numbers: Highway patrol, (800) 525-5555; fire department, (573) 223-4222. There is a helicopter pad at the park.

Visitor center: The cedar-sided stable-like visitor center has boulders and benches out front. Also in front is a small wildflower garden that includes butterfly weed, bergamot, black-eyed Susan, horsetail rush, scouring rush, spiderwort, purple coneflower, New England aster and mountain mint. Some trees near the visitor center also sport identification tags including a shagbark hickory, walnut and others.

Inside the visitor center are splendid interpretive displays that include a display about area minerals. In fact, the display has craggy samples of lead ore, iron ore, copper ore, barium ore, zinc ore and silver cobalt. This exhibit also discusses mining techniques, apparatus and history.

Settlers of the southeast Ozarks have a vibrant history that is told, in part, through the tools they used. The hulk of Mudlick Mountain and the surrounding domes of the Taum Sauk are panoramic and brutal if you were an early settler. Their most versatile tool was the ax. It was used for cleaning land, cutting trails, building shelters, cutting firewood, farming, hunting and sometimes, self-defense. Axes were made in many dissimilar shapes and sizes depending on their intended use. Starting in the middle 1800s, the crosscut saw was used by loggers to clear the land of virgin timber. At one time or another, these jagged-tooth saws cut almost all of the forests in the Ozarks.

Cultural history is also interpreted in the center, including the tragedy of the Civil War. The terrain of these beautiful mountains didn't escape the violence of the Civil War. Both Union and Confederate armies had headquarters in the area and scouting expeditions and raiding parties frequently clashed on the wooded hillside and rocky bluffs that provided ideal hiding places for bushwhackers.

Several battles were fought in the area including the Battle of Pilot Knob. On his way to the scene of the battle, Confederate General Sterling Price marched though the narrow shut-ins gorge call Stony Battery on Big Creek northwest of the state park. Hiding close by in a small cave were two Union spies. According to local lore, one of the spies was struck by a rock that was dislodged by moving heavy artillery. He is reported to have cried out, but his chorus was lost amid the rumbling of the weighty war wagons being heaved over the rocky paths. The Battle of Pilot Knob is also interpreted at the Fort Davidson State Historic Site at Pilot Knob.

Nearby are a number of Native Indian tools that include spear points, hammer stones, projectile points, stem-point spears, chert flakes, arrowheads, pottery chards, hoes, spades, bone tools, flake knives and large cup stones. Large animals like deer and elk were hunted with spears, but small animals like rabbit and squirrel were trapped. The characteristic Dalton point, a multi-functional stone knife, was used for killing and skinning animals. Sandstone mortars, cup stones and grinding slabs reflected dependence on nuts, berries and fruits as staple foods.

The first potters were the Woodland culture and they began to replace their large stone points and spears with bows and arrows and more highly crafted projective points. In addition to hunting, this later culture cultivated corn, squash, pumpkins and berries in the fertile bottomlands. Clay was being used to form containers, and pottery became an important household item of the Woodland culture.

The Mississippi Period (700-900 AD) cultures slowly developed a more sophisticated agricultural system and large permanent settlements of houses and farmsteads. These structures were made of woven rods and twigs. There is evidence that there was some interaction between the Woodland Indians and village farmers. Traces of village farm campsites have been found in the Wappapello Lake area and east of the Sam A. Baker State Park.

As the culture of the village hunters began to decline, the Indians became less reliant on farming and returned to the rigors of hunting and foraging. By the time the white man arrived, small nomadic tribes had already replaced these large permanent settlements.

Campground: Sam A. Baker State Park has more than 200 sites at two campgrounds and an equestrian campground with basic and electric sites. The park also has a special-use camping area. Services include reservable sites, a dump station, showers, water and laundry. There are some large mowed open spaces at the campground entrances.

For reservations, there is a required minimum stay for weekends and major holidays from May 15 through Sept. 15.

Campground No. 2's entrance is next to the visitor center. Site 103 is next to an open space that can be used for field games. A big RV rig can park on site 104. Most of the sites are shady, but site 106 gets plenty of sunlight. But next to it on site 107 there is considerable shade. Ten- to 14-inch caliper trees modestly separate many of the sites. There is a drinking fountain at site 108. Site 110 is best for small rigs and is shady. Site 111 can hold a big camping rig and features morning sun. Site 112 also gets morning sun and most of the sites in the section of the campground are backed up against the woods.

Sites in the 120s, 160s and 170s are near the cedar-sided showerhouse. The showerhouse has a kiosk, laundry and soft drink vending machines. Site 120 is immediately across from the modern showerhouse.

Sites 124-130 are against a grassy area. Sites in the low 140s are completely shaded. Site 152 is near the creek access and on the bend of the road. Sites 155-158 are small, shady sites and a small grassy spot in the middle of the micro-loop. Sites 157 and 158 are against a nature area. Sites 144-154 are heavily shady, as is site 160.

Sites that run down the middle of the loop are less private but ideal for families who want to keep an eye on small children. Sites 165, 169, 170-172, 174 and 177 have lots of morning sun. Many maples and a few cedars shade the road and create a mixed canopy over countless campsites. The CCC-era drinking fountains are another classic feature of the park.

Sites 180-196 have been renovated. They are sunny and have electrical hook-ups.

Campground No.1 is composed of three loops (sites 1-96). This campground has a single-lane boat launch and access to the St. Francois River. The hard-surface trail that connects the park is a great design element and well liked by visitors. The two campgrounds are almost a mile apart. Therefore, this campground is away from the park store.

Campground No. 1 is more open and grassy than the other campground. Site 1 is great for an anglers with a small boat. A two-foot-wide oak shades it. Site 3 has poison ivy growing up its oak tree and also has space for a boat trailer. Sites 138-139 are open and near a water bib. Other open sites are 4-6; they are near the river. In fact, sites 4-13 parallel the river and are an effortless walk from the river. Sites 9, 11 and 12 get a bounty of morning sunshine.

Overflow parking is across from site 14. For small RV rigs and tents, you can't do better than site 116 that is nestled under the pines. Sites 18-19 are duplexes are first-rate for families and friends camping together. Site 35 gets morning sun and can take a big RV rig. Site 36 is next to the small showerhouse that serves this loop. A giant sycamore also shades this area.

The park has 18 rustic cabins.

Site 40 has a wide road in front, making it easier for big RV rigs to back in. In loop 44-73 you'll find generally shaded sites. Sites on the outside of the loop will typically be backed up against some woods. Site in the 50s have somewhat more vegetation separating the sites. Sites 60 and 61 have a small mowed area next to them. Site 63 has morning sun and a water bib next to it. Sites in the 60s and low 70s are near the newer showerhouse that has an attractive timber-framed entrance. Site 72 is especially shady. Site 73 can hold a big RV rig. Sites 90-92 get morning sun. Sites in the high 70s and high 80s are backed up against a thin natural area that gives them some added privacy. Sites 88 and 89 are sunny in the morning. Sites 81 and 82 can take big rigs and are among the most private in the campground. Site 84 is shady and at the end of the loop near the hard-surface pathway. Sites 88-89 are popular for tents, allowing them to set up away from the park road.

Cabins: The cabins, dining lodge, store and canoe raft, kayak and bicycle rentals are also available. For more information about the concession facilities, call (573) 856-4223.

Sam A. Baker State Park has 18 rustic CCC-era cabins made of native stone and wood with modern conveniences.

Most have fireplaces, kitchens, full baths, heating and air
conditioning, outside grills, fire pits and picnic tables. They
are equipped with bedding, towels and kitchen utensils.
Cabins are available for rent April through October.
Reservations can be made April 1 or after by calling (573)
856-4223 or toll free at 1-800-334-6946.

There is a two-night minimum stay for all reservations
with a one-night deposit required. Deposits are refundable
with at least a seven-day cancellation notice. Upon arrival,
the deposit will be credited to the last day of the reserved
period. Deposits will be forfeited for early departure. Pets
are not allowed in the cabins by state statute. A doghouse
can be rented. A damage deposit is required for all pets.

Cabins 1, 2, 3, 4 and 14 have one bedroom with a queen
bed and a sofa sleeper, living room, air conditioning and
fireplace. Cabin 8 is handicapped accessible. Cabin 5, 6, 16
and 19 are one-bedroom cabins with two double beds, sofa
sleeper, fireplace and air conditioning. Cabins 9-12 have two
bedrooms with one queen bed in each bedroom and a futon
in the living room, fireplace and air conditioning. Cabins 15
and 17 are two-bedroom units with one queen and one
futon bed, fireplace and air conditioning. Cabin 18 has five
bedrooms with four queen beds and a full-size bed. There is
a sofa sleeper in the living room, fireplace and air
conditioning. Cabin 13 has an eye-catching porch and a
queen bed, shower, small refrigerator and fireplace.

Cabin 8 faces the woods. Most of the cabins have a
grassy side yard and hard-surface parking. Cabin 4 looks
down on the other cabins and a broad day-use area. All
cabins are within walking distance of the park store,
laundry and dining lodge. Bring your bikes and inline
skates. Cabin 14 is the sunniest of the group. Cabin 16 has
a shady backyard and sits above a small creek that runs
flush after it rains. Cabins 17 and 18 are at the end of the
loop. Cabin 18 is shady and has a first-class front porch that
overlooks the day-use area. The most private cabin is 19.

Park store/dining lodge: Sam Baker has one of the bigger
park stores in the system. It rents bikes and cabins. It also
sells ice, wood, camping supplies, candles, ice cream,
batteries, toys, key chains, footballs, flying discs,

volleyballs, floatation mattresses, T-shirts, soft drinks, buns, chips, coffee, canned goods, popcorn, cold beer, milk, film, flashlights, some fishing tackle and charcoal.

Next to the park store is the charming CCC-era dining lodge. The lodge has a small garden in front and a few of the trees are identified with small tags. The small garden has a number of wildflowers that are also identified including gay feather, few fever, purple coneflower, rose verbena, wild rose, goat's rue, Christmas fern, tickseed, Ohio buckeye, maiden hair fern, white prairie clover, mountain mint, spiderwort and other grasses.

The classic lodge has two benches and a stone walk that takes you inside where an oversized fireplace greets you on the left. A wall of windows faces towards a wooded area, stone patio and washed gravel creek. The vaulted ceiling, wood floors and great food are well known in the area. The Shut-ins Trailhead and Big Creek Overlook are behind the lodge.

The lodge is renowned for its Saturday night prime rib dinner, catfish buffet on Friday evenings and all you can eat buffet on Sundays.

Hiking: Mudlick Trail provides a journey into one of the oldest mountain regions of North America: the St. Francois Mountains. It is a moderate to very strenuous 12-mile loop trail, climbing from 415 feet above sea level in Big Creek Valley to 1,313 feet above sea level at the top of Mudlick Mountain. It is open to hiking, backpacking and horseback riding. Most of the trail is in the Mudlick Mountain Wild Area, one of the most noteworthy, undisturbed natural tracts in Missouri.

The trail begins by ascending the bluffs above Big Creek where three stone hiking shelters, constructed by the Civilian Conservation Corps in the 1930s, offer dazzling views of the surrounding countryside and the valley below. The trail then drops into Mudlick Hollow, a narrow rock-strewn valley interspersed with pools of clear water. The trail follows Mudlick Hollow for about three-fourths of a mile before beginning a gradual climb to the summit of Green Mountain. Horses may bypass the rocky Mudlick Hollow on the Hollow Pass Trail. Hikers may use the Hollow Pass Trail as a return route after visiting the scenic

New play structures have been built in many Missouri State Parks.

hollow. The view from Green Mountain is best during the fall and winter when the trees in the thick oak-hickory forest have shed their leaves.

Mudlick Trail has three entrance points. The trailhead is on the west side of Hwy. 143 across the road from the dining lodge. The remaining trailheads are in the equestrian camp. Equestrian campers can access the trail in Campground No.1. The equestrian trailhead for day users only is just north of the assistant superintendent's residence. Parking areas and water are available at all trailheads. During the winter, when most of the water lines are shut off, water can be obtained at the park office. Much of the trail is covered with old-growth oak, a forest with many 200-year-old trees.

Coming out of the forest, you will enter an igneous glade, which are treeless rocky openings that usually face south or southwest. The word glade is derived from "glad," which is what early explorers might have felt after coming into the sunny openings from the dark forest. Plants and animals that live on the glades must adapt to the severe conditions.

For example, the prickly pear cactus has thick skin to conserve moisture and collared lizards require intense sunlight to survive.

Vertical cliffs are common to the St. Francois Mountains, especially along the streams, rivers and along the hiking trails. Sharp ledges rise hundreds of feet above Big Creek. When rocks from these big ledges break away and accumulate at the base, they form talus slopes that spread over several acres. Ledges of these north-facing cliffs are often draped with ferns. One of the rarest trees in North America, the yellowwood tree, has been discovered at the base of the talus slope along Big Creek. Use the Shut-ins Trail to reach this area.

Short-leaf pine is Missouri's only native pine and can be found growing on the south-facing slopes. They are sometimes concentrated or mixed in with oaks and hickory. Pines are generally taller than oaks occupying the same area. In the park, short-leaf pines are found north of Big Creek. Some of the bottomland trees in the park reach 140 feet tall. Excellent examples of bottomlands forests and flowers can be seen along the Shut-ins Trail.

The park has several incomparable Ozark streams, including Big Creek. Many plants along the gravel bars have flexible stems and long roots to hold them in place. Wildflowers along the gravely creeks include garden phlox, vipers, bugloss, mistflower and Cardinal flower. Big Creek has about 30 species of fish including rock bass, silver jar minnow, shiners and many others.

Fishing: Fishing is available at multiple access points in both the St. Francois River and Big Creek. Day usage is from 8 a.m. to 10 p.m. Primary fish are bass, bluegill, sunfish and catfish.

Boating: There is a concrete boat launch at Campground No. 1 on the St. Francois River. It is open at all times except during serious flooding. There are no launch fees or motor restrictions; however, the size of the river limits use to smaller boats. Due to the river current shifting in recent years, the launch area is usually too shallow for anything but canoes and small boats.

Canoeing: Raft, kayak, tube and bicycle rentals are

The park has lots of fishing access points.

available at the park store. For more information, call (573) 856-4223. Rentals for float trips are available at the park store. The park store also has inner tubes for sale.

For a St. Francois River four-mile trip, put in at the boat ramp. You will float to the Highway 34 bridge. Float time is two to four hours - or take all day! The trip is offered Sunday through Friday at 11 a.m. and Saturday at 11 a.m. and 1 p.m.

The St. Francois River's 14- and 18-mile float trips put in upstream and float to the park's boat ramp. Approximate time is eight to12 hours, depending upon water level. It's offered daily at 9 a.m. There are also floats on the Big Creek.

Swimming: Swim at the multiple access points in both the St. Francois River and Big Creek. Day usage is from 8 a.m. to 10 p.m. Most of the swimming points are gravel, stone and sand. Yikes, the water can be chilly!

Nature: The nature/visitors center are housed in a distinctive historic building that was constructed as a stable in 1934 by the Civilian Conservation Corps. Visitors can enjoy a variety of hands-on exhibits that feature park wildlife, plants, geology and natural processes. Live snakes, a 150-gallon native fishes aquarium, and insect collections are just a few of the favorite exhibits. A detailed 3-D model of the park provides directions and orientation to trails and other park facilities.

Naturalists provide a variety of interpretive nature programs and a summer staff provides recreation and leisure programs at the park. Programs are provided on weekends in late spring and fall, and one or more programs are available on most days during the summer months. Programs may include evening amphitheater talks, hikes into the park's wild area or natural area, demonstrations of park plants and animals, outdoors skills instruction and much more. Call the park at (573) 856-4411 or check bulletin boards upon your arrival to find out what programs or activities are being offered during your visit.

When possible, naturalist staff will also conduct interpretive activities for schools and civic and youth groups. Call the park at (573) 856-4411 to schedule a visit or activity.

The nature center's winter hours from November through March are weekdays from 8 a.m. to 4 p.m. From April through Memorial Day weekend and Labor Day through October, the nature center is open daily from 9 a.m. to 4 p.m. From Memorial Day weekend through mid-August, hours are extended to 5 p.m. From mid-August through Labor Day, the nature center is open Sunday through Friday from 9 a.m. to 4 p.m. and Saturday from 9 a.m. to 5 p.m.

The nature study room in the visitors center has aquariums that house a revolving assortment of animals. They often contain prairie king snakes, rat snakes and corn snakes. Mounts include beavers, bass and river otters. The nature study room also features a colorful collection of butterflies that include the Monarch, Viceroy, painted lady, alfalfa butterfly, cloudless sulfur, dainty sulfur, zebra swallowtails, Eastern tiger swallowtail, dog-faced butterfly and many other insects and moths. The walking sticks are fun to examine in the six cases of insect specimens.

Civilian Conservation Corps: During the Great Depression of the 1930s, agriculture and industry were stagnant, banks were closed, business failures were common and unemployment was the highest in the history. In an attempt to end this economic chaos, President Franklin Roosevelt came up with a plan. His program would include putting thousands of unemployed men to work in the Civilian Conservation Corps. During its nine-year stint, more than three million men worked on a variety of projects including many in the state park. In the visitor center you can view some of the tools the men used.

The CCC had five barracks, officers' quarters, mess hall, infirmary and hospital. Although the workers had a strict daily routine, there was time for recreation. The camp's baseball diamond was located near the current park office. Boxing was also a popular sport and weekend bouts were often held at the boxing ring that is now the amphitheater.

The CCC did extensive work at the park during the 1930s. The stone buildings include the superintendent's residence, rustic cabins and lodge. The visitors center originally was constructed as a horse stable. Crews cleared land in the park and also built hiking trails, roads and fences.

The park's natural history is equally interesting. Lightning has often struck the trees on Mudlick Mountain. Many trees are not killed, but get stunted trunks and knobby scars from the strikes. Lightning can also eradicate limbs and cause fires. Violent windstorms such as tornados have taken a toll on some of the forests also. In some areas the natural disturbances have had an effect like clear cutting. East of the fire tower is stand of trees about 75 years old.

When trees are uprooted by wind, large deposits of soil cling to the roots, forming tip-up mounds. Trees on the south and southwest facing slopes are susceptible to drought and the soils are usually thin when trees are exposed to wind and direct sun. Animals can browse on small saplings and bucks polish their antlers on their bark. Birds such as the yellow-bellied sapsucker riddle trees with holes, feeding on sap and insects. Insects, fungus and bacteria also play a role in maintaining the health of the forest by recycling nutrients from decayed wood soils.

Mudlick Mountain has also been damaged by ice. The

weight of the ice and wind can break a tree's crown and limbs. After being stripped of limbs, the trees can resemble telephone poles.

Conical domes surround the area as part of the broad and deep St. Francois Mountains. Mudlick Mountain is an example of a dome that reflects the shape of the indigenous rock before it was subject to erosion. Its shape is also due to the way that ancient rock fractures the layers of rock sloped from the top of the hill to the rock of the side dome. As erosion continues, the hills become more dome-like.

The St. Francois Mountains contain a variety of habitats with characteristics that vary because of the rock type, moisture and exposure to the sun. The plants and animals have adapted to these characteristics. When plants and animals are grouped together, it's called a community. The state park contains examples including igneous glades, oak forest, pine forest, igneous cliffs, talus slopes, bottomlands forests, gravel washes and streams.

Day-use areas: Two picnic shelters can be reserved for a fee. If not reserved, the shelters are available at no charge on a first-come, first-served basis. There is one shelter in the main day-use area and the other is north of the Big Creek Bridge. Occupancy is 75 people per shelter.

There is a playground at the day-use area as well as Campground No. 2.

The park office offers free rentals of basketballs, volleyball and net, horseshoes, wiffle ball and other recreational equipment. Tubes for floating can be purchased in the park store. Also available in the park store are raft, canoe and kayak rentals.

Insider's tips: The campgrounds are usually filled on holiday weekends. Bring your bike; the park roads are rolling and wide. The labeled wildflowers at the lodge are a great way to sharpen your identification skills. The campground design is great, some of the best sites in the system. Campers with big rigs will find the design friendly. Sites are near needed facilities; and frankly, there are no bad campsites at Sam Baker.

Ask for a bird checklist. It covers a five-mile radius of the park and is keyed by season. Eleven types of sparrows have been identified in the park. Remember to rent a canoe or raft and bring your basketball, the full court is near the park store, but be careful if the ball rolls out into the park road.

Sam A. Baker State Park

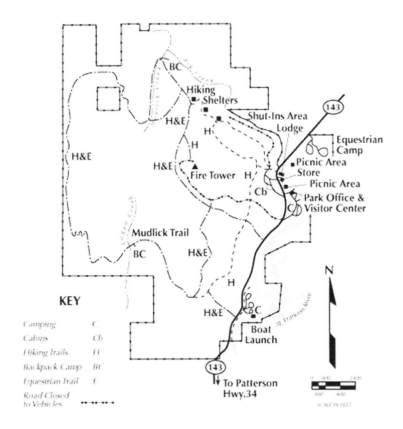

The author hugs a really, really big bur oak tree.

CHAPTER 40

Big Oak Tree State Park
Land: 1,029 acres

Big Oak Tree State Park is an oasis of majestic trees in the heart of abundant farmlands that extend to the horizon. Waving fields of corn and soybeans surround the W-shaped park that is home to many champion trees. The exceptionally rich soil that supports the farms and trees can reach 25 feet deep in this part of the state. Today, the park is the home of seven trees that qualify as state champions of their species and two registered as national champions for their huge size.

The park is one of the last virgin bottomland forests in the state. The 80-acre virgin tract is registered as a national natural landmark. But there is much hard work to be done to resuscitate the unit and to ensure future champion trees.

So, how do you measure a champion tree? Measure the circumference 4.5 feet from the ground. Measure the height to the top branches from the base of the tree. The crown is the average after obtaining the shortest and longest diameter. When all three aspects of the tree size are known, a point value is determined by adding the circumference in inches and the height and feet and one-fourth of the crown spread. Bigger is better, and there's some colossal trees at the park like you have never seen before.

The park protects 12 species of rare plants and animals, 250 kinds of plants, 25 mammals, 31 reptiles and seven amphibian species. Two wooden benches are along the 1.25-mile self-guided steel boardwalk. Trail guides are available in the interpretive center. Along the trail, you'll walk beneath a paw paw (Missouri banana), a stand of great cane, a burr oak with a 17-foot trunk, pumpkin ash, a bent tree, tip-up mound, bald cypress knees, wetlands, state champion black willow and much more.

On the 1.4-mile Bottomland Trail, which is sometimes flooded, are a number of state champion trees including a swamp chestnut oak, shumard oak and possum haw (also called deciduous holly). All the massive sentinels had a certain spiritual effect on me. How about you?

The park was established in 1938 and was largely made possible by private donations.

Information and activities

Big Oak Tree State Park
13640 South Hwy. 102
East Prairie, MO 63845
(573) 649-3149
www.mostateparks.com

Directions:

From St. Louis

Take I-55 south to the East Prairie/Matthews exit (Exit 58). Turn left/east onto Hwy. 80. Follow Hwy. 80 through

East Prairie. Turn right/south onto Hwy. 102. Big Oak Tree State Park is about 10 miles from the Hwy. 80/102 junction. The drive takes about 2.5 hours (154 miles).

From Memphis

Take I-55 north to the East Prairie/Matthews exit (Exit 58). Turn right/east onto Hwy. 80. Follow Hwy. 80 through East Prairie. Turn right/south onto Hwy. 102. Big Oak Tree State Park is about 10 miles from the Hwy. 80/102 junction. The drive takes about three hours (175 miles).

From Springfield

Take U.S. Hwy. 60 east. U.S. Hwy. 60 turns into I-57 as it crosses I-55. Stay on I-57 north to Exit 10 at Charleston. Turn right/south onto Hwy. 105. Travel about 10 miles down Hwy. 105 and turn left onto Hwy. 102. Follow Hwy. 102 south to Big Oak Tree State Park. It takes about 5.5 hours (277 miles).

The closest stores for gasoline and food are East Prairie and Charleston. Both are 15-20 miles from the state park.

Interpretive center: The tree house-like center is open 10 a.m. - 4 p.m. daily April to October.

The interpretive boardwalk begins below the center. It also can flood; call ahead in the spring.

The modern interpretive center, built 19 feet above the ground, does a great job of explaining the natural history of the area including information about the living swamp, home of the birds, and colorful graphics that depict the birds and mammals of the area. Pictures of rose-breasted grosbeak, Carolina wren, downy woodpecker, hooded warbler, Rufus-sided towhee (now called the Carolina chickadee) and others are on display.

Birders should consider a spring trip when they might spot many vivid migrants. Due to the park's location amid flat farm fields, the park attracts many migrating species at this time of the year. Other birds in the park include yellow-throated warbler, Northern parula warblers, hermit thrush, winter wren, thrushes, Acadian flycatcher, Mississippi kite, least tern and brown creeper during the winter. The park has about 150 species.

The first thing you see upon entering the tree-house

The intrepretive center is treehouse-like.

interpretive center is a 400-year-old sentinel oak cross-section. The section of the huge tree allows visitors to count the rings from the 1550s up to the 1900s. Surrounding the cross-cut section are historic photos and narrations about the times past that took place during this giant tree's life. The tree measured 140 feet tall (its waistline was 21 feet) and grew at the time of Elizabeth I, William Shakespeare, the Pilgrims, the Bill of Rights, Alamo, Civil War, Statute of Liberty, the movie Frankenstein in 1936, Albert Einstein's formulas, Halley's Comet, World Wars I and II and Disney World.

This tree was as high as 32 cars stacked on each other; 21 people standing on each other's shoulders or as tall as a 14-story building.

The overhead skylight cascades light onto the educational exhibits. The elevation of the center allows visitors to feel like they are a part of this cathedral of trees.

The center has a number of brilliant mounts that include barn owl, fish crow, great crested flycatcher, warblers, common flicker, wood duck, beaver, water snake, diamond-backed water snake, broad-banded water snake, red-eared slider and fox squirrel.

Many wetland plants are rarely encountered in other types of communities. The swamp once covered more than two million acres in this region. This area is characterized by fascinating flora like lizard tail, bald cypress, duckweed, pepper vine, birthwort, swamp privet, water locust, swamp cucurbits, buttonbush, resurrection fern, stinging nettle and poison ivy. Each of these plants has pictures and natural history descriptions at the interpretive center.

However, not long ago the park had more champion trees than today. Why is the number falling? In short, the big trees are falling and are not being replaced.

The champion slippery elm died of Dutch elm disease, and many old oaks have also fallen. Efforts are underway to manage the park in a manner that will allow new champions to flourish.

One of the park's burr oaks is 154 feet tall; a persimmon is130 feet; a pumpkin ash is 50 feet; a rusty black haw is 129 feet; a cottonwood is 114 feet; a swamp chestnut oak is 156 feet; and a black willow is 115 feet.

Bird, wildflower and woody plant checklists are available at the interpretive center. The wildflower checklist breaks out the list by color for ease of use.

Programs: A naturalist provides interpretive programs on a range of topics throughout the summer. Programs last 45 minutes to one hour. Contact the park for a current list of programs.

Living History Day is an annual event held at Big Oak Tree State Park on the second Saturday in September. Demonstrators show their skills in blacksmithing, weaving, spinning, quilting, woodcarving, herbs and making bobbin lace, among others. Music is provided throughout the day and concessions are available.

Fishing: Big Oak Lake provides 22 acres of fishing. The lake is stocked with catfish, bass, bluegill and crappie. The borrow pit or moat surrounding the lake is also available for fishing. Swimming is not allowed.

Boating: A small boat ramp provides access to the lake. The boat ramp is open all year, except during managed hunts. There are no launch fees. Electric motors only.

Day-use areas: One picnic shelter can be reserved for $30

The park is one of the last virgin bottomland forests in the state.

per day. If not reserved, the shelters are available at no charge on a first-come, first-served basis. Occupancy is 75 people. They have two large grills; electricity and water are on hand at the shelter. Ten picnic sites are scattered throughout the park. A newer play apparatus joins the flat mowed grove that is shaded by dozens of oaks.

Insider's tips: Take a ride on the nearby Dorena ferry. The ferry area along the flats of the Mississippi River is also excellent for watching shorebirds.

There are a lot of stinging nettles in the park. Never grab the hairy stem of the plant; it will cause lots of pain. Look for poison ivy vines that are as big as your leg.

Earthquakes? Yup, learn about the Missouri fault line and the 1811 New Madrid earthquake in the interpretive center. Check out the seismograph model that when working would monitor the Earth's crust.

Ninety percent of the park is deemed a Missouri natural area due to the rarity and value of the resource. Ancient Druids worshiped trees - I can see why!

Bring your bug repellant and long pants. A snowflake-like cottonwood seed can travel 10 miles on the wind.

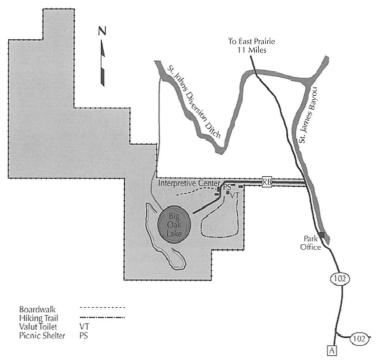

Boardwalk
Hiking Trail
Valut Toilet   VT
Picnic Shelter   PS

Big Oak Tree State Park

Intrepretive signs are scattered amoung the huge boulders.

CHAPTER 41
Elephant Rocks State Park
Land: 131 acres

The biggest granite boulder at Elephant Rock is 27 feet tall, 17 feet wide and 35 feet long. It's estimated to weigh at least 680 tons. Now, that's a big elephant! All the rocks are big, and if you use some imagination they look like a motionless line of elephants outside the circus big top.

The park gets packed on holidays and some weekends as kids and adults dance and hop from boulder to boulder. These "pachyderms" are fascinating to ponder, kind of like the big bang theory. The weathered labyrinth of rocks generally face two directions, northeast and northwest. At the point where the rocks intersect is the place with the biggest concentration of oblong rocks that have been visited for decades.

The state park contains a number of old quarries and interpretive signs that detail their history and backbreaking work. Much of the high-quality granite was used for buildings all around the country. Damaged stones, however, became road pavers that sold for 8 cents. At that rate, a good block maker could produce 50 blocks a day, earning four dollars. Not bad for 150 years ago.

The elephants of the Ozarks are worth the trip. Merely touching some of the oldest rock on the continent is a humbling reward.

The park opened in 1970.

Information and activities

Elephant Rocks State Park
c/o Fort Davidson State Historic Site
P.O. 509
Pilot Knob, MO 63663
(573) 546-3454
www.mostateparks.com

Park hours: From November through March, the park grounds are open from 8 a.m. to 5 p.m. daily. From April through October, the park grounds are open from 8 a.m. to 8 p.m. daily.

Directions:

From St. Louis

Take I-55 south to U.S. Hwy. 67, just south of the Festus (Route A) exit. Turn right (Exit 174) onto southbound U.S. Hwy. 67 and drive past Bonne Terre, Park Hills, Leadington and into Farmington. On the south side of Farmington is the Route W overpass. Exit onto Route W. Travel for 18 miles to a flashing stoplight at a three-way stop. Turn right onto northbound Hwy. 21 and travel two miles. The park entrance is on the right side of road. The trip is about 1.5 hours long.

From Jefferson City

Take U.S. Hwy. 50 east to U.S. Hwy. 63. Turn right and travel to Vichy. Turn left onto Hwy. 68. South of St. James at the junction of Hwy. 68 and Hwy. 8, stay to the left. You will be on Hwy. 8. As you leave Potosi, turn right onto Hwy. 21. About five miles south of Belleview on Hwy. 21 is Elephant Rocks State Park on the left side of the road. The trip is about 2.5 hours long.

From Springfield/Joplin

Take I-44 out of Springfield toward St. Louis. Exit at the St. James Overpass (Exit 195) and turn right onto Hwy. 68. South of St. James at the junction of Hwy. 68 and Hwy. 8, stay to the left. You will be on Hwy. 8. As you leave Potosi, turn right onto Hwy. 21. About five miles south of Belleview on Hwy. 21 is Elephant Rocks State Park on the left side of the road. The trip is at least 4 hours long.

Emergency numbers: Ambulance, (573) 546-2311; police, (573) 546-7321.

Don't take samples of the rocks, and there are no inline skating or skateboards allowed on the trails.

Elephant rocks: A hard-surface trail with interpretive signs meanders among some of the oldest rocks on Earth. The blind can use much of the trails. The pinkish granite rocks in the region are found as part of the Ozarks known as the St. Francois Mountains. The rocks making up these mountains were formed more than 1.5 billion years ago when molten magma beneath the Earth's thin crust cooled; over millions of years, the land uplifted, was level by erosion cycles, and was covered with sediments deposited by ancient seas. The granite rock was again exposed when the land uplifted and sedimentary rock was created.

The haystack-like rocks were once sharply angled. Through geological time, the exposure to wind and rain has rounded these huge rocks much like an ice cube becomes rounded as it melts. Also part of this landscape are oak and hickory woods, quilts of colorful lichen and carpet-like mosses that thrive in the shade. These species are characteristic of the hickory deciduous forest that covers much of the St. Francois Mountains.

Long before the rocky tract became a state park, visitors came to the area. In fact, many quarry workers carved their names and date in the rocks when they became master stonecutters. Local homes, government buildings, a U.S. customs office and gravestones were crafted from the granite quarries that opened in 1869. Massive granite

It's easy to see why they call them "elephant rocks." The big ones weight more than 680 tons.

deposits in the area also produced paved roads, huge blocks for piers for Mississippi River bridges and granite for the state capital buildings of Missouri, Iowa and Illinois.

Fat Man's Squeeze is a popular narrow point along the trail network that allows visitors to climb the rocks. The narrow path was formed along a joint fracture in the granite bedrock. You will walk between what someday might be two separate elephant rocks. Near the squeeze are the clear waters of the old quarry. The water is about 40 feet deep. Other small pools are home to reptiles and amphibians. Also in this area are some heavy steel rings that are embedded in the rock and were used for crane booms that removed giant granite slabs from the Earth.

Trails: Elephant Rocks Natural Area is easily viewed from the one-mile Braille Trail. Designed especially for people with visual or physical disabilities, the Braille Trail is the first of its kind in Missouri state parks. A short spur off of the trail takes visitors to the top of the granite outcrop, where they can explore the maze of giant elephant rocks. A second spur brings visitors to a point overlooking an old quarry.

Nature programming: It is best to contact the park naturalist, based out of Johnson's Shut-Ins State Park, at (573) 546-2450, for current information. Group programs can be arranged in advance for any time of the year by contacting the naturalist as well.

Day-use areas: Thirty picnic sites among the giant boulders provide ample opportunity for picnicking and exploration of the elephant rocks. A children's playground is also available to visitors, making a trip to Elephant Rocks State Park perfect for a family outing. The park has some tire swings, seesaws, climbers and many benches where adults can watch youngsters.

Interpretive kiosks near the parking lot and day-use area offer geological information about the rock formations, quarry activities and samples of tools.

Long hand-drills were used to remove the granite. The two-person drill was rotated after each blow. A block was broken away from its bed by a row of metal wedges, or plugs and feathers, which were driven into the predrilled

The haystack-like rocks are fun to climb on.

holes. As the plug was driven further into the feather, the
block would split off the formations. To avoid hauling extra
weight, blocks were cut to the approximate size and
desired shape before taking them from the quarry. The
granite is estimated to weigh 250 pounds per square foot.
Cranes with compound pulleys were used to maneuver the
blocks into the sled-stone boats and carts. In the 19th
century, steam power made the block moving easier.

The success of the commercial quarry depended on the
having good transportation to its consumers. It wasn't until
the completion of the St. Louis Iron Mountain and South
Railroad to the Arcadia Valley in 1870 that the quarries
became cost-effective. The quarries built spurs connecting
their sites to the railroad and transported the rock to the
main line with their own locomotives.

Three quarry companies operated in the region. Some
employed up to 500 men. One of the companies was in
existence for 63 years.

Climbing: Technical climbing is permitted in designated
areas. Repelling is by permit. Solo climbing is prohibited at
all times and all climbers must sign a waiver to climb.
Climbing permits can be obtained at the Fort Davidson

State Historic Site.

Insider's tips: In 1984, Missouri became the first state to dedicate a portion of its sales tax to fund the state park system. The 100-foot-long shady maze trail is splendid for upper elementary-age children. The day-use park can be packed on holidays. Look in the dark crevices for roosting bats that can eat 600 mosquitoes an hour once the sun goes down.

The Ozark Trail is south of the park and takes hikers through some of the most rugged and scenic country in the state. Someday, the Ozark Trail will be extended 900 miles from St. Louis to Fort Smith, Arkansas.

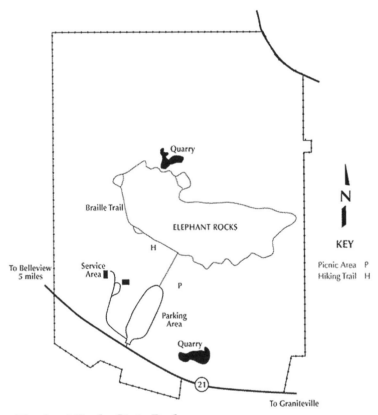

Elephant Rocks State Park

Grand Gulf State Park is a National Natural Landmark.

CHAPTER 42
Grand Gulf State Park
Land: 322 acres

Grand Gulf's canyon, which is often compared with the Grand Canyon, began like the rest of the Ozarks. The rock in which Grand Gulf was formed originated more than 450 million years ago when a shallow sea deposited thick sediments. As the land was uplifted, the waters receded.

Below the Earth's surface, water percolated through fractures in the rock, slowly creating caves. On the surface, streams also began carving the landscape. As the water table lowered more water drained away, leaving air-filled passages such as the one at Grand Gulf. In some areas surface streams, like Bussell Branch, were carved through the rock and connected with caves. In the areas where a cave broke through, the stream was diverted underground. This process continued over thousands of years. Caves collapsed. Geologists believe that the collapse of Grand Gulf occurred in the past. The rock continued to erode, weakening the roof of the cave until it collapsed and formed Grand Gulf.

After heavy rains, the chasm often fills with water. This water slowly drains underground and eventually appears at Monmouth Stream in Arkansas several miles away. This major collapsed cave system is often called the "Little Grand Canyon." The three-quarter-mile-long canyon is one of the largest natural bridges in Missouri.

The park is a National Natural Landmark because the site possesses exceptional value as an illustration of the nation's natural heritage and contribution to understanding man's environment. Grand Gulf was dedicated as a National Natural Lankmark in 1971 by the National Park Service.

Information and activities

Grand Gulf State Park
Route 3, P.O. Box 3554
Thayer, MO 65791
(417) 264-7600
www.mostateparks.com

Directions: Six miles west of Thayer, off Route W in Oregon County.

From West Plains

Grand Gulf State Park is 25 miles from West Plains. Travel south on U.S. Hwy. 63 to Thayer. Turn right onto Hwy. 19 and then right onto Route W, which leads into the state park.

From Arkansas

Grand Gulf State Park is 12 miles from Arkansas. Travel north on U.S. Hwy. 63 almost to Thayer. Turn left onto Hwy. 19 and then left onto Route W, which leads into the state park.

From Springfield

Grand Gulf State Park is 135 miles from Springfield. Travel south on U.S. Hwy. 60 to Cabool. Take U.S. Hwy. 63 south to Thayer. Turn right onto Hwy. 19 and then right onto Route W, which leads into the state park.

From Sikeston

Grand Gulf State Park is 118 miles from Sikeston. Travel west on U.S. Hwy. 60 to Poplar Bluff. Take U.S. Hwy. 67/160 west to U.S. Hwy. 160. Continue to Doniphan, then travel west on Hwy. 142 to Thayer. Turn north on U.S. Hwy. 63 and continue to the caution light at Hwy. 19. Turn left onto Hwy. 19 and then left onto Route W, which leads into the state park.

Emergency numbers: public safety, (417) 778-6111; ambulance, (417) 264-7228.

Grand Gulf is sometimes compared with the Grand Canyon.

Hiking: Grand Gulf State Park has four large overlooks connected by a one-fourth-mile boardwalk that takes you to the bottom of the canyon. Also, a 119-step descent to the bottom of the gulf can be accessed from the parking lot. There are a number of sheer rock cliffs along the path. Look closely and you can see the layers of rocks and small plants.

Once at the bottom, a small cascade runs, depending on how much rain has fallen lately.

Interpretive programs: Guided group tours of Grand Gulf may be arranged in advance with the tourist assistant. The tours feature park history and interpretive talks, and cater to the visitor's inquiries. Call the park office for information at (417) 264-7600.

The two valleys were passages before the roofs collapsed. Rain runoff from about 20 square miles drains into these valleys. The drainage basin covers Howell and Oregon counties.

Day-use areas: There are three picnic sites along the tree-shaded rim of the gulf available for day use. The park has no running water and only a vault toilet. There is no camping allowed on park property.

Insider's tips: Because of the many cliffs in the park, use caution at all times. Visitors must contact the park office before entering unmarked caves. A permit is needed. The mossy walk to the bottom of the canyon is worth the trek as you pass stunted trees and Alpine-like cliff dwelling plants. The best overlooks are less than 50 yards from the parking lot.

Grand Gulf State Park

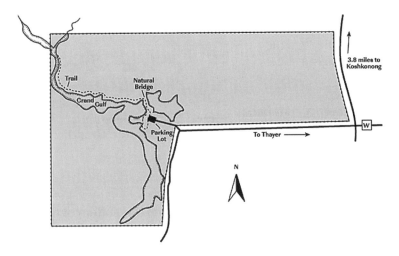

Some of the most beautiful scenery in the state is found along the upper reaches of the Black River.

CHAPTER 43
Johnson's Shut-Ins State Park
Land: 8,729 acres Water: Black River

The term "shut-in" refers to a steep, V-shaped, narrow gorge carved into ancient volcanic rock by swiftly flowing water. Johnson's has two miles of riverfront and limited public access. The park might be the most well known state park in Missouri and sometimes you must wait to get in at the main gatehouse. Each visitor receives a color-coded parking pass and crowds are tightly controlled. The strict control of the number of visitors was instituted a few years ago when the park was nearly loved to death.

Some call Johnson's Shut-ins "nature's water park." It's an easy quarter-mile walk from the park store to the remarkable gorge, where you may clamber among the smooth boulders and roaring waters of the clear East Fork of the Black River.

How was the gorge formed? A searing molten liquid called magma cooled and formed ahard, erosion-resistant mountains. Warm seas that buried them in sediments later covered these ancient mountains. One hundred million years ago, the last sea retreated and rivers scoured and carved downward through sediments, leaving the hard rock known as the St. Fransois Mountains. Today, streams and rivers are confined between two mountains that have formed canyon-like gorges and "shut-ins."

Some of the most beautiful scenery in the state is found along the upper reaches of the Black River and the terrain surrounding the state park. The upper Black River is gin-clear and a great smallmouth bass stream. This wild and rugged area, especially in the East Fork Wild Area, incorporates igneous and dolomite glades, upland ridges, steep bluffs, moist grassy meadows and bottomlands that are home to hundreds of plant and animal species.

A small part of the tract is fen. A fen is a permanent wetland that is fed by calcareous groundwater that creates boreal conditions much like those found in Canada. Unique plants grow here that include blue smooth violet, bottle gentian, swamp wood betony, sweet Williams and other boggy plants.

Information and activities

Johnson's Shut-Ins State Park
HC Route 1, Box 126
Middlebrook, MO 63565
(877) I Camp Mo Camping Reservations
(573) 546-2450
www.mostateparks.com

 Directions:

From St. Louis

Johnson's Shut-Ins State Park is about 130 miles from St. Louis; the trip will take at least two hours. Take I-270 south to I-55 south. When you get to the Festus area, take U.S. Hwy. 67 south to Farmington. At the second Farmington exit, turn right onto Route W toward Doe Run. Travel 17 miles on Route W. At the flashing red light, turn right/north onto Hwy. 21. Travel about one-half mile and turn left onto Route N. Go 14 miles on Route N to the park entrance on your left.

From Jefferson City

Johnson's Shut-Ins State Park is about three hours driving time from Jefferson City. Go south on U.S. Hwy. 63 to Hwy. 68. Take Hwy. 68 through St. James to Hwy. 8. Stay on Hwy. 8 to Potosi. At the intersection of Hwy. 8 and Hwy. 21, turn right/south onto Hwy. 21. Travel about 25 miles to Graniteville. Turn right onto Route N. Travel 14 miles on Route N to the park entrance on your left.

From Kansas City

The park is five to six hours from Kansas City. Take I-70 east to St. Louis, and follow the directions above.

Emergency numbers: Reynolds ambulance and sheriff (573) 648-2491; Ellington (573) 663-2511.

Park store: The hectic clapboard-sided park store sells a range of Johnson's Shut-Ins souvenirs such as T-shirts, books, postcards and more. The store also has grocery items, camping supplies, vending machine, frozen foods, sub sandwiches, chips and hot foods for a snack such as nachos, pizza and hot dogs. The store also has a book rack that sells a number of field guides to Missouri fauna and flora.

Store hours from Memorial Day weekend to Labor Day weekend are 8 a.m. to 8 p.m. daily. There are changing rooms at the store complex. A small outdoor deck and eating area are in front of the busy park store. There are also shady trees and a scattering of picnic tables around the parking lot and near the store and changing rooms.

Campground: Johnson's offers basic and electric campsites and a special-use camping area. Services include a dump station, showers, water and laundry. All campsites in this park are reservable. Water is not available in the park during the off-season. The campground has a sand volleyball court and an amphitheater with six rows of seats.

Loop 1-25 has electric sites. Site 3 gets some glorious midday sunshine. Site 5 also gets midday sun and is across from the sand volleyball court. Site 6 is shady and next to a natural area. Sites 7-9 have midday sunshine. One of the shadier sites along this section of the loop is site 10. There are 16 parking spaces at the modern showerhouse. Sites in

The riffles and eddys are great fun to play in.

the high teens and 20s are along a natural area. Sites in the low 20s are also near the volleyball court. Site 22 would be great for a big RV unit and is backed up against a natural area. Sites 23-25 are also near a natural area and received lots of afternoon sunshine. The front of site 24 is often sunny while the back of the site can be shady during much of the day. Most of the campsites have roofed picnic tables. The tables are great for staging your equipment and supplies.

The south concentric loops have eight pull-through sites and are about 40 percent shady, a bit less than the north loop. Site 43 is J-shaped and under some mature trees. Site 34 is one of the nicer pull-through sites shaded by a large sycamore and cedar. Site 37 is also a good pull-through and has a mix of sun and shade near a water bib.

For reservations, there is a required two-night minimum stay on weekends from April through October and major holidays from May 15 through Sept. 15.

Shut-ins: The riffles and eddies along the river increase in intensity as you approach the narrow, boulder-strewn shut-ins. It's like someone tossed slabs, rocks and car-sized boulders across the river, causing the water to increase its velocity as it courses through the maze called shut-ins.

The "rock garden" now attracts visitors who enjoy romping from boulder to boulder, sometimes "swimming" in the refreshing waters that ceaselessly struggle to find the least resistant path among the primordial river rubble. The swirling water isn't deep, but the rush and power of the white water are fun to wade. Sometimes you feel like you must stay close to the maze of boulders for security, other times you can stand in the hurrying water and let it flow against your legs. It's mighty refreshing on a hot day!

An observation deck looks down on the "swimmers" and gurgling river. They are fun to watch. Soon, first-time visitors will gain confidence and begin crossing the streams and stepping from boulder to boulder.

Hiking: The 2.5-mile Shut-Ins Trail provides access to the shut-ins. A gentle one-quarter-mile walkway leads to an observation deck overlooking the scenic upper pothole shut-in. Continuing past the lower chute shut-in, the trail becomes more rugged, looping through the East Fork Wild Area.

The Taum Sauk Section of the Ozark Trail is a 12.8-mile trail that leads hikers east to the adjacent Taum Sauk Mountain State Park. The Ozark Trail also leads west, passing through both the East Fork and Goggins Mountain wild areas into the Bell Mountain Wilderness in Mark Twain National Forest. Backpack camping is allowed along the Ozark Trail.

Regulations for backpacking the Ozark Trail from Johnson's to Taum Sauk:

You must be two miles from the trailhead and 100 feet from water sources, trails, public-use areas and scenic areas before setting up camp.

Open campfires are prohibited on the trail. Camp stoves are recommended.

To limit damage to the environment, camp in groups of six people or less.

Always stay on the trail, where provided, even if it's wet or muddy.

Carry out what you carry in.

A newly constructed 10-mile hiking and equestrian trail in the Goggins Mountain Wild Area climbs the ridgetops to Goggins Mountain. The 5,000-acre wild area includes all of

Goggins Mountain and three other igneous domes that are some of the most dramatic in the St. Francois Mountains. The area is heavily wooded with forests of oak and hickory trees, interspersed with rocky openings called glades. These glades provide opportunities for hikers and equestrians to stop and enjoy vistas of nearby mountains, including Bell Mountain and Proffit Mountain. The trailhead includes a parking area for 15 vehicles and trailers and a vault toilet. The trailhead is three-quarters of a mile down Highway MM. Highway MM is about 1,000 feet west of the entrance to Johnson's Shut-Ins State Park on Highway N, eight miles north of Lesterville.

Fishing: Fishing is permitted on the Black River. Smallmouth and largemouth bass, bluegill and perch are taken. No boats are allowed.

Swimming: Yahoo! Wading is one of the park's most popular activities. Swimming is allowed at the shut-ins area in the East Fork of the Black River only. A quarter-mile paved trail extending from the park office complex, where a bathhouse and restroom facility is located, can access the swimming area. Scuba diving has restrictions; obtain a permit from the park office. Remember, no diving! And don't swim in the shut-ins during floodwater passages.

Nature: The Taum Salk section of the Ozark Mountains is one of the most beautiful and rugged tracts along the Ozark Trail. Ask at the park office for a bird checklist that details more than 100 birds. The region has had about 900 plant species.

Birding and wildlife observation are best before Memorial Day and after Labor Day. The Shut-ins Trail is excellent for birding after you have passed the busy area. Look for ruby-crowned kinglet, red-eyed vireo, pileated woodpecker, Easter wood pewee, red-bellied woodpecker, cedar waxwing and whippoorwills.

Regularly scheduled evening programs are held at the amphitheater from Memorial Day through Labor Day. Group programs can also be arranged any time of year by contacting the park naturalist at (573) 546-2450.

Here are some examples of the types of programs done on a regular basis during the summer months at Johnson's

Wading is one of the park's most popular activities.

Shut-Ins State Park: Owl Prowl Spider Sniff, The Amazing Flying Rat - Not!, River Critters, The Roach Motel, The Demise of Frederick T. Frog, The Love Connection, Johnson's Shut-Ins State Park Slide Show, The Bear Necessities, Kid's Corner and Evening Skies.

Every year, debris from the comet Swift-Tuttle awes us with views of a meteor shower. Join park staff in the amphitheater to watch. This program is usually in late June. To inquire about the events listed above, please call (573) 546-2450.

Day-use areas: More than 15 picnic sites equipped with a grill and picnic table are located throughout the park. There are playgrounds in both the campground and main day-use area. Just inside the gate is an open space just past the pine grove.

Campers may check out recreational equipment like wiffle balls and bats, kick balls, soccer balls, bases, volleyballs and horseshoes.

Rock climbing and rappelling are allowed from the day after Labor Day to Memorial Day weekend only. A daily permit is required. For more information regarding climbing, contact the park office at (573) 546-2450.

Insider's tips: A horseback riding concession is near the park. Also, the park office publishes a handy directory of local private campgrounds, float trips, lodging and bait shops. A split-rail fence surrounds the Johnson Family cemetery that quietly rests on a shady knoll. Bring your aquatic shoes. There is large RV rig parking along the backside of the parking lot.

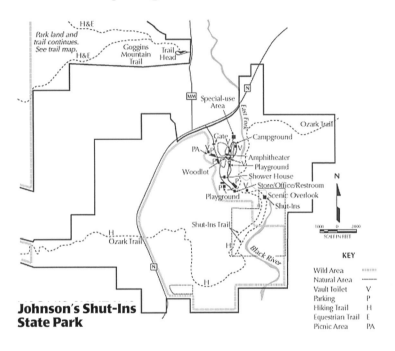

**Johnson's Shut-Ins
State Park**

Lake Wappapello State Park is in the Ozark foothills and features hiking, camping, cabins, boating, fishing and swimming.

CHAPTER 44
Lake Wappapello State Park
Land: 1,854 acres
Water: 8,400-acre Lake Wappapello

L ake Wappapello is in the Southeastern foothills of the Ozarks. Explored and settled by Spain, owned by the French and purchased by the United States in 1803, the area was originally inhabited by Cherokee, Delaware, Osage and Shawnee Indians. The lake was named after a Shawnee chief who hunted and explored the rugged area. Many years later, the first permanent white settlers came to lumber the forest in the early 1800s.

The rich foothills that circle the peninsula park are steep and clad in pine and hardwoods. In 1941, the U.S. Army Corps of Engineers finished a 2,700-foot dam on the St.

Francois River, creating the 8,400-acre lake where anglers, boaters, hikers and campers come to play.

The huge lake is huddled beneath long ridges of pine, hickory and oak. Along these ridges are hiking trails and campgrounds; at their base is a great place to view the park from a boat. In fact, a small boat or canoe is a great way to see the park's wildlife that includes white-tailed deer, bobwhites, quail, geese, cormorants, grebes, diving ducks, gulls, turkeys, beaver, squirrels and many other common animals.

Because of the diverse habitat surrounding the reservoir and vast public natural lands, you have a great chance of seeing dozens of interesting bird species, so bring your binoculars. The tract's short-leaf pines often contain pine warblers, kinglets, nuthatches, spring warblers and many types of sparrows. Along the wooded you might see various waterfowl, brown creepers, thrushes, shorebirds, raptors and bald eagles. The understory can have many types of warblers, vireo, Carolina wren, flycatchers, ovenbirds and others. About 60 species are recorded in the area each year.

Information and activities:

Lake Wappapello State Park
H.C. 2, Box 102
Williamsville, MO 63967
(573) 297-3232
1-800-ICAMPMO - campground, lodging reservations

The park office has a soft drink vending machine, ice and pay phone. It also is tastefully decorated and has one of the most complete brochure racks in the system. Souvenirs, firewood and a few camping supplies are sold at the information counter.

Directions:

From St. Louis

Take I-55 south to U.S. Hwy. 67, Park Hills exit, at Festus. Travel 77 miles or 1.5 hours to Greenville. Remain on U.S. Hwy. 67 south for 14 more miles. Turn left onto Hwy. 172 east. Follow Hwy. 172 five miles to a stop sign where you will turn left. Travel one mile and turn right onto Hwy. 172 east. Hwy. 172 ends in the state park.

From Jonesboro, Ark.

Take U.S. Hwy. 49 north about 24 miles to AR Hwy. 135. Turn left onto AR Hwy. 135 and travel about 22 miles to U.S. Hwy. 62, where you will turn left. Continue on U.S. Hwy. 62 for four miles before turning right onto U.S. Hwy. 67. Travel about 40 miles north on U.S. Hwy. 67 to Hwy. 172, where you will turn left. Follow Hwy. 172 for five miles to a stop sign. Turn left at the stop sign and travel one mile before turning right onto Hwy. 172 east. Hwy. 172 ends in the park.

From Memphis, Tenn.

Take I-40 west about 8 miles to Exit 277 at Blytheville/Jonesboro. Exit onto I-55 north and travel 16 miles to U.S. Hwy. 63N/Exit 23B. Merge onto U.S. Hwy. 61; it will turn into U.S. Hwy. 63N. Take the AR Hwy. 1/Stadium Blvd./U.S. Hwy. 49N exit toward Caraway Road. Keep right at the fork in the ramp and turn right onto U.S. Hwy. 49N. Travel 22 miles before turning left onto AR Hwy. 135. Travel another 22 miles to U.S. Hwy. 62. Turn left onto U.S. Hwy. 62 and continue for four miles before turning right onto U.S. Hwy. 67. Travel on U.S. Hwy. 67 for about 40 miles north to Hwy. 172. Follow Hwy. 172 for five miles to a stop sign. Turn left at the stop sign and travel one mile before turning right onto Hwy. 172 east. Hwy. 172 ends in the park.

From Springfield

Take U.S. Hwy. 60 east for 187 miles to U.S. Hwy. 67. Turn left/north onto U.S. Hwy. 67 and continue for about 9 miles to Hwy. 172. Turn right onto Hwy. 172 and continue for fivew miles to a stop sign. Turn left at the stop sign and travel one mile before turning right onto Hwy. 172 east. Hwy. 172 ends in the park.

Emergency numbers: Missouri Highway Patrol, 573-840-9500; Poplar Bluff Medical Center, 573-785-7721; Wayne Co. Sheriff, 573-224-3090; Park ranger, 573-297-3232.

Campground: From the top of the hill near the campground entrance, you can catch glimpses of large pleasure boats that ply the azure water. You also can walk down to the shoreline and sit in the sun. The park has two campgrounds.

The park has three boat launching ramps.

In the Asher Creek campground (sites 55-81, closes each year on Nov. 1 and opens April 1), the block showerhouse has an ice machine, bulletin board and soft drink vending machine. Campsites are on varying elevations in this campground. The shower house has two showers and two washers and dryers. Firewood is sold nearby and all of the camping pads have hard surface drives. Many campers bring fishing boats. Site 55 is backed up against the woods, while shoreline sites 57 and 58 are close together and great for related families to spend a week or a weekend. Shoreline sites have great access for fishing.

Sites 55 to 70 are reservable and most have great water views. Site 64 is mostly sunny. Site 65 is a pull-through and great for a small RV. Site 66 is below the showerhouse and across the narrow park road from the soft shoreline. Site 67 is a perfect waterfront site for a pop-up camper. Site 70 is near the water and open. Site 71 is a pull-through and near the small single lane boat-launching ramp. Site 75 is on the highest elevation in the campground and big enough for large RV rigs. Site 78 is shady and has a water view; in fact, all the sites have a full or partial water view.

Sites 65, 67, 69 and 71 are the only non-electric sites in the park. Sites 65, 67 and 69 are great tent sites.

The Ridge Campground has sites 1-54. Sites 1, 2,11-21,

26, 27, 29-49 are reservable. Eighteen of the sites are pull-throughs and all the sites have electrical hookups. Sites in the beginning of the area are nicely separated by vegetation. Site 4 is on varying elevations. Sites 1-9 are mostly shady and reasonably private. The shower house has soft drink vending machines, laundry and is near handicapped accessible sites 10 and 11. Sites 12 and 13 are good family sites. Pull-throughs in this area are 14, 15, 17, 19, 20, 26, 31, 32, 35-37 and 45. There are through-the-trees lake views from most of these sites also. It's a steep scramble down to the lake, but there is shoreline fishing access. Part of this campground is open all year.

Site 16 is great for a pop-up camper. Site 17 is near the vault toilet. On a slightly higher elevation is large and shady site 18. Sites 19 and 20 have a wooded view of the lake. Sites 23-25 are high, dry and shady and at the end of the loop that looks down on a narrow bay. These sites may be the finest in the park, but be careful backing into site 25 - it's steep on one side. A water bib is near site 29, which is handicapped, accessible. Site 30 is best for pop-up or tent campers. Many of the campsites in this area have picnic tables that are outlined by ground-mounted landscape timbers. Site 32 is near a vault toilet that is outlined by some large rocks and near a blue-colored water bib faucet. Site 36 is a pull-through on the curve of the hard-surface park road. All tent camping is on gravel pads and park staff recommends cushioning.

Loop 37-47 is private. Large RVs should be careful on site 40; it has a pad dip. Site 41 is a back in only. Site 42 is sunnier than many of the other sites. Site 44 is a wonderful semi-sunny site on a slight elevation change and it is private. Site 45 is a pull-through and private on both sides, but there is a site directly across the campground road. Sites 46 and 47 have varying elevations. For example, your RV rig can be on one elevation while your picnic table is on another grade level. They also have extra room for chairs and socializing. Site 50 can accommodate a large RV. Site 52 has a boulder punctuating the site. It's also shaded by a couple of nice maples. Site 53 allows tent campers to set up quite far off the road.

332 Missouri State Parks

Cabins: Lake Wappapello State Park offers beautiful two- and three-bedroom housekeeping cabins equipped with pots, pans, silverware, bedding and linens. Each cabin has a color TV/DVD player. The cabins are open from April through November 15. There is a two-day minimum rental with a three-day minimum rental on holidays. Two night's deposit is required to hold a reservation. Check-in is at 3 p.m. and checkout is at 11 a.m. There are no pets allowed in the cabins. Children age 4 and under stay for free.

The cedar lapboard sided cabins are a bit like small ranch-style houses. The cabins are on a peninsula and along a quiet road that is perfect for families with small children. Cabins 1-7 have a six-person maximum occupancy and cabin 8 has a 10-person maximum with infants and kids counted as occupants. Cabins have front and back porches, fire rings, grills and picnic tables.

The Allison Cemetery Trail surrounds the cabin peninsula. Each cabin has a porch and three windows on the front. There is enough room for boat trailer parking. Each cabin has a picnic table and charcoal grill. Oak, hickory and maples wave overhead, offering shade during much of the day. Each has a small side yard and a wooden deck built off the back of the house. Cabins are about 40 feet apart.

Cabin eight is north of the beach and not with the other seven cabins mentioned above. It has shutters and is clean and neat. The Allison Point boat ramp is near this large cabin and parking at the cabin for four to six vehicles, and boat trailers. To inquire about cabin availability or make a reservation, please call 1-8876-ICAMPMO. There are also four camper cabins in the campground. They offer electricity, air-conditioning and heat. Guests must bring their own linens and use the shower house for these cabins.

Hiking: All trails in Lake Wappapello State Park are identified with entrance signs and marked at intersections with colored directional arrows. Occasional colored markers is used to identify the trail where the route is not clear. Hikers are advised to watch closely for trail markers, especially where trails intersect old roads.

Allison Cemetery Trail - 3.5 miles

This trail, which is open to hiking use only, provides an easy walk on the ridge to Allison Cemetery and then meanders along the lake's edge to complete a 3.5-mile loop. There are three trailheads, one in the day-use area near the picnic shelter and the other on the north side of the road leading to the cabins. Cabin guests may access the trail at the end of the cabin road. The trail is signed in a clockwise direction with green arrows. Shorter hikes are possible by using connector trails that are identified with white arrows.

Lake View Trail - 1/2-mile

This short trail begins in the day-use area at SH #1 and provides excellent views of the lake. It is signed with blue arrows in a clockwise direction and is designated for hikers only.

Asher Creek Trail - 2 miles

The clockwise trail (red arrows) begins on the west side of the Asher Creek campground and crosses the hillside up Asher Creek Valley though some dry, rocky slopes and travels downhill to the water. This arm of the lake in the winter is a designated waterfowl refuge, making the Asher Creek Trail an excellent area for viewing wildlife. The trail follows higher ground on its return to the campground and passes through several stands of mature timber that include oak, musclewood, elms, river birch and hickories. The trail passes two connector trails that are used for shorter hikes.

Wappapello Backpack and Equestrian Trail - 15 miles

The Lake Wappapello Trail is used by hikers, backpackers, all-terrain bicyclists and equestrians. The single-track trail traverses 15 miles of varied and rugged Ozark terrain and may be accessed from Highway 172 near the west boundary of the park. The route is signed in a counterclockwise direction with yellow arrows. There are some excellent views of the lake from the hilltops. There is backpackers' camp on the northeast corner of the trail. Check with the park office for details.

The equestrian parking area is dry and hard-packed gravel. About 20 rigs could park in the staging area.

Biking: The 15-mile Wappapello Trail is best for experienced riders. The single-track trail has been featured in a book on mountain biking in the U.S. Riders will encounter downed trees, rocky terrain and some steep slopes. The trail is maintained with the U.S. Army Corps of Engineers and leaves parklands meandering along additional undeveloped public ground west of the state park.

Fishing: The sprawling lake is a popular fishing spot and offers a wide variety of species. Common species include crappie, largemouth bass and catfish. Fishing is allowed in all areas of the park except at or near boat ramps and the swimming beach. The facility allows night fishing at specific locations throughout the park. The best fishing months are May, September and October. Many angles do well in the late winter and early spring.

A state-sponsored crappie-tagging program might earn you from $10 to $100. If you catch a tagged crappie, merely write down the date, tag number, whether you kept or returned the fish, length of the fish, your name, address and phone number, and send it to the Missouri Dept. of Conservation, 2302 Cape County Road, Cape Girardeau, MO 63701. You might earn cash, but you are definitely helping research.

If you think you have caught a record fish, it must be weighed in the presence of Conservation Department personnel. Here are some of the state's record fish: largemouth bass, 13 pounds, 14 ounces; spotted bass, seven pounds, eight ounces; carp, 50 pounds, six ounces; walleye, 21 pounds, one ounce. The lake is a great black crappie fishery.

Record fish forms and information are available from the Department of Conservation, Fisheries Division, State Record Fish, P.O. 180, Jefferson City, MO 65102-0180, telephone (573) 751-4115.

Boating: The park has three boat launches. All are single-lane. They are at the Asher Creek Campground, the old marina and just past cabin 8 at the Allison Point day-use area. All are concrete ramps. There is a courtesy dock at the old marina launch. There are no launch fees or motor restrictions.

Swimming: The park offers a small swimming beach at the Allison Point day-use area. It opens on or about

The park has two campgrounds.

Memorial Day weekend and closes shortly after Labor Day weekend. The sandy beach area is surrounded by woodland. There is a large parking area, change house, picnic tables and modern playground nearby.

Interpretive programs: In season and when there is funding the park employs a naturalist that offers guided hikes and various programs. Many events meet at the park's amphitheater near the Ridge Campground.

Nature: The cherty ridges, slopes and hillsides contain a variety of trees characteristic of the southern Ozark plains and the southeastern coastal plains. These include a variety of oak and hickory, red buckeye, beech and tulip trees. Vegetation in the park comprises ferns and orchids in the shaded areas, and birdsfoot violets and pussy's toes on the sunny slopes. Mistletoe, which grows in the black gum trees and sycamores along the edge of the lake, is a special feature rarely found in Missouri.

Day-use areas: The park has three picnic areas and two playgrounds for visitor use, free of charge.

Picnic sites are in the Allison Point day-use area, near the Allison Cove boat ramp and near shelter house No. 1. Both shelters feature picnic tables and an outdoor grill, making a perfect venue for family gatherings and special outings.

Shelter No. 1, in the day-use area at the end of the main park road on a high ridge, has an 80-person occupancy and can be reserved for a fee. It is also equipped with electrical outlets.

Shelter No. 2 is 9in Allison Cove day-use area, has a 50-person occupancy and can be reserved for a fee. This shelter has a drinking fountain and nearby water bib. This day-use area also has a one-acre open field for games and family picnics. Shelter No. 2 sits above the lakeshore. If the shelters are not reserved, they are available at no charge on a first-come, first-served basis.

Picnicking at the shelter houses is accessible to persons with disabilities. For reservations, please call the park office at (573) 297-3232.

Children's playgrounds are at the Allison Cove day-use area and at Shelter No. 1.

Insider's tips: Bring your boat and fishing rod. The Asher Campground has many waterside sites with great shoreline fishing access. The park has lots of poison ivy - learn to identify it now! It also has many steep roads, drive slowly.

Plan to watch sunsets over the lake as the golden shafts of light make the waters shimmer. In addition to the state park, the extensive U.S. Army Corps-owned land around the lake offers trails, six campgrounds, 11 boat ramps, five courtesy docks, naturalist's programs, various lake access and several day-use areas.

Star gazing at Allison Point is excellent because artificial light is low and the area is wide open. The Wappapello Fire Department shoots off a wonderful fire works display over the lake each Independence Day. Boat views are great.

The unit is often busy in June and July, but it is a hidden get-away the rest of the year for those that enjoy lakeside recreation and water sports.

Lake Wappapello State Park

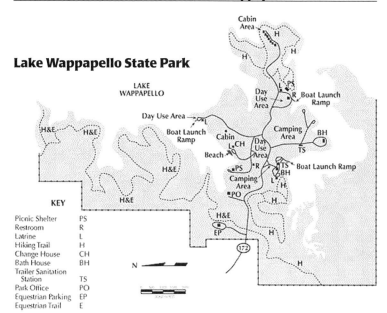

KEY

Picnic Shelter	PS
Restroom	R
Latrine	L
Hiking Trail	H
Change House	CH
Bath House	BH
Trailer Sanitation Station	TS
Park Office	PO
Equestrian Parking	EP
Equestrian Trail	E

Come for the fishing---learn about the history at Montauk State Park.

CHAPTER 45
Montauk State Park
Land: 1,396 acres   Water: Current River

Several springs produce more than 40 million gallons of water daily that nourish the Current River. The icy-cold river is stocked with trout each night. About 90,000 trout anglers annually visit the park to try their luck along the river.

Montauk is likely the best known of the three state parks that offer put-and-take trout stocking and a full-service hatchery. During the 1930s, the Civilian Conservation Corps built wonderful stonework and rustic architecture amid the steep ridges and splendor of this park. Much of the handiwork is listed on the National Register of Historic Places.

Clearly, Montauk is a trout angler's paradise, but it's also a great camping and hiking park. Foot trails, open spaces and shelters are scattered throughout the park. The beauty of the Ozark Highlands and steady flow of the river attracted pioneers in the 1800s and modern families today. With rolling and flat park roads, playgrounds and a multi-loop campground, visitors can also dine in the bucolic lodge, learn to fly fish or have a legendary ice cream treat at the old fashioned soda fountain.

Montauk has it all and is one of my favorite Missouri state parks.

The charming park opened in 1926 and about 450,000 people visit annually. Missouri's state park system began in 1917, one of the oldest in the nation.

Information and activities

Montauk State Park
R.R. 5, Box 279
Salem, MO 65560-9025
(573) 548-2201
(573) 548-2434 - cabin, motel rentals
(877) I Camp Mo: Camping Reservations
www.mostateparks.com

Directions:

From St. Louis

Montauk State Park is 140 miles from St. Louis. Travel west on I-44 to Rolla. Exit onto U.S. Hwy. 63 south. At Licking, turn left onto Hwy. 137 and follow it through town for three miles. Turn left onto Route VV and travel 10 miles to Hwy. 119. Turn right and enter the state park.

From Salem

Montauk State Park is 22 miles from Salem. Travel west on Hwy. 32 to Hwy. 119. Turn left onto Hwy. 119 and continue for 10 miles to the state park.

From Springfield

Montauk State Park is 110 miles from Springfield. Travel east on U.S. Hwy. 60 to Cabool. Turn left/north onto U.S. Hwy. 63. Ten miles north of Houston, turn right onto Route P and travel one mile to Hwy. 137. At Hwy. 137, turn left and travel one mile to Route VV. Turn right onto Route VV and continue 10 miles to Hwy. 119. Turn right and enter the state park.

Emergency numbers: ambulance, (573) 729-7400; sheriff, (573) 729-3241.

Park store: The park store operates out of the Dorman L. Steelman Lodge. The store features a complete line of fishing supplies including hand-tied flies made by local craftsmen. A large variety of souvenirs and gifts, groceries, milk, bread, charcoal, camping supplies and other essentials will help make your stay in the park more comfortable.

Store hours are listed below.

• November through Feb. 27: Friday from 4 p.m. to 6 p.m.; Saturday from 9 a.m. to 7 p.m.; Sunday from 9 a.m. to 2 p.m.

• Feb. 28: 8 a.m. to 11 p.m.

• March: 5:30 a.m. to 8 p.m. daily.

• April (Central Standard Time): 5 a.m. to 7:30 p.m. daily.

• April (Daylight-Saving Time): 6 a.m. to 8:30 p.m. daily.

• May: 5:30 a.m. to 9:15 p.m. daily.

• June and July: 5:30 a.m. to 9:30 p.m. daily.

• August: 6 a.m. to 9 p.m. daily.

• September: 6:30 a.m. to 8:15 p.m. daily.

• October (Daylight-Saving Time): 6:30 a.m. to 8 p.m. daily.

• October (Central Standard Time): 5:30 a.m. to 7:30 p.m. daily.

Campgrounds: All loops are open year-round and have water hydrants. The park has 125 electric sites and 31 non-electric sites. There are two showerhouses.

The campground showerhouses and coin-operated laundries are open seven days a week from Feb. 25 through October 31. Soap and bleach are sold in vending machines.

Campers can buy firewood from the campground woodlot. From Feb. 25 through October, the woodlot is open Sunday through Thursday from 6 p.m. to 7 p.m. and Friday and Saturday from 6 p.m. to 9 p.m. From November through Feb. 24, the woodlot is closed. During those months, wood is available on weekends from the dining lodge during its business hours. There also is ice for sale near the woodlot and showerhouse from February 25 through October 31. ice is available at the lodge during the winter season.

Montauk Hatchery.

For reservations, there is a required two-night minimum stay for weekends and major holidays from May 15 through Sept. 15. Remember to never drain your gray water on the ground.

Site 101 is adjacent to a marvelous sycamore tree and overflow parking. Many of the sites are backed up against the river for easy access. This section of the campground is airy. Site 118 is on the end of the loop and site 119 is probably the most private site on the loop both are in a forested area. Sites 120 and 122 are also private and shady.

Some say the campground registration center is "cute." A maple shades sites 201 and 202. A water hydrant is behind site 204. Many young trees have been planted to begin the slow process of replacing the big trees that are still offering shade. The campground has about a 50-50 mix of shade and sun. A huge sycamore provides shade for many of the sites in the low 200s. Sites 209-211, however, are sunny. The colorful playground apparatus is near site 214. Site 215 is also shady and great for small children. Sites 218-220 are another pair of sunny sites. A small rig would work well on site 225; a water bib is nearby.

Sites 302-303 are duplex sites and partly shaded by a

small sycamore tree. Sites on the outside of the loop are backed up against a natural area and the river. There is ample access to the river. Site 317 has sun in the front of the site during midday. Site 320 has a diminutive path down to the river. Site 332 is generally sunny. The fishing access for anglers with disabilities is at the end of this camping loop. The access is hard-surfaced and wheelchair-bound anglers could cast into the riffles from the elevated platform. Two benches are also featured at the access point that has bumpers and low rails. Site 328 is near the handicapped fishing access point. A handicapped camping site is also nearby.

Sites 336 and 338 are large shaded sites. However, most of the sites in this vicinity are big enough for large RVs. Sites in the low 400s are shady, and many are along the river. Sites 412 and 414 have immediate access to the cool-running stream. Site 415 is near the end of the loop. Site 419 often has a sizeable unit on it. Sites 420 and 427 get midday sun. Most of the sites on the interior of the loop have about 50 percent shade. Site 430 is big enough for a larger rig and is near the stable-like showerhouse, laundry and vending machines.

Lodging: Montauk State Park offers one- and two-bedroom housekeeping cabins with kitchens, sleeping cabins and 18 motel rooms. All cabins and motel rooms are air conditioned and heated. Linens are furnished in all types of lodging. Motel units 1 and 18 and cabins 11, 12 and 26 are accessible to persons with disabilities.

Cabins 3, 9 and 10 and cabins 22 through 33 have tub/shower combinations; all others are equipped with showers only. Queen-size beds are available in cabins 9 through 12 and 22 through 33. All motel rooms as well as cabins 3, 22 through 33 are equipped with televisions (limited reception). Cabins 15 and 26 through 29 have fireplaces. Cabins 13-15 are shingle-sided and feature a fieldstone porch.

Cabins 7 and 8 are near the river and mowed open space, plus have screened porches. These cabins are steps from the cold river and hungry trout. Cabin 3 has cedar siding and is behind the hatchery in the upper end of the park. It also has a handsome deck in front. Duplex cabin 11-12 has a view of the mill and is on a rise above Cabin 3. An open space for field games is nearby. Sycamores shade many of the cabins.

Cabins 16-17 are a duplex built into the hillside and don't have much outdoor play space. Duplex cabins 20 - 21 also have a small yard.

Motel rooms: Each of the 18 motel rooms has ceramic floor tile in the bathroom, wood furniture, wallpaper and a TV. Wall-mounted fishing rod racks are in motel rooms.

For additional information or to make reservations, please call (573) 548-2434.

Dining and lodge: The Dorman L. Steelman Lodge offers a store, fishing tackle, snack bar and restaurant. The 28-table dining room is a full-service restaurant serving breakfast, lunch and dinner. It also has pictures of trout, a vaulted tongue-and-groove ceiling, with exposed beams, colored glass in the walls and great food. The Saturday evening special is prime rib. Reservations are not necessary. A trip to the ice cream bar is a must when you visit the park. Six double-door-like windows look out into the woods. These are the best tables in the house.

Dining lodge operating hours are shown below.

- November through Feb. 27 - Friday from 4 p.m. to 6 p.m.; Saturday from 9 a.m. to 7 p.m.; Sunday from 9 a.m. to 2 p.m.
- Feb. 28 - 8 a.m. to 8:30 p.m.
- March - 7 a.m. to 8 p.m. daily.
- April and May - 7 a.m. to 8:30 p.m. daily.
- June through August - 7 a.m. to 9 p.m. daily.
- September - 7 a.m. to 8:15 p.m. daily.
- October - 7 a.m. to 8 p.m. daily.

In front of the lodge is a planting bed with identified wildflowers and other flora. Species include prairie drop seed, purple poppy mallow, white beard's tongue, birdsfoot violet, Jacob's ladder, Missouri black-eyed Susan, hawthorn tree, wild sweet William, Eastern blazing star and others. Also in front of the lodge are vending machines.

Inside the lodge are a fireplace and plenty of fishing trophies, plaques and artwork. Also in the lobby are a TV and comfortable chairs where fishing stories have been

The tower takes you to the treetops for a wonderful view.

exchanged for more than 40 years. Next to cozy lobby are the ice cream counter and store that features full-service trout fishing supplies, T-shirts, canned goods, milk, juice, break, soft drinks, toys, coolers, bike rentals, hats, candles, souvenirs and other useful items.

The fishing shop has a big assortment of fly-tying supplies, bamboo nets, rods, vest, rod repair supplies, hand-tied flies, reels, laptop fly-tying benches, fingerless gloves, socks, waders, insect repellant, Dutch ovens, yarn, fillet knives, Powerbait, glow balls, books, maps, trout bait with glitter, garlic-flavored bait, spinners and salmon eggs.

Flies for sale include duns, caddis, midges, wooly bugger, early brown stone, red St. Juan, sulfur emerger, pale morning dun, royal coachman, yellow Sally, black leech, dark Henderson, quill Gordon, Adams, red-quill, dun midge, pheasant tail, sow bug, ants, cinnamon ant, olive caddis, renegade, cream sparkle pupa, crayfish and many more. The Montauk special is a spinner with a woolie buck tail and red yarn.

The ice cream counter is a killer. Like an old stainless steel soda fountain, it offers all kinds of treats and you can sit at one of the 18 stools in front of the blue-green counter. My favorites, that's plural, were the chocolate chip ice cream cones, all-chocolate sundae and root beer float.

Conference space: The brown clapboard Searcy Building is the park administrative office and a roomy meeting space equipped with a kitchen and restrooms. The meeting room can be reserved for a fee for groups of one to 30 and for groups of 30 to 50. The meeting space was dedicated in 1972. To reserve the meeting room for business groups or family gatherings and to arrange catered meals, contact the lodge manager at (573) 548-2434 or (800) 334-6946.

Fishing and hatchery: The Rose Holland Trout Derby is held at Montauk State Park each year during the first full weekend in October. Various smaller trout derbies are held during the remainder of the trout season. Nearly 90,000 fishing tags are sold annually. It costs about $1.25 to produce a mature trout. The hatchery began operation in 1932 with many buildings added later.

The Missouri Department of Conservation sponsors

tours of the trout hatcheries. For a schedule of tours, contact hatchery personnel at (573) 548-2585.

The raceways and hatchery are near the old mill. Trout eggs are taken once a year by hand. Spawning occurs during October, November and December. Eggs are fertilized by squeezing milt from the male fish over the eggs. Female trout average about 3,000 eggs at the time of spawning. An ounce of eggs equals 320, if fertile. Fertile eggs are placed in jars, in the incubator room with fresh spring water flowing over them during incubation.

Each jar will hold about 50,000 eggs. Eggs hatch in 56-degree water in 21 days. They are then known as "sack fry." Due to the large sack, they aren't able to swim and they lay on the bottom for 10 days while the rich nutrients in the sack are absorbed. When the fry start feeding, they are placed in troughs and fed about 10 times a day. It takes one pound of feed to produce one pound of trout. Missouri hatchery trout ate 1 million pounds of feed during a recent season. After the fingerlings reach 4 inches long, they are fed twice a day. Only trout 10 inches or longer are released into the stream for anglers to pursue. Trout will grow to 12 inches in about 15 months. Trout are stocked in the stream each night just after the "stop fishing" siren is blown. It gives the fish several hours to get accustomed to the stream before the next day's fishing.

The fast-flowing, spring fed Current River contains both rainbow and brown trout. Trout season opens March 1 and lasts until Oct. 31. In between, there is a catch-and-release program for year-round angling fun at the park. License and daily trout tags are required.

Anglers have been successful using many types of flies and baits including crappie rigs, live bait, white rooster tails, Powerbait, glow balls, white jigs, orange power ball, white flies, yellow Cleo's and others. Access to the Current River abounds throughout the linear park.

Please release trout you don't intend to eat immediately. Avoid all excess handling by grasping them gently across the gill covers. Never put your fingers in the gill or eye sockets. Wearing a cotton glove will help. Carry a hook disgorger or needle-nose pliers to carefully remove the

Flyfishing classes are offered at the park.

hook. Never remove a hook from the fish's throat or stomach. Merely cut the line; the hook will rust away. Use hooks with the barb squeezed shut or barbless hooks for ease of releasing healthy trout.

Hiking: If you're interested in a relatively challenging walk, Pine Ridge Trail is ideal for you. Be sure to wear good hiking shoes with rugged "grippy" soles. There are two trailheads: one starts directly behind the old stone picnic shelter and the other is just beyond the naturalist's office. The trail does not make a complete loop, so if you decide to park at one end and walk the 1.5-mile trail, you will need to walk another three-tenths of a mile along the road to get back to your car. Most people start at the end by the stone picnic shelter. Although the beginning of the trail is steep, don't give up. Once you get to the top of the first long hill, the trail is pretty easy from then on. The beauty of the surrounding hillsides is worth it!

The trail begins by leading you through Montauk's Upland Forest Natural Area. This was designated in 1979 as a premier example of one of Missouri's special native ecosystems. The natural area is made up of about 40 acres of dry upland oak and pine forest. As you ascend the steep hill, take a few moments to look at the diversity of trees around you. As you approach the top of the hill, you will start to notice more and more huge shortleaf pine, Missouri's only native pine tree.

Once you leave the natural area, you will cross the highway and walk through a peaceful oak pine forest. This stretch of trail offers the best chance to see wildlife such as forest songbirds, whitetailed deer and wild turkeys. Listen for great horned owls and the loud knocking of pileated woodpeckers as they search for insects in the trees above you.

A prominent highlight of the trail is reached toward the hatchery end. Just before descending down a hillside to the end of the trail, you will be treated to one of the most beautiful views in Montauk State Park. The trees open up to a breathtaking view of Bluff Spring and Montauk Lake below, and Jack Pond Ridge across the valley. Look for great blue herons near the water, or (in the winter season) bald eagles soaring above.

The Montauk Lake Walk is one of the most popular places to walk in the park. You don't need hiking shoes, but we do recommend something more than sandals, since the road surface is gravel. It's excellent for small children and strollers. The hike starts at the naturalist's office, near the hatchery office. Just follow the gravel road that begins at the north end of the public parking area. Feel free to walk or ride your bicycles, but no motorized vehicles are allowed.

This walk is about three-fourths of a mile and makes a loop. There are other foot trails along the way if you want to extend your hike.

You will see a wide variety of sights within a short distance. Montauk Lake is actually an artificial wetland area created as a result of an old hatchery impoundment. This wet environment creates excellent habitat for beaver and other water-loving mammals, wading birds, wood ducks, water turtles, frogs and wetland wildflowers. Wildlife viewing is guaranteed on this hike!

A highlight on this hike is Bluff Spring, one of many spring outlets in the park. This particular spring provides all the water for the hatchery building and the spring branch. Look for the active beaver lodge in the middle of the large central wetland (it's a large mound of sticks and mud). Other highlights to look for, especially in late summer and early fall, are the mixture of colorful berries produced by trees, shrubs and vines, such as blackberries, raccoon grape, wild grape, greenbrier, spicebush, flowering dogwood, hackberry and Carolina buckthorn. Also, notice the beautiful large pink blooms of the rose mallow, a native wetland wildflower.

Whether you're out for a leisurely stroll or ready for a rugged hike through the Ozark hills, Montauk State Park has much to offer! Check the park program posters posted throughout the park for naturalist-guided hikes (offered March-October). Of course, feel free to walk Montauk's beautiful trails on your own. For more information on Montauk's hiking opportunities, contact the park naturalist.

The mill: The mill at Montauk State Park is more than 100 years old and has six-over-six windows and two millstones at the entrance. For 31 years, millers ground tons of wheat and flour. The community of Montauk included several general stores, a blacksmith's shop, schools, churches and houses scattered across the countryside. The mill used water power, and the turbine wheel was considered the most efficient power source. Parts of the mill still work.

At one time there were three mills in the Montauk valley before this one was built in 1896. Timothy Hickman built this mill away from the river to avoid flood damage. The lumber is stacked, so the walls are not hollow. No one knows why the mill was built this way, including international experts. The small front room that is now used as the nature study space was the bran bin. Bran was the left-over product of the wheat milling process. The bran was used to feed livestock. The small nature study room contains touch boxes, youth artwork, pressed leaves and wildflower collection and wall posters.

This historic site was a crucial part of the Montauk community into the 1920s. Free tours of the mill are given on weekends. Hours vary, depending on demand and scheduled group tours. New schedules are posted each week showing times and dates for available public tours.

For information regarding tours or to schedule a special group tour, contact the park naturalist at (573) 548-2225. There's some excellent day-use open space and a picnic shelter across from the mill.

Nature: From March through October, park naturalists offer a variety of interpretive programs, including nature walks, live animal demonstrations, evening programs, nature games, nature crafts, storytelling and mill tours.

Program schedules are posted on bulletin boards in the campground, picnic areas, the lodge, mill and naturalist's office. Programs are one hour or less (unless otherwise noted). Programs include a stream walk, fishing tips, mill tour, late night walk, black bear program and others.

An animal checklist is available from the park office. Unlike most lists, Montauk's list features butterflies, moths, dragonflies, damselflies, mayflies, stoneflies, beetles, "true" bugs and miscellaneous invertebrates.

Native flora and fauna include river birch, hawthorn, sycamore, Jack-in-the-pulpit, trillium, Solomon's seal, Jacob's ladder, dogtooth, pussy toes, wild ginger, yellow star grass, shooting star, Virginia waterleaf, tulip popular, black willow, dogwood, cherry, elm, sweet gum, Eastern redbud, mockery nut hickory, broad beach fern, bracken fern Christmas fern, grape fern, sensitive fern, honey locust, short-leaf pine and hackberry. Mammals include striped skunk, river otter, beaver, big brown bat, fox squirrel, mink, coyote, black-tailed Jackrabbit, raccoon, Eastern wood rat, shrew, prairie vole and red fox.

Also in the nature room is a three-ring binder that details the toads and frogs including the five-eighths-inch tree frog; Eastern narrow mouth toad that lives under flat rocks in dry woodlands and floodplains; 3-inch leopard frog that inhabit moist areas; the green frog, which looks like a bullfrog but is smaller and has a ridge of skin on its side and back that isn't found on bullfrogs, they are found along rocky creeks and sloughs. The tan and brown northern crayfish frog is Missouri's second largest species that often lives in crayfish burrows; the 1-inch Blanchard's cricket frog is a member of the tree frog family but can't climb; the 2-inch green tree frog is bright green but can turn dark green when the weather cools off.

Day-use areas: The park has two open picnic shelters just right for family reunions or corporate picnics. Both shelters have picnic tables, outdoor grills, a playground and restrooms. There also is a playground in the campground.

The "new" shelter can be reserved for a fee, accommodates up to 70 guests and is equipped with electrical outlets. The "old" shelter can be reserved for a fee and accommodates roughly 30 guests.

If not reserved, the shelters are available at no charge on a first-come first-served basis.

Insider's tips: Nearby Salem has a Wal-Mart superstore. There also is the Cahill County Store and Reeds Cabins about a mile from the park. Consider a "Thomas and Thomas" fly-fishing course that is offered at the park. Check the fishing tote board that details the weight and species caught for the season. It's next to the lobby in the lodge. A hard-surface walking path, which connects the lodge to the campground entrance and is lit for nighttime use. A base map is at the lodge. A hand-written note from Steve Fishing, manager, welcomes each overnight lodger in each motel and cabin.

A hummingbird feeder is often busy at the lodge. The corncob feeder that can be seen from the windows in the dining room gets amusing when squirrels take the stage. The park operates a courtesy freezer in case you want to freeze the lunker you catch while visiting the park. Coin-operated vending machines are at the hatchery rearing pools that offer the appropriate feed for the growing fish. Bald eagles often stay in the park from late October to February. Canoeing is not allowed at the park.

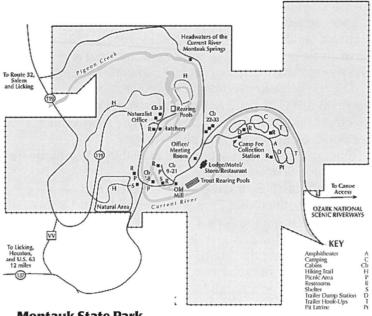

Montauk State Park

To Route 32,
Salem
and Licking

Headwaters of the
Current River
Montauk Springs

Pigeon Creek

Naturalist
Office

Rearing
Pools

Cb 3

Cb
22-33

Hatchery

Office/
Meeting
Room

Camp Fee
Collection
Station

Lodge/Motel/
Store/Restaurant

Cb
9-21

Trout Rearing Pools

Old
Mill

Current River

Natural Area

To Canoe
Access

OZARK NATIONAL
SCENIC RIVERWAYS

To Licking,
Houston,
and U.S. 63
12 miles

KEY

Amphitheater	A
Camping	C
Cabins	Cb
Hiking Trail	H
Picnic Area	P
Restrooms	R
Shelter	S
Trailer Dump Station	D
Trailer Hook-Ups	T
Pit Latrine	Pt

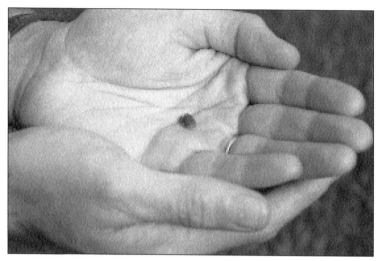

A newborn toad at Morris State Park.

CHAPTER 46
Morris State Park
Land: 161 acres

Morris State Park's 161 acres are located almost exclusively in Crowley's Ridge. Crowley's Ridge was named after Benjamin Crowley, a participant of the War of 1812 and one of the first settlers of the area. It rises above the Bootheel area of southeast Missouri in a natural range of low hills. Morris State Park preserves significant natural and cultural features within this region. Many plant species in the park and region cannot be found anywhere else in Missouri.

The ridge was a primary route of transport and commerce for the people of the region for centuries. In 1999, Jim D. Morris, a Springfield businessman, donated 161 acres in this area to the Missouri Department of Natural Resources so it could be protected for future generations to enjoy. The uniqueness of the region, the unusual soil types and rare plant species make this a prime area for research and the application of natural and cultural preservation techniques vital to the department's mission.

The ridge towers 100 to 250 feet above the Mississippi River valley, yet it is built of many thick layers of gravel and sand that were washed in from the ancient Ozarks when this region was a long Gulf of Mexico bay. When the ocean receded and torrents of ice age meltwater stripped most of the sediments from the Bootheel region, Crowley's Ridge was left behind. Ferocious winter storms added up to another 50 feet of wind-blown dust. Some of these layers are seen throughout the park.

The ridge harbors more than 300 types of plant species, some of which are native in Missouri only to Crowley's Ridge. The uplands contain white, post and red oaks up to 26 inches in diameter. The middle to ground level layers of the forest contain such species as sassafras, red maple and dogwood. The moist, rich and lush hollows are teeming with ferns and shade-tolerant wildflowers beneath American beech, sweet gum and tulip poplar trees, species more typical of moist eastern forests than the dry Ozark ones nearby. Rare species and some of the plants restricted to the southeastern portion of Missouri include the red buckeye and Hercules club, both under story trees, as well as overcup, cherrybark and willow oaks. Several sedges and grasses in this park are not found in any other state park in Missouri. Most are found in the rare sand forest, acid seeps and remnants of the former Malden Prairie, which are prized features of this park.

Because the Missouri Department of Natural Resources wants to preserve the park's natural integrity, only minimal development of the park will occur. A two-mile-loop hiking trail allows visitors to take a closer look at this unique natural feature of our state. The trail extends through a large portion of Crowley's Ridge, taking visitors to the lowest point of the ridge and near the park's predominant feature - a very large soil exposure depicting the natural erosion of the ancient alluvial soil layers typical of the ridge. The trailhead features an accessible walkway that leads to an overlook.

Information and activities

Morris State Park
c/o Hunter-Dawson State Historic Site
P.O. Box 308
New Madrid, MO 63869-0308
(573) 748-5340
www.mostateparks.com

Directions: West of Malden, five miles north of Campbell on Route WW in Dunklin County. The park is in the Bootheel area of southeast Missouri.

Hiking: The two-mile Beech Tree Trail offers hikers a meandering passage along part of Missouri known as Crowley's Ridge. The region's unique soil types feature more than 300 types of plants, a few native only to Crowley's Ridge. The trailhead includes an accessible walkway that leads to an overlook, which offers views of the surrounding forest.

Insider's tips: Morris State Park offers a trail, vault toilet, small parking area only, and interpretive kiosk.

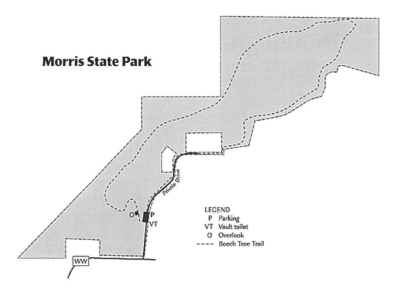

Morris State Park

LEGEND
P   Parking
VT Vault toilet
O   Overlook
---- Beech Tree Trail

Ninety-minute cave tours are led by trained naturalists at the park.

CHAPTER 47

Onondaga Cave State Park
Land: 1,316 acres   Water: Meramec River

Undulating woodlands and rambling pastures dotted with cattle and horses mark the many routes to this state park that is recognized as Missouri's underground treasure chest. Although Meramec State Park has more caves than Onondaga, this show cave is one of the Midwest's most popular destinations. Some say you can't visit the park without a cave tour. I agree!

The cave not only represents millions of years of geologic history, but also the human story of hucksters, roadside attractions, Route 66 nostalgia, nasty local politics and other colorful cultural events. In 1904, the St. Louis World's Fair organizer convinced cave owners to open the cave to the public. Visitors were loaded on the Frisco Railroad, then onto big-wheel buggies to get to the park to tour the stunning cave. This was the beginning of the cave's fame and an attraction that flourished in the 1950s and '60s under the ownership of Lester B. Dill. Dill was known as "America's No. 1 Caveman." Ever the showman, Dill built the attraction and also gave the land for the park before his death in 1980.

A stream flows through the cave and the Lily Pad Room, an underground pool with ceiling and floor structures that sprout from circular underwater formations. You can see it all on the .9-mile guided tour. For a more adventurous tour, try the Cathedral Cave and probe the darkness with lanterns.

Equally beautiful are some of the overlooks from ancient bluffs above the Meramec River. A park brochure details the sometimes zany history of the cave, property disputes, conflicts, failed mining and amusement park-like promotion during the middle of the last century.

Information and activities

Onondaga Cave State Park
7556 Highway H
Leasburg, MO 65535
(573) 245-6576
(877) I Camp Mo; Camping Reservations
www.mostateparks.com

Directions

From St. Louis

Onondaga Cave State Park is 90 miles from the St. Louis Arch; the trip will take about 1.5 hours. Go west on I-44 to Exit 214. Head south on Route H for seven miles. You will pass through the town of Leasburg, population 323. The paved section of Route H ends in Onondaga Cave State Park just before the visitor center. Do not cross the Meramec River.

From Jefferson City

Allow 1.5 to two hours for the trip. Go south on U.S. Hwy. 63 to Rolla. Turn east on I-44 to Exit 214 (Leasburg). Head south on Route H for seven miles. You will pass through the town of Leasburg. The paved section of Route H ends in Onondaga Cave State Park just before the visitor center. Do not cross the Meramec River.

From Springfield/Rolla

Onondaga Cave State Park is about 130 miles from Springfield and should take about two hours. The trip from Rolla is about 45 miles and 45 minutes. From both, go east on I-44 to Exit 214 (Leasburg). Head south on Route H for seven miles. You will pass through the town of Leasburg. The paved section of Route H ends in Onondaga Cave State Park just before the visitor center. Do not cross the Meramec River.

Emergency number: 911 system.

Visitor center and cave tours: Open 9 a.m.-5 p.m. daily. The 90-minute naturalist-led cave tours are offered daily from March 1 to Oct. 31. The visitor center opened in 1989 and offers some superb displays. You must purchase your cave tour tickets from the gift shop inside the visitor center.

A circular garden in front of the stone visitor center has double oak entrance doors which are your gateway to the cave tour and lessons in natural history. The nature classroom in the center features aquariums with live native reptiles, mineral displays, bird and mammal mounts and educational posters.

The gift shop is one of the more complete in the system featuring mineral samples, T-shirts, postcards, jewelry, plaques, beanie toys, candy, limited camper supplies, soap, insect repellant, signs, books, sky finders, soft drinks, rubber snakes, refrigerator magnets and children's miner helmets.

Across the foyer from the gift shop is the waiting room for the cave tours with four rows of chairs and bat posters that describe their natural history. Bats amount to nearly a quarter of all the mammal species. 42 of these species live in the United States and Canada. American bats come in an amazing variety. Some are highly colored and exceptionally marked, while others have huge ears and unusual faces that are adapted for their navigational system to detect insects and avoid obstacles.

Bats send out high-frequency sound through their mouths, relying on sensitive ears to hear the reflected echoes. Worldwide bats are the primary predator of night-flying insects. Individual bats, among them the myotis, the most abundant of American species, can catch up to 600 mosquitoes an hour. Large colonies of free-tailed bats can eat up to a half-million pounds of insects nightly including countless crop-damaging insects. Long-nose bats of the Southwest are vital pollinators of desert plants.

Most bats typically give birth to a single young in May or June. Babies nurse and learn to fly in an amazing three weeks. In the fall, most bats migrate south or find suitable places to hibernate until spring warms the air and fills it with insects.

Aside from bats, the museum in visitor center also teaches about the many zones of caves and the inhabitants that call it home. It also had a display on groundwater and its importance to the region.

Onondaga Cave

"Onondaga Cave is a highly scenic cave because of the great abundance and quality of its cave formations. Stalactites, stalagmite columns, rhinestone dams, cave coral, draperies, flowstone and soda straws extensively decorate the cave...Massive draperies are intricately deposited and deeply folded, while simply formed soda straws hang by the thousands from the ceiling."
— National Natural Landmark, 1980.

Caves also attracted early businesses and settlements. For example, gristmills in the Ozarks were often placed at springs that flowed from caves. These springs provided reliable sources of water power and the mills provided meal and flour from local crops. Settlers were first attracted to the area by the pure water near Onondaga Cave.

The Crestwell family came to the area in 1850 and built a mill near Saranac Spring upriver on the Meramec River. In the late1800s, the property was sold to William and Artressa Davis, who dammed the spring flowing from the cave and built Davis Mill just outside the entrance. After discovery of the cave, a property dispute developed

Floating the Meramac River is popular in kayaks, canoes, tubes and johnboats.

between the Davises and the cave's discoverers, Christopher Eaton and John Eaton. The cave owner managed to obtain title to the mill following William Davis' death in 1899. Artressa Davis spent the rest of her 95 years suing the owner of the cave. The mill was torn down in 1946, three years after her death.

One of the most interesting displays in the center is about hand mining, where you can view a variety of nasty-looking tools were used about 100 years ago.

Campground: The campground was completely renovated in 2003 and features hard-surface pads, park road, contours and showerhouse. A connect channel and day-use area welcome campers to the rolling grounds that are often filled on holidays and many mid-summer weekends.

The quiet Meramec River flows near the campground. A mostly flat campground has many mature trees across the tract. The campground also has some sunny loops, streams and open spaces for field games.

Firewood is sold throughout the day by the campground hosts. The wood shed is next to the showerhouse.

Hiking: The park has four trails that cover 8 miles along wooded hollows and ancient bluffs.

The Blue Heron Trail (half mile, blue arrows) is an easy and scenic hike that skirts the north side of an oxbow lake formed by the meandering Meramec River. The steep hillside reflects in the clear waters of the lake. It also winds past the spring that leaves the cave where a mill once operated. The deep pool formed by the spring is quiet. Dolomite bluff and rocky slopes can be covered with flowering wildflowers during the spring.

The Deer Run Trail (2.75 miles, green arrows) is accessed near the amphitheater where hikers will find a moderately difficult trail along mossy hills, cedar-choked glades and panoramic overlooks. It takes about an hour-and-a-half to hike. The overlooks of steep-walled bluffs and rocky outcroppings are worth the rugged effort.

Cave: Graffiti that mars many caves is a great concern. Organized cavers have helped pass both state and federal protection laws. Their creed is, "Take nothing but pictures, leave nothing but footprints, kill nothing but time."

Boat ramp: The small hard-surface ramp closes at 10 p.m. and has parking for about 20 vehicles and trailers. A vault toilet is near the single-lane launch. This part of the Meramec River is popular with canoeists.

Floating: Old yellow school buses ferry paddlers up and down the Meramec River to launch points. In fact, across the river from the park is Ozark Outdoors *(www. ozarkoutdoors.net),* a lively livery. The operation rents canoes, kayaks, johnboats and tubes. There also are riverfront camping, showerhouses and a camp store. The rustic outdoor stores features rental office, snacks, ice cream, camper supplies, limited grocery supplies, firewood, lunch meat, nachos, sunglasses, film, ice, aqua shoes, sun block and paddling information.

Nature: The scenic bluffs and wooded hills are viewed best from a quietly paddled canoe. Along the river, nature viewers might spot red fox, raccoon, more than 40 songbird species, beaver, two species of heron and lots of turtles. The Blue Heron Trail meanders by springs, rugged bluffs and rocky outcrops. Here you might find nesting songbirds. Seed-eating birds love the ancient cedars that line some of the bluffs in the park.

Day-use areas: Near the campground are a half-court for basketball, vault toilets and plenty of open mowed spaces. Shoreline fishing is also a popular activity at the park. All of the day-use areas are clean and well-equipped with tables, grills and parking.

Insider's tips: There are firewood vendors along Route H. Skippy's Rt. 66 Restaurant and Chat & Chew Restaurant in Leasburg only five miles from the park. The log buildings are very cool. Missouri has more than 5,000 caves. Try a swim in the Meramec.

Onondaga State Park

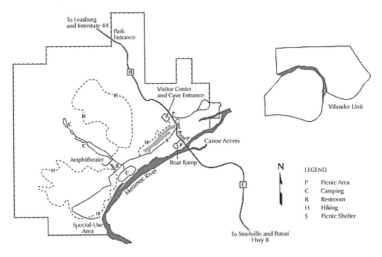

The mountainous doom at Taum Sauk Mountain State Park.

CHAPTER 48
Taum Sauk Mountain State Park
Land: 7,551 acres 1,772 feet above sea level

You can get really high at Taum Sauk Mountain State Park. The twisting drive up to the park is like a mini-Pike's Peak climb. From the zigzagging road, you can see the mountains undulating off to the horizon.

The park entrance sign is also interesting. The lime green letters against a brown field alert visitors that they are in for an exceptional experience. The vistas reveal natural areas that don't have any hint of the hand of man.

The major attraction at Taum Sauk Mountain is its unspoiled wilderness. Much of this area has been carefully developed to retain its rugged features.

How Taum Sauk got its name remains a mystery. Some think that it received its name from the Native American Chief Sauk-Tom-Qua. Others believe the name is derived from the Sauk Indians. The Sauk were known to occasionally travel down the Mississippi River where they probably visited the area. There was "Tongo," an Indian name for "big," which may have been shortened to "Taun" and them Americanized into "Taum." So, Tongo Sauk meant "big Sauk." The name fits since it refers to the highest point in the state.

Information and activities

Taum Sauk Mountain State Park
c/o Johnson's Shut-ins State Park
HCR 1, P.O. Box 126
Middlebrook, MO 63656
(573) 546-2450
www.mostateparks.com

Directions:

From St. Louis

Taum Sauk Mountain State Park is about 120 miles from St. Louis (South County); the trip will take about two hours depending on traffic. Take I-270 south to I-55 south. When you get to the Festus area, take U.S. Hwy. 67 south to Farmington. At the second Farmington exit, turn right onto Route W toward Doe Run. Travel 17 miles on Route W. At the flashing red light, continue through the intersection and head south on Hwy. 21. Travel about 9 miles south on Hwy. 21 until you come to Route CC. Turn right and travel about five miles to the state park.

Emergency numbers: Reynolds County sheriff, (573) 648-2461; ambulance, (573) 648-2491. Iron County Sheriff (573) 546-7321.

Camping: Taum Sauk Mountain State Park offers basic campsites and a special-use camping area. Water is available. Campsites are available on a first-come, first-served basis.

Hiking: A gentle walk from the parking area heads visitors to Missouri's highest point, 1,772 feet above sea level. The area also looks down upon the state's deepest valley. The Taum Sauk Mountain overlook offers a view of the far-reaching mountainous topography to the north.

Interpretive reader boards are at the visitors' overlook, providing a thorough history of the expanse.

Beginning near the parking lot is the rugged, three-mile Mina Sauk Falls loop trail, which takes visitors to the state's tallest waterfall, cascading 132 feet over volcanic rock. The best time to view the falls is after heavy rainfall, particularly in the spring and fall.

The legend of Mina Sauk Falls is interesting. It's said that Chief Taum Sauk's daughter, Mina Sauk, was in love with an Indian brave from an enemy tribe, the Osage Indians. When the Chief found out, he forbade the two lovers from seeing each other. Mina Sauk refused to obey, so the tribe made plans for her lover's death by lining the cliff with spear-carrying warriors. They threw the brave from the clifftop, watching him bounce from ledge to ledge. Mina was so angered she jumped off the cliff after him. The "Spirit God" brought a great bolt of lightning on the mountain, splitting it open and forming the cascading falls as we find them today. Water gushed out of the falls, washing away the blood of the young lovers. Blood-red flowers known as "Indian pinks" are found there today.

A mile beneath the falls along the Taum Sauk section of the Ozark Trail rests Devil's Tollgate. This eight-foot-wide passageway takes visitors through 50 feet of volcanic rhyolite rising 30 feet high. This geological phenomenon is the result of a vertical fraction of volcanic rock. The crack allowed a big chunk of rock to fall, leaving the space known as "The Tollgate."

There are many legends associated with Devil's Tollgate. One of them says that the tollgate was formed when a gigantic monster was chasing an Indian maiden. According to the story, a large rock wall cut off the maiden's escape. The monster struck the wall with a bolt of lightning, splitting it into two parts, which allowed the young Indian girl to escape.

Another legend says the tollgate got its name from an old military road that passed through the rock. A wagon train that came down the road couldn't fit through the passageway and the wagon had to be taken apart, carried through the narrows, reassembled and reloaded. This was

The tower has seven levels and overlooks the treetops.

such a hassle that the constricted passage became known as "The Devil's Tollgate."

The 33-mile Taum Sauk Section is one of the most charming and rugged sections along the entire Ozark Trail. It traverses several mountains, including Bell Mountain, Goggins Mountain, Proffit Mountain and Taum Sauk Mountain. These mountaintops have incomparable assets ranging from wide glade vistas to rock-strewn streams and the cascading Mina Sauk Falls. The trail crosses several significant creeks and rivers, including Padfield Branch, the East Fork of the Black River, which has a footbridge, and Taum Sauk Creek. The Ozark Trail connects Taum Sauk Mountain State Park to Johnson's Shut-Ins State Park, which is 12.8 miles to the west. Backpackers may use this trail and it takes 10 to 11 hours to hike.

The Ozark Trail will eventually connect St. Louis with the Ozark Highlands Trail in Arkansas.

Nature: The mountainous domes contain woodlands of white oak, post oak and short-leaf pine. Many of the rocky openings, called glades, are home to unusual desert-adapted plants and animals including rain dew plants, America goldfinch, fast-moving Eastern collared lizards, Indian grass, little blue stem, prairie blazing star, ashy sunflower, scaly blazing star, rattlesnake master and white wild indigo. Clearly, this plat of fauna and flora suggests links to the tall grass prairies that lap the edge of the Ozarks in earlier times.

The lichen grasshopper is nearly impossible to see in the glades due to its coloration and adaptation to the dry environs. One of America's most endangered plants, Mead's milkweed, thrives on some of the region's rocky dry glades. The Eastern wood rat is also at home in the glades.

The top of Taum Sauk Mountain is actually quite flat, but the tract has probably the maximum diversity of natural life in Missouri. A clear Ozark stream cuts though the state's deepest valley and rich ecosystem.

Broad-winged and red-shouldered hawks are often seen soaring along the ridges and linear valleys. Other interesting birds you may find are pileated woodpeckers, American kestrel (look for the bobbing tail), yellow-breasted chat, field sparrows, great-crested flycatcher, ovenbird, scarlet tanager and others.

The park managers use prescribed burns to preserve these glades and woodlands. Look for dwarfed Bonsai-like trees that cling to the windy mountainside.

Day-use areas: The shady main picnic area is at the overlook. Drinking water and a vault toilet are nearby.

The main overlook that is outlined by a green rail has several reader boards that identify mountains in the distance. The interpretive signs detail their height and distance. For example, Buford Mountain is the southernmost of five knobs and reaches 1,740 feet. William Buford is buried at its base with the inscription: "Just bury me by Buford Mountain and Belleview Valley here below. And when my horses and hounds can join me, together we'll roam Buford Mountain and the Belleview Valley of our dreams."

Belleview means "beautiful valley" in French. Many French explorers passed through this area that was "covered in grasses that bent in the breeze like a huge meadow blooming in the harvest surrounded by towering hills which seems to smile upon the valley," said settler Williams Woods. The area also has salt licks that attracted deer and elk, and those who hunted them.

Iron Mountain can also be seen from the overlook. Many say its has some of the purest iron ore on the continent. It was an important mining area for 123 years, until 1966. After the top of the mountain was removed, the ore was excavated and later mined from underground. Standing on the edge of what looked like a crater, visitors saw miners so far away they looked like small boys.

A special-use area is available for use by nonprofit organized youth groups. Reservations are required by calling the office at Johnson's Shut-Ins State Park at (573) 546-2450.

Lookout tower: A hard-surface road meanders up to the seven-level lookout tower. The wood steps take you up to wonderful views from at least tree level of the surrounding mountains. The top floor is closed.

Insider's tips: Check out the many nearby float trips; many leave from Lesterville. Several private campgrounds are also around Lesterville. From the main overlook, you can see Elephant Rock in the distance. Missouri's longest plank road (five miles, now State Road W) was used for shipping iron ore. Travelers were charged seven tolls along the eight-foot-wide wooden road.

General Ulysses S. Grant described the nearby Arcadia valley as "one of the most beautiful places I've ever been with plenty of cool water available, making ice cease to being a luxury, and enough altitude to ensure cool weather."

Shepard Mountain is five miles as the crow flies from the park.

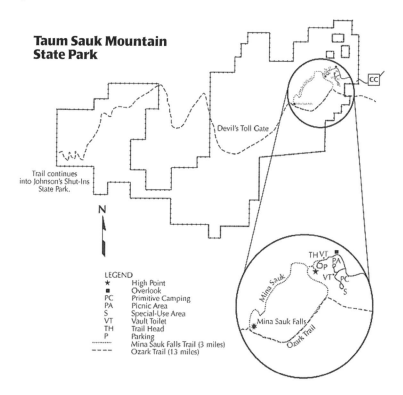

Taum Sauk Mountain State Park

Devil's Toll Gate

Trail continues into Johnson's Shut-Ins State Park.

N

CC

THVT
PA
P
VT
PC
S

Mina Sauk Falls

Ozark Trail

LEGEND
★   High Point
■   Overlook
PC   Primitive Camping
PA   Picnic Area
S   Special-Use Area
VT   Vault Toilet
TH   Trail Head
P   Parking
.... Mina Sauk Falls Trail (3 miles)
- - - - Ozark Trail (13 miles)

Trail of Tears State Park Visitor's Center.

CHAPTER 49

Trail of Tears State Park

Land: 3,415 acres

Water: Mississippi River and lakes

The razorback ridges and quiet hollows look much the same as they did when the Cherokees passed through them in1838 during one of America's sorriest moments. These towering river bluffs and deep ravines were witness to the tragic event called the "Trail of Tears."

This beautiful region was a place of unthinkable human misery when the Cherokee Nation was uprooted from their homeland in a forced 800-mile march that killed an estimated 4,000 people. The gruesome trek ended in Indian Territory, today known as Oklahoma.

The park's environs are much like the Appalachian Mountains. Here, the trees are bigger than those found in the Ozarks and the overall diversity includes rich ground cover, magnolia trees, bottomlands and river breaks that is as scenic as any place along the great Mississippi River.

The unit is a wonderful birding park. The diversity of habitat, from mud flats in the river bottomlands to winding valleys and oak/beech ridges, offers great places to watch birds and other wildlife. Bring your binoculars to see tanagers, woodpeckers, wood thrush, vireos, thrashers, mockingbirds and shorebirds. Also, look for mammals that might include whitetailed deer, raccoons, opossum and bobcats.

Information and activities

**Trail of Tears State Park
429 Moccasin Springs
Jackson, MO 63755
(573) 334-1711
(877) I Camp Mo; Camping Reservations**
www.mostateparks.com

Directions:

From St. Louis

The park is about 2.5 hours from the St. Louis area. Travel south on I-55 to Exit 105 (Fruitland/Jackson). Take Hwy. 61 north for one mile. Turn right onto Hwy. 177 and continue for seven miles. At the four-way stop in front of the Procter and Gamble plant, turn right to stay on Hwy. 177. Continue for another 2.8 miles. The entrance to the state park is on the left, just before the Hwy. 177/Route V intersection.

From Jefferson City

The park is about four hours from the Jefferson City area. Travel east on U.S. Hwy. 50 until it ends at I-44 (just past Union). Take I-44 east to Hwy. 141; proceed south to I-55. Take I-55 south to Exit 105 (Fruitland/Jackson). Travel north on Hwy. 61 for one mile. Turn right onto Hwy. 177 and continue for seven miles. At the four-way stop in front of the Procter and Gamble plant, turn right to stay on Hwy. 177. Continue for another 2.8 miles. The entrance to the state park is on the left, just before the Hwy. 177/Route V intersection.

From Springfield/Joplin

The park is about five hours from the Springfield area. Travel east on I-44 to U.S. Hwy. 65. Take U.S. Hwy. 65 south to U.S. Hwy. 60. Travel east to I-55 near Sikeston. Take I-55 north to Exit 105 (Fruitland/Jackson). Travel north on Hwy. 61 for one mile. Turn right onto Hwy. 177 and continue for seven miles. At the four-way stop in front of the Procter and Gamble plant, turn right to stay on Hwy. 177. Continue for another 2.8 miles. The entrance to the state park is on the left, just before the Hwy. 177/Route V intersection.

From Carbondale, Ill.

The park is 2 hours, 15 minutes from Carbondale. Travel south on U.S. Hwy. 51 to IL 146. Stay on IL 146 crossing the bridge to Missouri. Turn right onto Hwy. 177 and continue for 12.3 miles. At the stop sign at the junction of Hwy. 177 and Route V, turn right to stay on Hwy. 177. The entrance to the state park is on the right almost immediately after turning onto Hwy. 177.

From Memphis, Tenn.

The park is about 3.5 hours from Memphis. Travel west on I-40 to I-55. Take Exit 277 toward Blytheville/Jonesboro and merge onto I-55 heading north. Continue on I-55 for 170 miles to Exit 105 (Fruitland/Jackson). Travel north on Hwy. 61 for one mile. Turn right onto Hwy. 177 and continue for seven miles. At the four-way stop in front of the Procter and Gamble Plant, turn right to stay on Hwy. 177. Continue for another 2.8 miles. The entrance to the state park is on the left, just before the Hwy. 177/Route V intersection.

Emergency numbers: 911 system or (573) 243-3551.

Visitor center: From November through March the visitor center is open 10 a.m. to 4 p.m. on Saturday, and 12 noon to 4 p.m. on Sunday. From April through September, the tan stone visitor center is open Monday through Saturday from 9 a.m. to 5 p.m. and Sunday from noon to 5 p.m. During October, the center is open Thursday, Friday and Saturday from 9 a.m. to 5 p.m. and Sunday from noon to 5 p.m. Restrooms are off the lobby.

The well-designed visitor center has a diorama of the park and a variety of brochures in the lobby. Also in the

The visitor's center has dioramas, an auditorium, seasonal exhibits and history displays.

lobby are animal mounts that include indigo bunting, cedar waxwing, bobcat, striped skunk, American kestrel, bluebird, great flycatcher and others. A small glass display details native plants that include showy orchids, pennywort, tulip popular, purple trillium, baneberry, toothwort, beach drops, American beech, maiden hair fern, bloodroot, bluebell, ginger, wild sweet William, common violet, Dutchman's breeches, wild geranium and others. A souvenir area is also in the lobby that sells postcards, guidebooks, natural history books, finger puppets, Trail of Tears books, maps and other nature-related items.

It takes about an hour to read and view all of the freestanding and backlit exhibits.

The auditorium in the visitor center has aquarium tanks, audio-visual equipment and animal mounts that include a whitetailed deer, green-winged teal, snow goose and a mallard. There's seating for 30 in the small auditorium that is filled with teaching aids, presentation stage and live animals in the tanks. My favorite poster was the guide to the skies that details cloud types.

The seasonal exhibits are a great way to understand the constantly changing needs and habitats of Missouri's flora and fauna. For example, the summer tanager is only in the United States during the warm season and spends the winter in South America. It is often confused with a cardinal, but it doesn't have a crest or black around the face and neck. The large pictures and touch boxes contain feathers, seeds, rocks and other materials that give visitors a chance to use all their senses while learning about the cultural and natural history of the region and state.

A mount of a reclining bobcat is a popular display, as well as a nearby herbaceous plant exhibit. A tree identifier test allows visitors to learn about range, color, leaf shape and twigs. Trees you will learn to identify include Ohio buckeye, serviceberry, American bladdernut and others.

Aside from all of the great natural history displays are information and a chronology of the Trail of Tears, which began in February 1838 when 15,665 people of the Cherokee Nation were forced to move, resulting in a deadly march west. The chronology also details Jacksonian politics, pioneer impact, transportation, other tribes involved and post-migration lifestyles.

Be sure to watch the interpretive videos that includes the 13-minute "The Trail of Tears" and 30-minute video that teaches visitors how to trace their Indian heritage. There are also three-ring binders that offer incredible detail about the Trail of Tears history for those who enjoy a more complete picture of the era and human pain of this government-sanctioned event. The books are at a desk where you can sit. You'll learn about other tribes including the Kickapoo, Sauk, Illinois, Fox, Shawnee, Delaware and others.

Campground: Trail of Tears State Park has basic, electric and electric/water/sewer campsites and a special-use camping area. Services include reservable sites, two dump stations, showers, water and laundry. For reservations, there is a required two-night minimum stay for weekends and major holidays from May 15 through Sept. 15.

The campground is tucked amid some steep-wall valleys and overlooks that view the Mississippi River breaks. It is one of the most wooded campgrounds in the state park system.

A water tower greets campers at the entrance to the basic campground. Walls of vegetation and 12- to 20-inch diameter trees nicely separate sites. Most of the picnic tables at each site have a roof.

Site 21 is private and has a view of the steep valley. Sites 23 and 25 are great sites for two families to spend a weekend next to each other. They are also near a vault toilet. Site 29 is next to a small open area and ideal for a family that wants to spread out a little bit in a sunny area. Another sunny site is No. 30. The modern showerhouse is across the hard-surface park road. A child's level wash sink is a great design component in the showerhouse. The moderate Lake Trail also is accessed here.

Loop 31-45 is wooded and shady. A few of the sites in this loop are pull-throughs. Site 33 is on a knoll and the sites in the 30s (33-36) are a great area for families and friends to cluster. Sites 37 and 39 are also great for two families camping next to each other. These sites are also near the toilet facilities. At the end of the loop is the most private, site 43. You can back a medium-sized rig into this notched-out site. Site 45 is wide, graveled, private and shaded by some medium-sized oaks. This is my favorite site in this loop and would be great for kids due to its privacy and few vehicles passing by. It's also near a water bib.

Loop 46-54 has some smaller sites that are ideal for pop-up campers. Maples and ash trees shade sites in the 40s. Site 48 is a pull-through and near the water bib. On a higher elevation is site 49, which can host a small RV or a tent. Sites 50 and 51 are on the curve that can handle medium-sized RV units and are near the vault toilet. Site 52 is shaded by a 16-inch oak. Site 53 is private and quiet and best for a smaller unit. Site 54 is a pull-through with a view of the densely wooded valley, but it is only for a small-sized unit.

Sites in the Mississippi campground have hard-surface pads and electrical hookups. Most of the sites in this small area can accommodate large RV rigs. Sites 1 and 2 are sunny. They have great views of the river and barge traffic that seems ever present. Site 4 has no shade but a great view. Sites 5-11 are tightly spaced but offer good river views. Firewood is sold near site 11, and site 7 has shade. Some sites on the outside of the loop are backed up against a wooded area. Near site 15 are a hose bib and drinking fountain. Campers in this area might look out to the Mississippi and easily imagine Huck Finn and Jim happily paddling along the banks of the huge river.

Hiking: Trail of Tears State Park offers 14.5 miles of trails. No bikes are allowed on any of the trails.

The Peewah Trail (10 miles, red, moderate) derives its name from an Indian word meaning "come follow in this direction." This trail offers visitors access to the most remote areas of the park. Winding through Indian Creek Wild Area, this trail is open to hikers, backpackers and equestrian riders. The trail is divided into four sections by following various loops of the trail. The green section takes visitors to an overlook along the Mississippi River and is about 1.5 miles round trip. The yellow loop is 3.4 miles and meanders along the Mississippi for a short distance. The red loop is a little less than six miles.

The Sheppard Point Trail (two miles, rigorous) is a loop trail that ascends to a beautiful bluff overlooking the Mississippi River. The trail is open only to hikers due to the rugged terrain. The gravel parking lot can hold six cars and is about 150 yards from the Bushyhead Memorial.

The picturesque Lake Trail (two miles) winds around the basic campground and along Lake Boutin.

The Nature Trail (.5-mile) is the shortest trail in the park located behind the visitor center. Visitors have spotted whitetailed deer, cottontail rabbits and gray squirrels while hiking along this easy trail.

Nature: Park naturalists offer a variety of programs from Memorial Day through Labor Day that might include an owl prowl, sensational snakes and sniper secrets. Music and outdoor education programs are often featured at the amphitheater.

Swimming: Visitors can swim at the beach on Lake Boutin from 7 a.m. to 8 p.m. daily. There is no lifeguard on duty. The 40-yard-wide swimming beach is outlined by a series of orange floats. The view from the beach is terrific. The undulating hills are dressed with oaks, hickorys and maples. Above the beach at Lake Boutin is a day-use area that has picnic tables, grills, nearby phone and vault toilet.

Fishing: The Mississippi River offers catfish, perch and

Inside the visitor's center are many interpretive displays.

carp. Twenty-acre Lake Boutin is stocked with bass, bluegill and catfish. Day usage is from 7 a.m. to 10 p.m. April through October; 7 a.m. to 9 p.m. November and March; and December through February 7 a.m. to 6 p.m. Sunday through Thursday and 7 a.m. to 9 p.m. Friday and Saturday.

Black bass has a limit of six for 12 to 15 inches; crappies, 30 per day; and channel catfish, four per day. There is a lot of shoreline fishing access on the lake. Local anglers reported that live bait and dough balls are best during the summer. Spinners and jigs work well for bass in the spring.

Boating: The park has two hard-surface boat launching ramps. One accesses 20-acre tree-lined Lake Boutin (electric motors only, somewhat steep incline) while the other ramp gets you on the Mississippi River (the ramp becomes unusable when the river level reaches 17 feet or less). This two-lane Mississippi River launch is hard-surfaced, but the parking lot is gravel. Shoreline fishing is allowed near the launch and Mississippi camping area.

Day usage is from 7 a.m. to 10 p.m. April through October; 7 a.m. to 9 p.m. November and March; and 7 a.m.

to 6 p.m. Sunday through Thursday and 7 a.m. to 9 p.m. Friday and Saturday December through February.

Day-use areas: The plaque at the Bushyhead Memorial details Otahki, a Cherokee princesses burial place. Her real name was Nancy Bushyhead Walker Hilderbrand, a sister of Rev. Jessie Bushyhead who was a leader of a group of Cherokee on the Trail of Tears. The term "princess" was a courtesy title given at the time by local residents. The Cherokees have a democratic form of government and do not recognize royalty so there is no such thing as a Cherokee prince or princess. The memorial marks the area believed to be Nancy's grave. Nancy's husband, Louis Hilderbrand, and brother erected a wooden cross on this grave, which burned 35 years later. Local residents then mounded rocks and erected an iron cross. Today, the memorial not only recognizes Nancy Bushyhead but also all the Cherokees that were forced to march from their homelands to the Indian Territory along the route known as the Trail of Tears.

There are lots of day-use and picnic sites in the park. There are two picnic shelters. If not reserved, the shelters are available at no charge on a first-come, first-served basis. There are five popular picnic decks that overlook the small lake.

Greens Ferry Shelter is the smaller of the two shelters. This shelter is near the Bushyhead Memorial and can seat about 40 adults. It has vault toilets, a fireplace and six tables. It can be reserved. A sidewalk takes visitors to the Bushyhead Memorial and plaque that commemorates the Trail of Tears.

Wescoat Shelter can seat about 100 people. It has modern restrooms, water, electricity, lights, two fireplace grills, 14 tables and a playground nearby. (Warning: The road sometimes floods from March through June limiting access). Wescoat Shelter can be reserved. The area is a large mowed open space that is great for field games.

Near the Wescoat Shelter is an interpretive sign that details more of the Trail of Tears plight. It says, "It was January, we arrived in a snowstorm, there before us struggled the great Mississippi caught up in the grip of winter running full of huge jagged rocks crushed down on the river hitting each other with mighty shocks." - James Mooney

Two playgrounds are in the park. One is next to Wescoat Shelter, and the other is in the lake picnic area.

Insider's tips: Bring your bike. The winding park roads with expansive views are delightful places to pedal. Be cautious of the railroad tracks. Try the half-mile-long trail that begins behind the modern visitor center. Missouri has about 1,000 bald eagles during the winter. Some of the trees in the park are more than 150 feet tall. The view from Shepards Point is magnificent.